SOUTHERN HEAT

HEAT

New Southern Cooking
LATIN STYLE

The Taunton Press

SOUTHERN HEAT

HEAT New Southern Cooking LATIN STYLE

ANTHONY LAMAS & GWEN PRATESI

The Taunton Press

⊤ The Taunton Press

63 South Main Street
PO Box 5506
Newtown, CT 06470-5506
Email:tp@taunton.com

Editor: Carolyn Mandarano
Copy Editor: Li Agen
Indexer: Barbara Mortenson
Art Director: Rosalind Loeb Wanke
Jacket/Cover design: Stacy Wakefield
Interior design and layout: Stacy Wakefield
Photographer: Roger Pratesi
Food and Prop Stylist: James Herrin

The following names/manufacturers appearing in *Southern Heat* are trademarks: Abita®, Angostura®, Anson Mills®, Bourbon Barrel Foods®, Cabot™, Captain Morgan®, Carta Blanca™, Cavender's®, Chihuahua®, Chili's℠, Coco Rèal®, Corona®, Dos Equis®, Duke's®, Finest Call®, FoodSaver®, Gosling's Black Seal®, Goya®, Grand Marnier®, Hellmann's®, Juanita's Foods®, Kahlúa®, Knox®, Korin®, La Costeña®, Le Creuset®, Lodge®, Luxardo®, Magimix®, Mailbu®, Master of Mixes®, Myer's®, Old Forester®, Old Overholt®, PolyScience®, RealFruit™, Sailor Jerry®, Swanson®, Tabasco®, Tapatio®, Thermapen®, The Perfect Purée®, Vitamix®, Waring®, Woodford Reserve®, Ziploc®

Library of Congress Cataloging-in-Publication Data

Lamas, Anthony, author.
  Southern heat : new Southern cooking Latin style / Anthony Lamas & Gwen Pratesi ; Roger Pratesi, photographer.
    pages cm
  Includes index.
  ISBN 978-1-62710-915-4
  1. Cooking, American--Southern style. 2. Cooking, Latin American.
  I. Pratesi, Gwen, author. II. Pratesi, Roger, illustrator. III. Title.
  TX715.2.S68L34 2015
  641.5975--dc23

                    2015026690

Printed in the United States of America
10 9 8 7 6 5 4 3 2

DEDICATION

From Anthony: To my mama, Irene Lamas, who always kept a hot meal on the table and a roof over our heads. She taught me to always believe in myself and reach for my dreams.

To my wife Samantha, who is my backbone and not only an amazing wife but an amazing mother to our young boys. Thank you for accepting me for who I am and loving me unconditionally.

To my three boys, who remind me of what really matters in life.

To all of my family and friends in Kentucky and across the country. I love you all and thank you for your continued support. Buen provecho!

From Gwen: To my husband, Roger, who is my partner in life, work, and love. Without his support, none of this would have been possible.

To my Tibetan Terrier, Beamer, who has been a constant companion for many years.

› ACKNOWLEDGMENTS ‹

FROM ANTHONY I would like to thank all the people who made *Southern Heat* a reality and helped me to bring the flavors of my life to home cooks everywhere.

I met Gwen and Roger Pratesi when they came to Louisville in 2011 during their first culinary adventure. We hit it off immediately and haven't looked back. Gwen and Roger have become great friends, and they both have put a lot of energy—and trips back to Louisville—into making this book. Gwen, thank you for taking my recipes and making them work for the home cook and for recognizing my passion for my craft and weaving that into the book. I'm grateful for the many hours you have spent on this project, and I'm proud of what we have created together. To Roger Pratesi, thanks for capturing the journey through your beautiful photos and for supporting Gwen through this process.

My entire team at Seviche, especially James Moran, my right-hand man (my Asian brother), who kept a handle on the kitchen while I was away working on this book. To Madeline Doolittle, who has been with me through the ups and downs in business and my personal life. She keeps me sane by helping me organize my thoughts and get them out on paper. She's like a sister to me, and I feel lucky to be able to collaborate with her on many projects. Steve Rappa, my friend of 19 years, for his contribution to the Sweet Endings chapter. He takes my vision and flavors and creates delicious desserts at the restaurant and has done the same with the dessert recipes in this book. To my general manager, Hap Cohan, who holds down the front of the house, and my business partners George and Charlie Wagner—without you what we do would not be possible.

To all the farmers and artisans who dedicate their lives to creating incredible products for us to cook with. You all are rock stars. I have so much respect for your hard work and thank you for sharing your products with me.

Last but not least, thanks to Carolyn Mandarano and the entire Taunton Press team for believing in my vision and allowing me to express myself.

FROM GWEN *Southern Heat* has a short list of very dedicated people who worked on the book. Many thanks go to Anthony for sharing his personal story and culinary talent and for having the patience to work through the recipes in the book with me. Thanks also to Steve Rappa for his dessert recipes and to the farmers and artisans featured in the book who shared their life experiences with us.

I want to thank my husband, Roger, who worked on this project with me for several years and was the photographer for the book, and James Herrin, our food and prop stylist.

There would be no *Southern Heat* without our editor, Carolyn Mandarano, who believed in our project and allowed us quite a bit of creative freedom in the book. We thank her and the rest of the team at The Taunton Press for seeing our vision through to the end.

› CONTENTS ‹

THE FLAVORS OF MY LIFE

MY FOOD IS a lot like my personality—serious and playful; my flavors are bright and bold with a lot of love and passion mixed in, and, of course, a bit of Latin spice to heat things up. The recipes in *Southern Heat* are a reflection of my life's experiences, from the Latin flavors of my heritage, my time growing up in southern and central California, my culinary training on the West Coast, and the local Southern →

3

ingredients from Kentucky, where I now call home.

MY EARLY FOOD MEMORIES

Born to immigrant parents in southern California, my father is of Puerto Rican descent and my mama is from Mexico. Mama was 15 years old when I was born, and I have three younger sisters. She was a wonderful home cook and made traditional Latin and Mexican dishes using her own blend of herbs and spices. The dishes would fill the house with intoxicating aromas. Those that simmered overnight kept me awake in anticipation of the next day's meal. One of the most memorable is her Posole (p. 217). Other family favorites are included in the chapter Mi Casa es Su Casa, beginning on p. 202.

During my early childhood, my family left Los Angeles to avoid the street gangs that I started to hang out with and purchased a small 10-acre farm in central California. That's where I began to hunt, fish, and raise animals. I also fell in love with the fresh fruit and produce grown in the area. My uncle and grandfather moved to central California with us and opened a restaurant called Lamasty, a play on our name, where I got my first experience working in a restaurant.

With our close proximity to Mexico, my family would travel south, over the border, where we would eat fresh fish and seafood from the *mariscos* stands along the beach. While the other kids played on the beach, I would walk in the sand with the surf lapping over my feet while eating freshly grilled octopus with hot sauce or ceviche with crisp cucumbers and freshly squeezed lime juice. I was six or seven then, but even now, I can still taste the refreshing and bright flavors of sea salt and citrus with the subtle texture of the fish.

At the fruit stands in Mexico, women would cut up all kinds of fresh fruit, like watermelon, pineapple, mangos, and papaya. They would include cucumber and jícama, adding a crunchy texture and refreshing and unexpected flavor. The fruits were well-chilled and sometimes topped with a sweet, thickened tamarind syrup or fresh coconut pieces. They were served sprinkled with a spicy topping that included chili powder and salt and finished with a squeeze of fresh lime juice. It was an ex-plosion of flavors in my mouth. I prepare this salad for my two younger boys today. It's a favorite in our home, and I've included a recipe for you (see Barrio Fruit Salad on p. 208).

As a young boy, I also visited the taco stands in Ensenada and Rosarito Beach in Baja, California, with my family. Grilled fish tacos, with fish caught fresh from the ocean, were topped with Pico de Gallo or salsa, shredded cabbage, and a sauce or crema. The Mexicans' answer to the American fried fish sandwich, these, in contrast, were fresh, light, and full of bright and spicy flavors. These food memories are so vivid for me.

FAMILY AND FARMING

When we moved to central California, I traded in my Vans®, the shoe of choice for skateboarders in LA, and a boogie board for cowboy boots and Wranglers®. It was an easy transition, as I had always enjoyed the time we spent vacationing in this part of California. I embraced living in one of the largest agricultural areas in the country, where we were surrounded by thousands of acres of olive groves and orange, avocado, and almond trees. Farming became a way of life. We raised chickens, cows, goats, and pigs. It was exciting to pick oranges fresh from the trees to make our own juice, and I set

> Even as a kid, I viewed food differently. Eating was an experience for me, not just sustenance.

up an avocado stand, selling the ripe green fruit just as other kids would sell lemonade.

My first job working with animals was with a veal rancher. At age 13, I began to see and understand the best and worst of farming. Later in my teens, when I was in FFA (Future Farmers of America) and studied agricultural science in high school, I learned how to raise a healthy animal and impact the outcome of the meat by controlling its muscle structure through exercise. Happy animals are healthier and taste better. This was the first experience that would inspire me, later in life as a chef, to support smaller farmers who raise only cage-free and humanely raised animals. I appreciate the extra work it takes to properly raise these animals, and I'm willing to pay the extra cost to serve ingredients that are truly superior in taste and quality.

I spent much of my free time outside of school at Lamasty. The bus would drop me off after school so that I could help my uncle in the kitchen. I would wash dishes, do some prep work, and spend time with family. I knew that working in a restaurant was a great trade and a way to pay the bills, but I never considered it for a career.

My extended family and their friends would often get together and throw big parties, and we'd cook whole animals outdoors. It doesn't take much for a Latino to have an excuse to party, so I grew up with gatherings like these with great food and lots of people. I have always loved to grill foods and was the adventurous one at these outings, eating some of the raw animal parts or taking a big bite out of a fresh jalapeño.

I spent quite a bit of time during my early teenage years with my

younger cousin, Mando, who is like a brother to me. During the summers I would stay with my godmother, my mama's sister (Mando's mother) in Riverside, California, for two to three weeks. My aunt Yolanda (or Nina as I called her, which is slang for godmother in Spanish) would take us to the grocery store and give us each five dollars to spend as we wanted. My cousins ran to get candy, cookies, and cupcakes; I went straight to the butcher's counter, asking for the best cut of meat I could afford. I craved real food instead of all the processed things that most kids wanted. I would carefully select my steak and then spend time preparing it with a great rub and cooking it over an open fire to bring out all the flavor.

Mando used to laugh at me when we were kids because I viewed food so differently than he did; eating was an experience for me, not just sustenance. Mando would get upset because I always took a longer time to eat, but even back then, food was something special to me and I wanted to linger over every bite.

I worked a variety of jobs during high school, from selling fast food to flipping burgers at Chili's[SM]. I was into music and continued my involvement with FFA. Like most teenagers, I spent a lot of time trying to find myself during those

years. My mama and her husband had divorced earlier in my youth, I had a heartbreaking breakup with my first girlfriend, and was feeling lost and confused. I was seriously thinking about enlisting in the army, but I also applied to a few places for a job as a cook. One of those places was the Culinary Apprenticeship Program at the Coronado Bay Resort in San Diego, California. I was accepted, and the move turned out to be a pivotal point in my culinary career.

DISCOVERING MY GIFT

Jeff Tunks, the executive chef at Coronado Bay, was my culinary mentor. He gave me direction and encouragement; he was tough and pushed me to be better. It was here that I learned to create dishes with layers of unique flavors and textures.

Most important, I learned to trust my instincts when cooking. Jeff told me I had a gift—and I believed him. I could imagine a new dish in my mind and when it came to actually making it, I would do so by sight, taste, and smell. Even now, I don't read or follow recipes —I taste the dish as I prepare it to know whether it's right. I believe you need to feel your food.

I worked hard to develop my craft and skills. I also came to love the local ingredients and started cooking with a Pacific Rim flair that was popular at that time.

After three years at Coronado Bay, I followed a girl back to Kentucky and started a life in Louisville. I was young, a new father to my son Nicolas, and living in a strange new place. It wasn't long after the move that my girl and I separated, but I remained committed to providing for Nicolas and being an active father in his life.

While it's not the same as central California, the region surrounding Louisville is a large agricultural area and the people are proud of the land and the traditions. The rolling hills, fertile soil, and horse farms reminded me a bit of home, and I embraced the culture and a different way of life. Although the ingredients were different than what I was used to—grits, collard greens, paw-paws, and country ham were new to this California Latino—I was excited to cook with them and put my spin on these traditional foods. I also learned two important things about Kentucky: This is bourbon country and home to the greatest 2 minutes in sports—the Kentucky Derby.

THE EARLY YEARS IN KENTUCKY

I was called the "California Kid" by Chef Kathy Cary when she hired me at Lilly's (now called

Lilly's Bistro), my first job in Louisville. She gave me creative freedom with food, and the dishes I prepared started to get noticed by diners and critics. I also met friend and fellow chef Steve Rappa at Lilly's; he is now my pastry chef at Seviche.

Other than where I worked, I knew no one; I had no car and no belongings. I rented a small third-floor apartment, with absolutely no furniture, not far from where I worked on Bardstown Road, so that I could walk to work. I would take Nicolas with me to the grocery store, the restaurant, and other places in a little red wagon. To this day, some of my regular customers at Seviche still remember those days with me toting

Nicolas down Bardstown Road in that little wagon.

It was during these first few years in Louisville and after the split with Nicolas' mom that I met my wife, Samantha. She was not familiar with Latin or West Coast flavors, so I introduced her to new foods. I remember the first time she bit into a taco at a taqueria in Los Angeles. I saw the look on her face as her eyes rolled in the back of her head with excitement and she smiled as a little salsa verde slid down the side of her mouth onto her chin. I knew right then I was in love. Over the years, Samantha has kept me grounded. The life of a chef is intense. It involves long hours, travel away from home, and a lot of bourbon.

I was called the "California Kid" by Chef Kathy Cary when she hired me at Lilly's, my first job in Louisville. I also met friend and fellow chef Steve Rappa at Lilly's; he is now my pastry chef at Seviche as well as a great friend.

She has been by my side for all of it. I know I wouldn't be telling this story if it wasn't for her.

After we married, I merged another culture into my cooking repertoire. Samantha is half Jewish, and her family's heritage has inspired me to create unique twists on traditional Jewish dishes—matzo ball soup with jalapeño and lemon, and latkes with a spicy lemon crema instead of the traditional sour cream.

SPICING UP THE SOUTH

Over the course of the next few years, I solidified my reputation in Louisville. When Jicama, my first restaurant in Louisville, had been open for just one year, I was invited to participate in the Woodford Reserve Challenge, a cooking competition featuring Woodford's unique bourbon. I was pitted against some of the best chefs in Kentucky, but I won the challenge with my Southern-Latin dishes.

I closed Jicama and reopened as Seviche, A Latin Restaurant, in the same location. This was 2005 and the food scene all over the country was exploding. Cooking with local ingredients was the buzz, combining flavors from different cultures was the rage, and creating an experience with food was becoming the norm. I grew up around food being cooked in this style—it was all I knew. My food has been described as bold, bright, and fresh. For me, great food is about the layering of flavors, the balance of ingredients and textures, and building dishes using the best ingredients.

MY COOKING AND FOOD PHILOSOPHY

I've learned many things over the years, but at the top of the list is that cooking is a creative expression. Cooking for me is emotional, but as I said, it's also about layering flavors and balancing ingredients and textures. There are a few critical elements in creating great flavors.

Seasoning each ingredient individually as you go, rather than seasoning all of the ingredients together, creates layers of flavor. If you season and taste as you work through a recipe, you will create that perfect balance and each ingredient will shine.

Citrus and spice require more salt. I always suggest that you taste and add it to your prefer-

ence, but you will find that many recipes will require more salt than you would expect to create the right balance of flavors. Salt is the most underused ingredient.

We all define "hot" or "spicy" very differently. When creating dishes, the amount of heat in some components will be tempered by the other components of the dish when plated; you'll understand this when making Chicken Tinga (p. 113). You'll think the sauce is extremely hot and spicy, but it will mellow out when combined with the chicken and rice.

Caramelizing proteins and vegetables provides another flavor boost. If you walk into a professional kitchen, you will find that most of the chef's cast iron or stainless pans are sitting over very high heat, where the flame is climbing up the sides. Searing foods is the first step in creating great dishes—it will seal in the juices and add intense flavor.

You will find that my dishes pair several components to create layers of flavor on the entire plate. Putting the right proteins, sauces, and side dishes together is the best way to create that "party in your mouth" I've become known for. One example of this is the Macadamia-Crusted Sea Bass with Cranberry–Scallion Couscous and Passion Fruit–Habanero Sauce (p. 150). The flavors and textures blend together perfectly. There is subtle texture and flavor from the fish combined with crunch and saltiness of the nuts. The residual heat and slightly sweet yet tangy flavors of the passion fruit sauce dance on the roof of your mouth and in your throat. The final layer of flavor and texture comes from the couscous, with a slight sweetness from the dried cranberries and crunchy texture from the chopped scallions.

I'm passionate about using the best and freshest ingredients that I can source—and I encourage you to be the same. Nothing is more inspirational than local farmers showing up at my back door with beautiful fresh vegetables and produce picked hours ago at their farms, freshly laid chicken eggs, and meats and poultry raised on local farms. I have a number of farmers who grow ingredients especially for me, and I'm committed to taking whatever they grow. If I can't use the harvest immediately, I preserve it so that I'm still able to feature local products on my menu, even in the winter months.

I like to say that farmers, not chefs, are the rock stars. I could not do my job if it weren't for these amazing farmers and artisans and the beautiful products they supply. In fact, several of them are featured in the pages that follow. Farm to table is not a culinary style, it's a way of life; it's the way I was raised and the philosophy I live by now. It's better for us and the environment.

Time management plays just as large a role in cooking. Think ahead and plan meals, especially when entertaining. Read through the recipe before starting, and look for aspects of the dish you can prepare ahead. This is a restaurant technique that you can do at home to minimize what has to be done at the last second. There are tips in the recipes for preparing components ahead of time and then combining and assembling them just before serving. This also helps create layers of flavor. Use these strategies to minimize stress when preparing meals. More than anything, cooking should be fun.

> Farm to table is not a culinary style, it's a way of life. It's the way I was raised and the philosophy I live by now. It's better for us and the environment.

THE LATIN AND SOUTHERN PANTRIES

Following are some of the ingredients you will need to create the recipes in *Southern Heat.* Most of these will be available in your local grocery or specialty stores, but look through Resources (p. 277) for some of the more unusual items, which can be ordered online.

Latin Pantry Staples

HOT PEPPERS

There are many varieties of peppers, with new ones being created all the time, as well as many heirloom varieties being revived. The good news is that more of these varieties are becoming widely available with the growing interest in spicier dishes. Most home cooks can easily find jalapeños, poblanos, and habanero peppers, which I use in many of my dishes.

When working with peppers, wear gloves and do not touch any part of your body that you don't want irritated, especially your eyes. Also, do not put your face close to a pot while cooking peppers. While the aroma may be intoxicating, you can burn your eyes and face. When working with really hot peppers, like habaneros, and especially when cooking with them, you need to have excellent ventilation and open all the windows and turn up the exhaust fan. The fumes from hot peppers can take your breath away!

Below is a list of the peppers I use in my cooking.

› **Aji amarillo:** A yellow pepper that turns bright orange when ripened, these peppers are very hot (50,000 SHU) but also sweet. Because of this combination, some people eat them raw.

› **Aji panca:** This pepper turns a deep red, almost burgundy color, when fully mature. It has very little heat, particularly when the seeds and membranes are removed. Aji pancas are dried and are best known for their use in Aji panca paste, which is available in many Latin markets. We make an Aji panca sauce (p. 230).

› **Ancho chiles:** The most popular dried pepper in Mexico, these are the dried form of a poblano pepper and can be used in place of Pasilla chiles.

› **Chipotles in adobo:** Chipotles in adobo are dried and smoked jalapeños that are packed and canned in a smoky adobo sauce. With both heat and smoky flavor, these are added to many dishes to amp up the flavors. Because these peppers are hot, they are typically used in smaller amounts (like 1 to 2 tablespoons) in some recipes, so I recommend that you purée them and store the mixture in small zip-top bags in the freezer.

› **Guajillos:** The name for this commonly used dried pepper translates to "little gourd," referring to the rattling sound the dried seeds make inside the pod when shaken. With a hint of sweetness, the smoky and earthy undertones in this pepper pair well with many dishes and in sauces like Salsa Rojo (p. 242). Because of the thick dried skins, these peppers will need to be soaked prior to using; however, if grinding them in a rub, they can be used as is. They have a heat index of 2,500 to 5,000 SHU.

› **Habaneros:** Habaneros, a popular chile pepper, are the hottest chile we use in this book, with a level of heat ranging from 100,000 to 480,000 SHU. While most habaneros are red or yellow, some unique varieties have different hues and with varying levels of heat. The black (or chocolate, named because of its brown color) habanero is rated between 425,000 and 450,000 SHU and is not as smoky as the traditional habanero.

We use both fresh habaneros and dried habanero powder in the recipes. While you can substitute a fresh Scotch Bonnet pepper for a fresh habanero in a pinch (they have a similar ranking on the Scoville Scale), there really is no substitute for habanero powder. Ground cayenne will provide heat, but the

unique floral and citrus element of habanero powder cannot be replicated.

› **Padrons:** The Pimento de Padron peppers rank "0" on the Scoville Scale, with almost no level of heat. Occasionally you will find the one surprising odd hot pepper that will hit 2,500 SHU; it's a little like playing Russian roulette. Be prepared to expect the unexpected. These peppers are delicious when served blistered and lightly seasoned with extra-virgin olive oil and kosher or sea salt and are perfect with my refined version of the rustic Mexican dish Elote (p. 90).

› **Pasillas:** A popular dried chile that ranges from 250 to 4,000 SHU, the name for this pepper translates to "little raisin." Dried from the Mexican Chilaca pepper, the rich, smoky flavor of a pasilla makes it ideal for using in salsas and sauces, like the traditional Mexican *mole*. It is one of the two dried peppers (along with Guajillos) in my Salsa Rojo (p. 242). As with most dried peppers, it will need to be soaked prior to using in sauces.

› **Shishitos:** These Japanese peppers are similar in appearance and taste to a Padron pepper. Most of these peppers range in heat from 100 to 1,000 SHU. One in eight Shishitos will leave you with a hot surprise, but that's half the fun in eating them.

ACHIOTE (OR ANNATTO)

Achiote is a spice ground from seeds of the fruit from the achiote tree, which is found in the Caribbean and Latin America. The seeds are available in many spice shops and are usually called annatto seeds. The powder from the seeds is also made into a paste, Achiote paste, commonly used in Latin dishes primarily for its vibrant color. I've included a recipe for a homemade spice mix called Sazón, which includes achiote (p. 248). Goya® also makes the spice blend. If you prefer to buy it premade, be sure to get the Sazón with Culantro and Achiote.

CHAYOTE SQUASH

Originating in Mexico, Chayote squash are lime green-colored, pear-shaped, and mild. Known as mirlitons in French Creole cooking, some describe the flavor of this squash as a cross between a cucumber and an apple. To prepare the squash, peel the outer skin, cut in half, and then remove the "seed" or pit in the middle.

EPAZOTE

A very pungent Mexican herb, epazote should be used sparingly. It is a key ingredient in my Posole Spice Mix (p. 242). While small

ABOUT PEPPERS AND HEAT

PEPPERS CAN BE UNPREDICTABLE. Even peppers of the same variety can be quite different in taste and heat. The heat of a pepper depends on a number of factors, including where it originated, where it's now grown, the time of harvest, and the condition of the soil. Over time, the heat level of many varieties has changed due to the migration of the plants, seeds, and the changes in the environment. Many times, peppers that used to be considered mild are now quite hot and vice versa.

The best way to measure the level of heat, or capsicum, in peppers, is by referring to the Scoville Scale. This tool lists different varieties of peppers with their heat range from a low of "0," or no discernible heat, to a high of 2,200,000 SHU (Scoville Heat Units) for a Carolina pepper.

If you're uncertain about the heat of a pepper or how much heat you can tolerate, add just a little to the dish at first, then taste and add more until the heat is the right level for you. I ate fresh jalapeños right off the vine as a young boy, but I don't recommend trying that to start. Most of the heat resides in the seeds of the pepper, so if you want to make a dish hotter, add some or all of the seeds. Also remember that what seems hot by itself will be balanced out by the rest of the ingredients in the dish, like rice or proteins. Citrus and salt also balance heat, and they are common ingredients in many of my recipes.

amounts of this strong herb are fine, large amounts can be toxic. Epazote is usually found in Latin markets where herbs and peppers are displayed in plastic bags. Look for the El Guapo brand.

MASA FLOUR

This flour is made especially for tortillas. It is ground from dried masa, a corn that's been specially treated with a solution of lime and water (a similar process for preparing hominy) and then rinsed and dried.

MEXICAN CHORIZO

Mexican chorizo is raw, seasoned, crumbly meat that can be found in ground form or in sausages. Ancho chile powder is one of the main ingredients in this spicy sausage and what gives it its red color. Mexican chorizo is not the same as Spanish chorizo (a cured meat), and the two are not interchangeable.

MEXICAN OREGANO

Mexican oregano is much stronger and less sweet than the Mediterranean oregano that you may be more familiar with. It holds up to the other bold spices in Latin cooking, like cumin and coriander, and pairs well with the heat from the hot peppers. Dried Mexican oregano is available as buds and in a ground form. I use both in my recipes.

For me, great food is about the layering of flavors, the balance of ingredients and textures, and building dishes using the best ingredients that are seasoned at each step.

Southern Pantry Staples

BENTON'S BACON

Known as the King of Bacon, Allan Benton is a Southern legend. Benton's bacon and highly regarded hams are super smoky and quite different from any other. Flavoring dishes with country ham, ham bones or hocks, and bacon has long been a Southern tradition. With the popularity of Southern foods and anything pork or bacon across the country, Benton's Bacon has almost become a household word. Their bacon and hams can be ordered by phone from their location in Madisonville, Tennessee (see Resources on p. 277).

CAROLINA GOLD RICE

This Southern specialty is unique in its taste, structure, and qualities. Originally brought to the American colonies from Africa and Indonesia, this rice, almost lost in the early 20th century to other rice grains, was a staple along the coastal regions of South Carolina from the late 1600s through the 1800s and played a large role in the development of the cuisine of Charleston and in Lowcountry cooking. A revival of this rice began in the mid 1980s in coastal wetlands around Charleston. Depending on how the rice is cooked, it can either be fluffy (like traditional long-grain rice), sticky (like Asian sticky rice), or it can be used in creamy dishes, such as risotto, just as you would Arborio rice. Carolina Gold Rice is not aromatic, so it lends itself well to other flavors. Carolina Gold Rice

can be ordered through Anson Mills® (see Resources on p. 277).

COUNTRY HAM

There are a number of excellent country ham producers in the South, and while their production methods might seem similar, each creates a unique tasting ham, and the resulting flavor in a dish can vary greatly. Benton's creates very smoky hams, while Nancy Newsom of Newsom's Country Hams (see Resources on p. 277) makes a product that has a more subtle flavor and texture resembling that of a traditional Spanish ham or prosciutto. Southern cooking methods have always relied on tasty pig products (such as country ham and bacon) to season dishes, like collard greens and other vegetables, but today chefs create unique and complex flavors in dishes using country ham and bacon.

SEA ISLAND RED PEAS

Another heirloom food from South Carolina that was originally brought into the country from Africa, this field pea is a variety closest in appearance and taste to black-eyed peas, yet it is far more delicious. A companion crop to Carolina Gold Rice, it is no wonder these two ingredients pair so beautifully. The rich flavor and creamy texture make these peas wonderful on their own, and they can be cooked in either water or chicken or pork stock to elevate the flavor. Sea Island Red Peas can be ordered through Anson Mills.

SORGHUM

A popular sweetener in the South, sorghum is also delicious in savory dishes. Thanks to Southern chefs and local artisans, like Matt Jamie of Bourbon Barrel Foods® (see Resources on p. 277), people who never heard of sorghum are dis-

covering this unique syrup. Some Whole Foods Markets also carry Muddy Pond Sorghum, which is made in Muddy Pond, Tennessee.

STONE-GROUND GRITS

Different from quick or instant grits, stone-ground grits are sold by a number of small mills in the South. These grits are made by crushing the dried corn kernels the old-fashioned way, between two stone wheels. Kernels ground by this method produce both grits and cornmeal. Stone-ground grits take longer to cook than quick grits, but the resulting texture is substantial and they are full of flavor. Not all stone-ground grits are the same. The size of the grind, the corn used, and whether or not the hull remains in the grits all influence texture and flavor. I use grits from Weisenberger Mill in Midway, Kentucky (see Resources on p. 277).

COOKING IN A CONVECTION OVEN

ALL THE RECIPES IN *SOUTHERN HEAT* were prepared using convection ovens. Convection ovens circulate the heat better and produce more even cooking and baking results than non-convection. Many home kitchens are fitted with convection ovens, but if yours is not, adjustment to convert to non-convection cooking or baking is simple. Increase the temperature by 25°F and increase the cooking time by 10 to 20 percent, depending on your oven. As with any oven, be sure the temperature is accurate by using a good oven thermometer.

NIPS
& NIBBLES

DRINKS &
SMALL BITES TO GET THE
PARTY STARTED

I LOVE SMALL BITES or nibbles. In fact, my favorite way to dine when I go out is to be casual, sitting in the bar area and ordering a drink and three or four appetizers or small plates—*apertivos,* as we call them at Seviche. It's the perfect way to try different flavors and dishes without committing to one large entrée.

We serve a lot of small plates and appetizers at Seviche. Some of the most requested ones are our Kentucky Bison Empanadas (p. 35) or Crispy Chicken Liver Anticuchos with Aji Panca (p. 26). I also like to send out a few *bocaditos,* or one-bite snacks, to guests who are celebrating a special occasion or to friends as a way of saying thank you. Some of the recipes in this chapter can be made into these single bites, such as the Lamb Albóndigas with Jalapeño–Mint Pesto (p. 19). Along with the recipes in First Courses (starting on p. 50) and Ceviche, Cebiche, Seviche (starting on p. 72), these dishes are great to serve for your →

In both the Latin and Southern cultures, food is a cause for celebration. Gathering together at someone's home and sharing food and drink is the greatest expression of hospitality.

own special occasions or when entertaining at home.

This chapter is the perfect way to introduce you to the flavors, cooking methods, and recipes that combine my Latin heritage with West Coast influences and Southern ingredients. In both the Latin and Southern cultures, food is a cause for celebration. Gathering together at someone's home and sharing food and drink is the greatest expression of hospitality. Marrying Latin and Southern cuisines has been effortless since there are many similarities in the way both cultures look at food and entertaining.

I know that hosting parties at home can be stressful, so many of these recipes can be prepared ahead and then finished right before guests arrive. The beverages included here are simple and straightforward, and a few can be made in large batches. Cocktail parties, where guests are standing and grazing, are some of the easiest and most successful parties. The recipes and tips will help you create a perfect menu with an interesting mix of flavors and textures.

Some suggested pairings for entertaining: On a hot summer's day for a casual party, serve pitchers of chilled Bourbon Mojitos (p. 24) along with

Charred Gulf Shrimp Cocktail with Horseradish Chimichurri (p. 44) and Lamb Albóndigas with Jalapeño–Mint Pesto (facing page). If your guests prefer wine, choose a low-alcohol white that will pair nicely with the bit of heat and spice, such as Sauvignon Blanc, Riesling, or Chenin Blanc. When entertaining in the fall, winter, or holiday season, Perfect Cherry–Pineapple Manhattans (p. 37) are great served with a soul-satisfying and decadent Pork Belly with Sorghum–Chipotle Glaze (p. 22). For wine enthusiasts, pair the pork belly with a Rasteau or red wine from the Rhône River Valley.

LAMB ALBÓNDIGAS WITH JALAPEÑO—MINT PESTO

This popular appetizer at Seviche combines ground lamb from Border Springs Farm in Patrick Springs, Virginia, with the Latin and Caribbean jerk flavors of my housemade Posole Spice Mix and fresh ginger. If you haven't liked lamb in the past, try it in this recipe—the bold, bright flavors of the seasoning stand up well to the flavor of the lamb. I like to give my lamb dishes a lot of love, so I season them well. If you would prefer to use beef, then you can substitute it for the lamb, adjusting the seasonings to your taste. You can make the meatballs several hours ahead, cover, and refrigerate until ready to bake. (For longer storage, freeze on the baking sheet, then transfer to a zip-top bag and freeze for up to 1 month.) This recipe is also easy to double when entertaining a larger crowd.

The lamb from Border Springs Farm is very mild with grassy notes. While you can use lamb available at your local market, finding lamb that is young—and mild—is the first step to an extraordinary dish. Be careful of older lamb, as it takes on a stronger and almost mutton flavor, primarily because of the hormones in the animal. Know your farmer or ask your butcher where they source their lamb and ask how the meat is harvested. As an alternative, if you can't find local lamb, purchase milder tasting lamb, which comes from New Zealand and Colorado.

MAKES 13 TO 14 MEATBALLS · SERVES 4 TO 6

1 pound ground lamb

1 teaspoon minced garlic

1½ teaspoons Posole Spice Mix (p. 242), rubbed with hands to make finer

2½ teaspoons kosher salt

Juice and finely grated zest of ½ lemon

⅛ teaspoon lemon oil (see Resources on p. 277), or additional lemon zest

1½ teaspoons finely minced fresh ginger

1 large egg, beaten

2 tablespoons fine homemade dried breadcrumbs (omit if you eat gluten-free)

Jalapeño—Mint Pesto (p. 233)

Position a rack in the center of a convection oven and heat the oven to 350°F. Line a baking sheet with parchment.

Combine all of the ingredients except the pesto in a medium bowl and use your hands to mix gently but thoroughly. Measure out 1½ ounces of the mixture (use a digital scale to check) and roll between your hands to form a perfectly shaped meatball; place on the prepared baking sheet. The meatballs will be approximately 1¾ inches in diameter. Continue until you've used up all of the mixture. You should have 13 to 14 meatballs.

Bake the meatballs for about 15 minutes, until browned and cooked through but not overdone. The internal temperature should not be higher than 160°F. Transfer the meatballs to a plate and serve with the Jalapeño Mint Pesto. For a fun presentation, I like to thread 2 meatballs on a 4-inch bamboo skewer, drizzle with a little of the pesto, and then serve.

CHEF'S TIP > To check for proper seasoning before rolling the meatballs, put a small amount of the meat in a skillet heated with just a little neutral-flavored oil. Cook until the meat is lightly browned, then taste and adjust the seasonings as needed.

5 PEPPER MICHELADA

A Michelada is a traditional Mexican cocktail that is very popular on the West Coast. There are many versions of this drink, all of which traditionally include a combination of Clamato® or tomato juice, beer, citrus, and spices. Micheladas are refreshing and make a great accompaniment to dishes like Baja-Style Fish Tacos (see p. 147), especially when hosting a casual summer party. For this version, I use my Chef-Inspired 5 Pepper Bloody Mary Mix that I helped create especially for Master of Mixes®. The flavor of this mixer is bold, bright, and peppery and pairs perfectly with the fresh citrus in the cocktail. The Chile Salt is colorful on the rim of the glass and elevates the flavor with each sip of the drink. The true essence of the cocktail is captured with the fizziness created by the activity of the brewer's yeast in the beer. If you want to prepare a nonalcoholic drink, substitute a nonalcoholic beer for the Carta Blanca™. If you want a milder Michelada, use the Classic version of the Bloody Mary mix instead of the 5 Pepper.

This recipe is for one cocktail, but you'll have enough Chile Salt to make 1 dozen drinks.

MAKES 1 COCKTAIL

Lime wedges and slices	3 ounces Chef-Inspired 5 Pepper Bloody Mary mix (or your favorite Bloody Mary mix)
Chile Salt (recipe below)	
¼ lemon, juiced	⅓ cup ice
¼ teaspoon celery salt	Mexican beer (I like Carta Blanca)

Rub a lime wedge over the rim of the serving glass. Spread some Chile Salt on a small flat plate, turn the serving glass upside down in the mixture, and twist it in the salt so it adheres to the rim of the glass. Put the lemon juice, celery salt, and Bloody Mary mix into the glass, pouring it in carefully so that it doesn't drip on the salt coating. Add the ice and top off with the beer. Squeeze the juice of 1 lime wedge into the glass, then stir gently. Garnish with a lime slice.

CHILE SALT

MAKES ABOUT 4½ TABLESPOONS

1 tablespoon celery salt	½ teaspoon chili powder
1½ teaspoons sea salt	¼ teaspoon dried cilantro
¼ teaspoon paprika	¼ teaspoon dried chives
¼ teaspoon chile de arbol	½ teaspoon dried lemon rind (optional)

Stir together all ingredients in a small bowl.

CHEF'S TIP ❯ Carta Blanca beer is a smooth, medium-bodied American-style premium lager that is golden in color with low hops. It has more body than Corona™ and less than Dos Equis®, two very popular Mexican beers.

PORK BELLY WITH SORGHUM—CHIPOTLE GLAZE

Pork belly is succulent, rich, fatty, and incredibly tender. This is the part of the pig that is used to make bacon. With the popularity of this cut of pork and the interest in home-curing meats, pork belly is now widely available at many local butcher shops and in grocery stores.

While this dish requires a little planning and special equipment you might not have in your kitchen, it really only involves three simple steps: First is a 24-hour brine, second is sealing the meat in a vacuum sealer like FoodSaver® or Ziploc® vacuum seal bags, and third is cooking in a temperature-controlled hot-water bath for 24 hours with an immersion or thermal circulator (sous vide).

The sous vide technique keeps meat at an even temperature for an extended period of time, in this case 24 hours, breaking down fibrous tissues and making the pork incredibly tender while infusing it with more flavor from the brine in the vacuum-sealed bag. Time aside, this small plate meal can be made ahead of time; the Sorghum–Chipotle Glaze (facing page) can be made in advance as well. Warm up the glaze and trim and sear the meat right before serving. Serve with Spiced-Up Southern Greens (p. 102) for a flavorful and impressive dish. The sweetness of the smoky pork glaze and the succulent pork pair beautifully with the tanginess and slight heat of the greens.

SERVES 6 TO 8

FOR THE BRINE	3 whole cloves
2 quarts water	3 juniper berries
1 cup granulated sugar	
½ cup kosher salt	One 2-pound pork belly
1 tablespoon black peppercorns	Sorghum–Chipotle Glaze (facing page),
3 bay leaves	for serving

In a large nonreactive saucepan, combine the brine ingredients and bring to a boil, stirring to dissolve the sugar and salt. Remove from the heat, let cool to room temperature, and transfer to an airtight container. Refrigerate until chilled, 4 to 6 hours. The brine and pork belly should be the same temperature.

Put the pork belly in a nonreactive bowl or dish and pour the cooled brine over the top, making sure the meat is completely submerged. Cover with plastic wrap or a tight-fitting lid and refrigerate for 24 hours.

After 24 hours, remove the meat from the brine, rinse well, and pat dry. Place in a vacuum-seal bag large enough for the pork belly and vacuum-pack the meat. Use a vacuum-seal system such as FoodSaver, Waring® vacuum pack bags, or Waring Pistol Vac to vacuum-seal the pork belly. Using a sous vide, such as Anova or PolyScience®, bring the water temperature in a 5- to 6-gallon stockpot to 170°F. Place the vacuum-sealed meat in the pot, ensure it is fully submerged, and place plastic wrap over the top (not covering the sous vide circulator) in order to reduce evaporation.

After 24 hours, remove the bag from the water bath and submerge in an ice bath to stop the cooking. Once cooled, remove from the ice bath. If you're not going to cook the pork belly immediately, you can leave it in the bag or remove it and wrap it tightly in plastic and refrigerate. (The pork can sit in the refrigerator for up to 3 days before cooking.)

When ready to cook, cut the pork belly in half across the width, then cut it lengthwise into ¾- to 1-inch slices, trimming the fat as desired. Heat a dry cast iron or other large skillet over high heat until hot but not smoking. Add the pork slices so they're laying flat and sear until the first side is brown and crispy, 4 to 5 minutes. (If necessary, cook in batches.) Flip and cook on the other side for about 4 minutes, until both sides have a nice brown crust. Serve immediately drizzled with Sorghum–Chipotle Glaze. If you like, plate the pork in individual servings over Spiced-Up Southern Greens (p. 102).

CHEF'S TIP ❯ This recipe is the only one in the book that requires an immersion circulator, or sous vide. My intent in including this recipe was to introduce you, the home cook, to this tool with a recipe that is made fabulous through the use of the technique. Immersion circulators were once only available to chefs because the equipment was expensive. Thanks to companies like PolyScience and Anova, home cooks can now purchase their own immersion circulator at a very reasonable price.

SORGHUM—CHIPOTLE GLAZE

. . . .

MAKES ½ CUP

½ cup sorghum
1 tablespoon Chipotle in Adobo Purée (p. 114)

2 tablespoons Grade A dark amber or Grade B pure maple syrup

Combine the ingredients in a small bowl and whisk until smooth. Cover and keep at room temperature until ready to serve (or for longer storage, cover and refrigerate for several days). You can also warm the glaze slightly in a saucepan over low heat before serving.

CHEF'S TIP ❯ Sorghum, a traditional Southern ingredient, is made from the sorghum cane plant and is a lighter and sweeter syrup than molasses. Although sorghum is grown in a number of rural areas across the country, there are only a few major sorghum producers in the United States today, and they're located primarily in the South. At Seviche, we buy sorghum from Bourbon Barrel Foods® in Louisville (for more on Bourbon Barrel Foods, see pp. 246–247).

. . . .

BOURBON MOJITO

The first week of May is one big party in Louisville, all focused on a 2-minute horse race, the Kentucky Derby. And nothing says Derby more than the traditional Mint Julep. A Kentucky Latino's answer to the Mint Julep, my Bourbon Mojito is less sweet and more refreshing than the traditional Kentucky cocktail, and it can be enjoyed year-round, especially on a hot summer's day. My version is made with Woodford Reserve® bourbon, but you can use your favorite bourbon. If you like, mix up a batch in a pitcher when entertaining a crowd and serve over ice followed by a splash of club soda.

MAKES 1 COCKTAIL

1 tablespoon granulated sugar	1½ ounces sweet and sour mix (I use Finest Call® or homemade)
3 to 4 leaves fresh mint	Soda water or club soda
½ lime, sliced	Sprig of fresh mint, swizzle stick of fresh sugar cane (if available), and a slice of fresh lime, for garnish
2 ounces Kentucky bourbon	

Muddle together the first three ingredients in a cocktail glass. Add the bourbon and sweet and sour mix and shake well with a cocktail shaker over the top of the glass. Pour into an ice-filled tall cocktail or mixer glass (12 to 14 ounces) and top with a splash of soda water or club soda. Garnish with a swizzle stick of fresh sugar cane, a sprig of mint, and a lime slice.

PASSION FRUIT CAIPIRINHA

I love the slightly sweet and tangy flavor of passion fruit. It's not widely used on restaurant menus, but its flavor is unique and refreshing. Cachaça, the base ingredient of Brazil's national drink (the Caipirinha), is a distilled spirit made from sugar cane. This cocktail pairs well with an appetizer that has a bit of spice or heat, like the Kentucky Bison Empanadas (p. 35) or Crispy Chicken Liver Anticuchos with Aji Panca (p. 26).

It's best to use unsweetened passion fruit purée for this cocktail (I use The Perfect Purée® of Napa Valley; see Resources on p. 277). Most Latin markets carry some form of passion fruit purée, but many contain added sugar, so be sure to check the label. If you use sweetened purée, then you'll need to adjust the sugar to taste.

½ lime, sliced, plus an additional slice for garnish	2 ounces soda water or club soda, divided
1½ tablespoons superfine sugar	1½ ounces Cachaça (I prefer Cachaça 51)
	1 tablespoon unsweetened passion fruit purée

Muddle together the ½ lime, sugar, and 1 ounce of the soda water or club soda in a cocktail glass until the mixture is cloudy. Add the Cachaça and passion fruit purée and fill to the top with ice. Top with a cocktail shaker and shake just until the sugar has dissolved. Finish with the remaining soda water or club soda and garnish with the reserved lime slice.

VARIATION > Add some of your favorite fresh herbs such as thyme, rosemary, mint, or basil for a more complex flavor, just as you would add mint to a mojito. If you like, substitute 6 smashed, fresh raspberries for the passion fruit purée to make a Raspberry Caipirinha. You can also make the cocktail with 1½ ounces vodka instead of the Cachaça. It won't be a Caipirinha, but it will be delicious and refreshing.

COCO LOCO LAMAS

My personality is a little spicy and a little sweet with Latin flair, so I came up with a drink that fits that description. Some people think I'm a bit loco (I say passionate!), thus the name of this cocktail. I enjoy rum in cocktails as well as in other recipes, like Banana–Rum Pudding with Toasted Coconut (p. 255), so I'm happy to see rum making a comeback on restaurant menus. I hope this trend continues, but if not, we'll start our own with this drink.

This tasty concoction can be served as small shots or a single cocktail served straight up in a chilled glass or over ice. You'll find this drink reminiscent of those you sip while relaxing on a white sandy beach on the shores of the crystal blue water of the tropics. If you can't take that vacation this year, then make a Coco Loco Lamas and be transported to the Caribbean.

1 ounce Malibu® rum	Juice of ½ lime
1 ounce spiced rum (I like Captain Morgan® or Sailor Jerry®)	1 ounce piña colada mix or Coco Reàl® Cream of Coconut
3 ounces orange juice (preferably freshly squeezed)	Slice of fresh pineapple, for garnish

Fill a cocktail shaker with ice. Add all of the ingredients except for the slice of pineapple and shake vigorously for 20 seconds. Pour into shooter glasses, a chilled martini glass, or over ice in an 8-ounce cocktail glass and garnish with the pineapple.

CRISPY CHICKEN LIVER ANTICUCHOS WITH AJI PANCA

This recipe is a perfect example of taking a traditional Latin dish, Anticuchos, and preparing it with a Southern favorite, fried chicken livers. Anticuchos originated in Peru and are usually served skewered and made with inexpensive cuts of meat, such as organ meats. Organ meats are very economical to prepare and are often overlooked. In fact, one of my favorite dishes is liver and onions.

This is one of the most popular appetizers at Seviche. In fact, many people say they are the best damn chicken livers they've ever had. The bite-size pieces are double dipped in buttermilk and a mixture of flour and spices, which makes them extra crispy, and then they're topped with a simple garnish of sautéed shallots. Paired with a flavorful dipping sauce of Aji Panca, which has just the right balance of heat and spice, you will become a convert, too. I have converted many chicken liver haters into chicken liver lovers with this dish.

To make a really festive serving plate for entertaining, garnish the chicken livers with cooked and sautéed *choclo* (Peruvian corn) or in-season roasted yellow corn kernels and, if desired, Country Ham Chipotle Demi-Glace (p. 238) and micro celery or celery leaves. Purchase small (4-inch) bamboo skewers for serving the livers to make your own authentic Anticuchos.

MAKES ABOUT 16 PIECES · SERVES 6 TO 8

FOR THE CHICKEN LIVERS	FOR THE TOPPING
1 cup all-purpose flour	2 tablespoons unsalted butter
2 teaspoons smoked Spanish paprika (pimentón)	4 medium to large shallots, thinly sliced
1 tablespoon kosher salt	Pinch of sea salt
2 teaspoons freshly ground black pepper	1 tablespoon red-wine vinegar
2 cups buttermilk	Aji Panca Sauce (p. 230)
1 pound chicken livers, cut into about 16 pieces	*Choclo* or roasted yellow corn kernels, Country Ham Chipotle Demi-Glace (p. 238), and micro celery or celery leaves, for garnish (optional)
Canola oil, for frying	

MAKE THE CHICKEN LIVERS

Combine the flour, pimentón, salt, and black pepper in a shallow container or bowl and set aside. Pour the buttermilk into another shallow container and add the chicken livers. Cover and refrigerate the chicken livers for 1 hour.

When ready to fry, pour about 1½ inches of canola oil into a cast iron skillet or Dutch oven and heat to 350°F (attach a candy thermometer to the side of the pan to check the temperature). Remove the chicken livers from the buttermilk, then dredge in the flour mixture, shake off the excess, and quickly return them to buttermilk; dredge again in the flour and shake off the excess. Place on a wire rack until ready to fry. Add the livers to the hot oil and fry until they're brown and crispy and float to the surface, 1½ to 2 minutes. Work in batches, if necessary, so that the livers are not crowded in the pan; be sure the temperature of the oil remains at a constant 350°F. If needed, increase the heat to bring the oil back to temperature after adding the livers. Drain the cooked livers on paper towels and fry the remaining livers, if you cooked in batches. Keep warm.

MAKE THE TOPPING

While the chicken livers are frying, melt the butter in a medium skillet over medium-high heat until the foaming subsides. Add the shallots and season with a pinch of sea salt. Cook, stirring occasionally, until the shallots are lightly caramelized, about 5 minutes. Deglaze the pan with the vinegar and remove from the heat.

TO SERVE

Arrange the chicken livers on a serving platter. Top each with a few pieces of caramelized shallot and drizzle with Aji Panca (or serve Aji Panca in a bowl along-side the livers). If you like, garnish the plate with *choclo* or roasted yellow corn kernels, Country Ham Chipotle Demi-Glace, and micro celery or celery leaves. Serve while still warm.

FRIED GREEN TOMATOES WITH LEMON—HABANERO MISSISSIPPI COMEBACK SAUCE

Green tomatoes are a topic of intense debate in the South. Are green tomatoes really green or are they red tomatoes that just aren't ripe? Well, the answer is both. Purists seek out varieties that are green when mature, such as Green Zebra, Green Pineapple, or Green Giant. But when a true green tomato matures, it becomes too soft to use in this quintessential Southern dish. So regardless of whether you use a mature green or an unripe red tomato for frying, it must be firm.

My version of this Southern dish uses a traditional buttermilk dip for the batter, but we also spice things up with a Latino twist on another beloved Southern recipe, Mississippi Comeback Sauce. Stacked on a plate and topped with the subtly spicy sauce, the presentation is playful and the final result is an elevated version of a classic summertime favorite. →

SERVES 4

FOR THE LEMON–HABANERO MISSISSIPPI COMEBACK SAUCE

1 cup buttermilk

1 cup sour cream (not low-fat)

¼ cup mayonnaise (not low-fat)

¼ teaspoon habanero powder, plus more as needed

½ teaspoon ground oregano

¼ teaspoon garlic powder

¼ teaspoon onion powder

1 teaspoon freshly ground black pepper

1 tablespoon kosher salt

1 tablespoon tomato paste

Juice and finely grated zest of 1 lemon

FOR THE FRIED GREEN TOMATOES

2 large eggs

2 cups buttermilk

3 large green tomatoes, firm but not too hard, sliced ½ inch thick

2 cups fine day-old breadcrumbs, toasted, or plain dry packaged breadcrumbs

1 teaspoon kosher salt, plus more as needed

½ teaspoon ground white pepper, plus more as needed

Canola oil

Micro greens, for garnish (optional)

MAKE THE SAUCE

In a small bowl, whisk all ingredients together until thoroughly combined. Taste for seasonings. For a bit more heat, add a little more habanero powder to taste. Cover and refrigerate for at least 1 hour before serving. Any leftovers will hold for several days.

MAKE THE FRIED GREEN TOMATOES

Lightly beat the eggs in a shallow dish, then whisk in the buttermilk. Arrange the tomatoes in the dish and let soak in the egg and buttermilk mixture for ½ hour. In another shallow dish, combine the breadcrumbs, salt, and white pepper. Mix well and set aside.

Meanwhile, pour 2 inches of canola oil in a large cast iron skillet or Dutch oven. Heat the oil to 350°F (attach a candy thermometer to the side of the pan), checking the thermometer to make sure it stays at this temperature throughout the frying process.

Remove a tomato slice from the egg and buttermilk mixture, letting excess liquid drain off, then dredge in the crumb mixture. Repeat, placing the tomato slice back into the buttermilk mixture and then quickly dredging again in the crumbs. Shake off the excess crumbs and quickly add the tomato to the hot oil. Repeat with the remaining tomato slices.

Fry the tomatoes for 1 to 2 minutes on the one side, or until the coating is nicely browned. Flip the tomato slices over using a large spoon or spider and fry on the second side until crispy and brown, another 1 to 2 minutes. Be sure to fry just a few slices at a time and don't crowd the pan; otherwise the temperature of the oil will drop and the fried tomatoes will not brown properly and be oily. As you add tomatoes, be sure the temperature of the oil remains at a constant 350°F. If not, adjust the heat as needed. Carefully remove the tomatoes with a large spoon, spider, or spatula and

drain on paper towels. While hot, season them with a little bit of salt and white pepper. Repeat until all the tomatoes are fried.

TO SERVE

Stack three fried green tomato slices in the center of a serving plate and garnish with micro greens, if desired, and drizzle with the Lemon–Habanero Mississippi Comeback Sauce. Serve more sauce on the side, if you like.

CHEF'S TIP > The Lemon–Habanero Mississippi Comeback Sauce makes a pint. It will keep, covered, for several days in the refrigerator and makes a great dipping sauce for chicken wings; it's also a delicious salad dressing. This sauce is so good you just might find yourself dipping your finger in the leftovers and enjoying it all by itself.

MEET SARA CRAVENS DUNCAN ❯
DUNCAN FARMS, BOSTON, KENTUCKY

FROM ANTHONY

Sara is a local farmer who supplies Seviche with fresh eggs. We're probably the largest buyer of her eggs, taking about 20 dozen every time she visits. There is something special about cracking open and tasting a fresh egg that's been laid just hours before by a farm-bred, free-range hen. Even my line cooks notice the difference. You can see and taste the richness of the beautiful golden yellow yolks; there is nothing that compares to these eggs when you're cooking. They make an incredible difference in our flans, custards, ice cream, and puddings; even our guests notice the flavor and texture of our desserts that can only be attributed to these amazing eggs.

FROM SARA

When people ask me what I used to do before my husband and I owned the farm, it's usually quite a surprise. I was in the military for 2 years in the mid-'60s and then I worked for the federal government for 15 years. During that time I worked in fire control for the M60 series and Abrams tanks. I also handled EEO (equal employment opportunity) complaints and was elected by three states to serve as the National Women's Representative for the union organization, the American Federation of Government Employees (AFGE).

In November 1997 I was diagnosed with breast cancer and had a complete mastectomy and reconstruction the following year. In March 1998 I was offered a buyout from the government and had only considered it, until one day on my way home from work I had a car accident. I remember thinking, as I slid down a hill heading toward a semi truck, that life was too short to be doing this, so I opted for the buyout. I decided I'd had enough and wanted to work from home, so my husband and I purchased some land and started Duncan Farms. I haven't regretted the decision once.

When we first bought the farm, which is about 5 acres, we also raised rabbits and sold them to local chefs. There are a lot of issues with raising rabbits, though, so we got out of that business and now focus exclusively on our girls—our egg-laying chickens. We sell our eggs to a number of local chefs, including Anthony, and we also sell them at several local farmers' markets year-round.

We keep approximately 1,200 chickens at the farm, which are allowed to roam free. They eat from the pastures and fields, where they find their natural foods, as well as the feed we provide. They lay their eggs in the coop, but the truth is, you can find eggs almost anywhere. A favorite spot is in the tool shed on a shelf, preferably with some straw as bedding. You can walk along a path and find a hen scratching a hollow in the dirt where she'll settle in to lay her egg. Life is good here for the hens—it's natural.

We raise two breeds of hens: the Araucana, which lays beautiful blue-green eggs, and the other is a cross between a Rhode Island Red and White Rock Hen. That breed lays the more traditional brown egg. We're currently in the middle of some expansions for the farm, both in the number of chickens we have along with purchasing some equipment, such as egg washing machines. This will eliminate some of the work that is currently done by hand.

I much prefer our life on the farm to the job I used to have. It's the hardest work I've ever done, but we have our girls, our land, our pond, and our geese that greet you when you arrive. It's a simpler life that is filled with fresh air, no boundaries, and old-fashioned hard work.

GEORGIA PECAN—ENCRUSTED BRIE

My customers go crazy for this dish when it's on the menu—and they go even crazier when we take it off! The flavors of the pecan crust with the melted brie are delicious; it's almost like dessert. You can serve the brie alone or topped with fruit preserves, like a spicy fig jam or Peach–Habanero Preserves (p. 197). At Seviche, we pair the brie with a quick and simple Habanero Pepper Jelly (p. 34), which gives it a nice balance of sweetness and heat.

We garnish the brie with fresh seasonal berries or figs and crackers in the spring and summer. It is also festive to serve during the holidays. You can prepare and coat the brie up to a day ahead and then refrigerate it. You can also brown the brie before guests arrive, pop it in the refrigerator, and then place in the oven to warm right before serving. If you make the Habanero Pepper Jelly, it also can be prepared ahead of time and then served at room temperature with the warm brie.

SERVES 8 TO 10

2 cups pecan halves	Nonstick cooking spray
½ teaspoon kosher salt	1 small wheel of brie (a little over 1 pound), still firm and not ripe, cut into quarters
½ cup granulated sugar	
½ cup light brown sugar	
1 teaspoon freshly grated nutmeg	Canola oil
1 teaspoon ground cinnamon	Fruit preserves, fresh berries, or figs, for garnish
1 cup all-purpose flour	
2 cups half-and-half	Habanero Pepper Jelly (p. 34; optional)
2 large eggs, lightly beaten	Flatbreads or crackers, for serving

Place the pecans, salt, both sugars, nutmeg, and cinnamon in a food processor and pulse until the nuts are almost completely chopped (you want small pieces, but not too fine). Place the mixture in a shallow dish and set aside.

Place the flour in a shallow dish. In another shallow dish, combine the half-and-half and the eggs and whisk well. Line a baking sheet with parchment and spray with nonstick cooking spray; set aside.

Position the dishes so that the liquid is first, then the flour, and finally the nut mixture. With two hands, keeping one wet and the other dry, place two pieces of brie in the liquid. Let them soak for about 5 minutes, turning to coat them well. Make sure the rind is saturated. Working with one piece of brie at a time, remove it from the liquid and then dredge in the flour with a dry hand, coating it well and shaking off excess flour. Dip the brie back into the liquid with your wet hand, coating well again with liquid. With your dry hand, dip the brie piece into the nut mixture and turn to coat well, packing it on heavily and patting the mixture on the brie to make sure it sticks all over. Place the nut-coated piece on the prepared baking sheet. Continue the process with the other three brie pieces, then refrigerate for at least an hour and up to 1 day. →

When ready to cook the brie, pour enough canola oil in a cast iron skillet or Dutch oven until it thoroughly coats the bottom and comes up the sides about ½ inch. Heat the oil to 300°F (clip a candy thermometer to the side of the pan). Line a baking sheet with a clean sheet of parchment and spray with nonstick cooking spray. Gently add the brie pieces to the hot oil, in batches if necessary so they don't crowd the pan, and cook until the first side is lightly browned, about 1 minute. Carefully turn the brie pieces over and cook for about another minute until each piece is evenly browned. Remove and drain on paper towels, then place on the prepared pan. Continue cooking the remaining brie pieces, then refrigerate them for about 30 minutes before finishing in the oven. This will keep them firm so they hold their shape before baking. You can prepare the brie up to this point, cover lightly, and refrigerate for up to 12 hours before baking.

When ready to serve, heat a convection oven to 350°F. Bake the brie until it has warmed through but is not melting out of the nut coating, 10 to 15 minutes, checking after 10 minutes. Arrange slices of brie on a platter and serve immediately, garnished with fruit preserves, fresh fruit, or Habanero Pepper Jelly and flatbreads or crackers.

CHEF'S TIP ❯ A food processor makes short work of mixing, cutting, and chopping ingredients. I have used a Magimix® by Robot-Coupe for most of my professional career. Now the company has models available for the home cook. You'll find a reliable, high-powered food processor will simplify everything from making pie crust or empanada dough to shredding cheese, slicing vegetables, and chopping nuts.

HABANERO PEPPER JELLY

1 cup granulated sugar	1 teaspoon honey, plus more to taste
1 cup red-wine vinegar	½ teaspoon crushed red pepper flakes
1 habanero, trimmed, seeds and membranes removed, and finely minced (¾ to 1 tablespoon)	

Combine the sugar and vinegar in a medium saucepan and bring to a boil, then add the habanero, stirring to thoroughly combine. Continue to boil until the mixture is reduced by half, syrupy, and coats the back of a spoon, 5 to 7 minutes. Let cool, then transfer to a small bowl and whisk in the honey and red pepper flakes.

CHEF'S TIP ❯ If preparing the Habanero Pepper Jelly ahead, you might need to warm it and thin with a little water or red-wine vinegar before using.

KENTUCKY BISON EMPANADAS

Empanadas are the Latin version of the American turnover, and the flavor possibilities are endless. We make several types of empanadas at Seviche, but this one is always the most requested. Bison meat has become very popular due to its health benefits and lower fat content than beef. Bison has a very mild flavor, so we season it with just a little bit of heat. We serve these empanadas with ether Salsa Verde (p. 243) or Latino Butter (p. 236). If you like a spicier sauce, then serve them with the Salsa Verde.

One of our other popular empanadas is a vegetarian version made with wild mushrooms and fresh goat cheese from Capriole Goat Cheese (for more about Capriole, see pp. 62–63) that is served with Sun-Dried Tomato Chimichurri. You can also make dessert versions.

I've included a recipe for homemade empanada dough, but there are several brands of frozen dough rounds that are quite good (like Goya®) and are readily available at most grocery stores (see the tip on p. 36). The recipe is easy to double for a large party, and you can make these ahead of time and store in the refrigerator or freezer until ready to bake. We fry our empanadas at the restaurant (and you can fry these as well); however, this baked version is excellent.

MAKES 16 TO 20 TURNOVERS

FOR THE DOUGH
3 cups all-purpose flour, plus more for dusting
½ teaspoon kosher salt
1 large egg, slightly beaten
12 tablespoons cold unsalted butter, cut into ¼-inch cubes
7 to 8 tablespoons ice water

FOR THE FILLING
1 tablespoon extra-virgin olive oil
¼ Spanish onion, cut into ¼-inch dice (½ cup)
1 teaspoon chopped garlic

1 pound ground bison
1½ teaspoons kosher salt, plus more as needed
1 tablespoon Adobo Rub (p. 245), plus more as needed
3 tablespoons chopped fresh cilantro

Nonstick cooking spray
1 large egg, beaten with a little water, for brushing
Salsa Verde (p. 243) or Latino Butter (p. 236), for serving

MAKE THE DOUGH

Put the flour and salt in the large bowl of a food processor and pulse a couple of times to blend. Add the egg and butter pieces and pulse until the mixture resembles coarse meal. With the machine running, add the ice water and continue to process just until the mixture comes together, forming a ball.

Turn the dough out onto a wooden cutting board or work surface that has been lightly dusted with flour. Shape into a large disk (7 to 8 inches), cover tightly with plastic wrap, and refrigerate for at least an hour and no more than 8 hours.

When ready to roll out the dough, cut the disk in half, rewrap one half, and return it to the refrigerator. Line a baking sheet with parchment. On a wooden board or work surface lightly dusted with flour, roll out the other half of the dough to a ⅛-inch thickness. Cut into rounds using a 4-inch-diameter cutter. Place the dough rounds on the prepared baking sheet, keeping them covered with a kitchen towel so they don't dry out. Reroll the dough scraps into a ball, roll out to ⅛-inch thickness, and cut out more rounds. Repeat with the remaining dough. You should end up with 16 to 20 rounds. Refrigerate until ready to fill.

MAKE THE FILLING

Heat the olive oil in a large skillet over medium-high heat until hot but not smoking. Add the onion and sauté for about 1 minute, and then add the garlic and bison, breaking up the meat with a wooden spoon. Sprinkle with the salt. Cook the mixture for 3 to 4 minutes, or until the meat is lightly browned, continuing to break it into small pieces. Stir in the Adobo Rub and cook for another minute, then taste for seasonings and adjust the salt and/or Adobo as needed. If there are any juices in the pan, turn up the heat and cook until there's no additional liquid. The dough will curb the spiciness of the mixture, so you may want to add additional spice and salt, to taste. Transfer to a medium bowl. Stir in the cilantro, cover, and refrigerate for at least 10 minutes to cool.

FILL AND BAKE THE EMPANADAS

Line a baking sheet with parchment and spray with nonstick cooking spray. Remove the pan of dough rounds from the refrigerator. Spoon about 1 heaping tablespoon of the bison mixture onto the center of one round, then fold the dough over to form a half circle. With a finger or pastry brush, lightly wet the outside edge of the round with water (this will help to seal the dough). Crimp the edges with your fingers or the tines of a fork to seal. Arrange the filled empanada on the prepared baking sheet. Continue with the other dough rounds. (The filling makes a little more than what you'll use for the empanadas. Save the leftovers for a bison taco or two.)

At this point, the empanadas can be lightly covered with plastic wrap and refrigerated for several hours until ready to bake. They can also be placed in the freezer on the baking sheet and, once frozen, transferred to a zip-top bag for longer storage.

When ready to bake, heat a convection oven to 350°F. Brush the empanadas with the egg wash, then bake for 12 to 15 minutes, or until golden brown. (If baking chilled or thawed empanadas, adjust the baking time.) Transfer to a serving platter and serve immediately with Salsa Verde or Latino Butter.

CHEF'S TIP ❯ If you use the Goya prepared dough rounds (which are 5 inches in diameter), you'll need to increase the amount of filling for each empanada as well as the baking time. If the homemade dough rounds shrink a little before filling, simply roll them out slightly or press them out with your fingers.

PERFECT CHERRY—PINEAPPLE MANHATTAN

One of the oldest and best known cocktails, the Manhattan is truly a classic. For our spin on this drink, we add a little pineapple juice and a bit of sweetness from homemade Bourbon Cherries (p. 194). After numerous taste tests—a very tough job, indeed!—we decided that the balance of sweetness to bourbon was perfection. You will become addicted to the Bourbon Cherries, if you make them, and will be using them in everything from cocktails to desserts, but you can substitute Luxardo® cherries and use a small amount of the juice from these specialty cherries. You want to use a thick and sweet cherry syrup for this drink, not maraschino cherry juice.

This cocktail was the winner of the Woodford Reserve Challenge in 2003, along with the dish it was paired with, Pork Loin with Chipotle–Orange Bourbon Glaze (p. 133).

MAKES 1 COCKTAIL

2 ounces Kentucky bourbon (I like Woodford Reserve)	Generous splash of sweet vermouth
1¼ ounces unsweetened pineapple juice	1 drop Angostura® bitters
Juice of ¼ lime	⅛ teaspoon juice from Bourbon Cherries (p. 194) or Luxardo cherries
2 teaspoons simple syrup (2 parts granulated sugar to 1 part water)	1 Bourbon Cherry or Luxardo cherry, for garnish

Chill a martini glass. In a cocktail shaker half filled with ice, combine all of the ingredients, except the cherry. Shake several times and then strain into the chilled glass. Garnish with the cherry and serve immediately.

PICKLED JALAPEÑO PIMENTO CHEESE

You'll be hard-pressed to find a Southern chef or home cook who doesn't have his or her own version of pimento cheese. Many of these recipes have been handed down through generations and are top secret. Sometimes referred to as the "pâté of the South," every pimento cheese I've ever tasted has been just slightly different from the others. It's hard to believe there are so many combinations and twists on just a few simple ingredients. This recipe is my spin on this widely popular Southern staple.

Of course, there's a bit of spice and heat in my version. The pickled jalapeño adds a little crunch for texture. If you want the pimento cheese a little hotter, add another chopped pickled jalapeño or another pinch of smoked serrano chile powder or hot paprika. Smoked serrano chile powder has more flavor, but you can substitute hot paprika, if necessary. I like Cabot's™ pepper Jack cheese for this recipe, as it adds a nice peppery flavor compared to others I've tried.

¼ cup (2 ounces) cream cheese, softened (not low-fat)

¼ cup mayonnaise (Duke's® or Hellmann's®, not low-fat)

1 cup (4 ounces) grated sharp Cheddar cheese

½ cup (2 ounces) grated pepper Jack (I like Cabot)

1 pickled jalapeño with seeds, chopped (La Costeña® is a good brand)

1 tablespoon chopped scallions (white and light green parts)

¼ cup chopped canned pimentos (or fresh roasted red pimento peppers)

⅛ teaspoon smoked serrano chile powder or hot paprika, plus more as needed

⅛ teaspoon garlic powder

⅛ teaspoon onion powder

¾ teaspoon freshly ground black pepper

Pinch of kosher salt, plus more as needed

Crackers or toasted baguette slices, for serving

In a small bowl, blend together the cream cheese and mayonnaise. Add the rest of the ingredients and stir to combine. Adjust the salt and chile powder as desired. Cover and refrigerate for a couple of hours before serving to let the flavors come together. Keep in mind that the spice and heat will intensify as the cheese sits. Serve with crackers or toasted baguette slices. The cheese is best when served the same day.

PISCO SOUR

Pisco Sour, a Peruvian cocktail, is made with pisco, a type of pomace brandy that is produced in the winemaking regions of Peru and Chile. Many Latin chefs have a version of this cocktail on their menus since it's such a classic drink. Unique in flavor and attractive to serve, it takes about 100 good shakes to get the egg white perfectly frothy. We've counted numerous times, so we know! Top with a dash of bitters and serve this refreshing drink to guests at the beginning of a special evening where you've prepared a Latin-inspired meal with one of my ceviches (see the chapter beginning on p. 72) or one of my signature dishes, like Moqueca (p. 154), a beautiful Brazilian seafood stew.

MAKES 1 COCKTAIL

1 large egg white

½ lime, sliced

1½ tablespoons granulated sugar

2 ounces pisco

1 cup ice cubes

Angostura bitters

Chill a martini glass. In a cocktail glass, muddle the egg white with the lime slices, sugar, and pisco. Pour into a cocktail shaker filled with the ice. Cover and shake 100 times to froth the egg white. Pour into the chilled glass and top with a dash of bitters.

RIVER OYSTERS (OSTIONES) A LA LAMAS

I love oysters and will eat them no matter how they're prepared. Some of my favorite oysters come from Rappahannock Oyster Co., located on the coastal waters of Virginia (for more on Rappahannock Oyster Co., see pp. 124–125). The company cultivates several varieties of oysters with a different taste and brininess in each. I prefer their signature Rappahannock River Oysters for this dish because of their sweet, buttery, full-bodied flavor.

Rappahannock River Oysters are medium size and have deep shells, making them ideal for this preparation. However, you can substitute other deep-shell briny oysters, such as Blue Point, Malpeques, or Wellfleets. Use cold-water oysters, which are firmer and meatier than warm-water oysters.

My Latin and Southern spin on the classic Oysters Rockefeller uses smoky Benton's bacon, Manchego cheese, and roasted poblano peppers. Make the topping mixture a day ahead. Several hours before serving, prepare and top the oysters. You can then refrigerate them until you're ready to bake and serve.

MAKES 1 DOZEN

1 ounce smoky bacon (like Benton's), finely chopped	2 ounces grated Parmigiano-Reggiano cheese (or use all Manchego)
¼ small Spanish onion, cut into ¼-inch dice (½ cup)	1 roasted poblano, trimmed, peeled, seeds and membranes removed, and chopped (p. 97)
¾ teaspoon kosher salt	2 ounces fresh spinach, roughly chopped
¼ teaspoon ground white pepper	1 dozen medium-size, deep-shell, briny oysters, scrubbed clean (I like Rappahannock River Oysters)
½ ounce Pernod	
1 cup heavy cream	
1½ to 2 teaspoons cornstarch slurry, (p. 118), as needed	Sea salt and water, for cleaning the oysters
	Ice cream salt, as a base for baking
2½ ounces grated Manchego cheese, plus more for garnish	Fine breadcrumbs, for topping
	Lemon wedges, for serving

In a medium skillet over medium-high heat, sauté the bacon for about 2 minutes, until it renders some fat, then add the diced onion. Continue cooking over medium heat until the bacon is lightly browned but not overcooked and the onion is softened, 4 to 5 minutes. Season with the salt and white pepper. Off the heat, add the Pernod and light to cook off the alcohol. Add the cream and return the skillet to the heat. Bring the mixture to a low boil, add the cornstarch slurry, and cook until the mixture thickens, stirring constantly, about 30 seconds. Add more slurry, if necessary, so that the mixture is the consistency of a heavy cream sauce. Stir in the grated cheeses and roasted poblano; mix thoroughly. Transfer the cream mixture to a medium bowl, add the spinach, and mix well. Cover and refrigerate for at least 4 hours and preferably overnight. The mixture will thicken and appear semi-solid.

Several hours before serving, clean and scrub the oysters. To do this, remove the oysters and connective muscle from the shells (see the tip on p. 42). Reserve the oysters and discard the muscle. Wash the shells in salted water, using a mixture of 1 part sea salt to 8 parts water (this replicates ocean salinity). Drain. Rinse the shells to remove any sand or grit.

Lay out the oyster shells on a baking sheet with sides that's covered with a thick layer of ice cream salt. Mound enough salt to keep the shells from tipping over. Put one oyster in each shell and top with 1½ tablespoons of the cream mixture, covering the oyster completely. Refrigerate for about 1 hour.   →

When ready to bake, heat a convection oven to 400°F and top each oyster with a sprinkle of breadcrumbs, pressing the crumbs into the cold mixture so that the bread-crumbs are secure. Make sure the oysters are level on their salt bed, then bake for 11 to 12 minutes, or until the oysters are golden brown, bubbly, and heated through.

Top each oyster with a pinch of grated Manchego and serve immediately with lemon wedges.

CHEF'S TIP ❯ To clean an oyster, wrap one hand with a towel and hold the oyster. Starting at the narrow tip of the hinged end, pry open the shell with an oyster knife. Slide the knife under the oyster and against the shell to remove the oyster and cut the muscle (discard the muscle). Reserve the oyster and dip the shell into salted water to remove the grit.

SPICY DEVILED EGGS WITH PICKLES

No barbecue or casual summer get-together in the South would be complete without deviled eggs. It's one of those starters or side dishes that everyone loves to snack on. Chances are you'll find most folks will have two or three halves on their plate and perhaps even sneak back for one more, so be sure to make plenty.

This version of a summertime favorite adds some crunch with the addition of finely diced dill pickles and celery. It creates an unexpected and interesting layering of flavors and textures. And, of course, there's a little heat from habanero powder, adding another different yet delicious spin. If you put up your own dill pickles, then use them in this recipe; otherwise, store-bought pickles will be fine.

MAKES 16 HALVES

4 dill pickle spears (homemade or store-bought), cut into ⅛-inch dice, divided

1 stalk celery, cut into ⅛-inch dice, divided

8 large eggs, hard-cooked, peeled, and cut in half

½ teaspoon kosher salt

½ teaspoon freshly ground black pepper

2 tablespoons mayonnaise, or more to achieve the desired consistency

1 teaspoon Dijon mustard

½ teaspoon granulated sugar

Pinch of habanero powder or ground cayenne

1 tablespoon minced fresh curly parsley

Paprika, for garnish

Add half of the diced pickles and half of the diced celery to a small bowl and mix to combine. Cover and refrigerate until ready to serve.

Remove the yolks from the hard-cooked eggs and put them in a small mixing bowl. Add the rest of the ingredients, except for the paprika. Mix well to blend thoroughly

and then check for seasonings. Place the mixture in a large zip-top plastic bag, scrape it into one corner, then cut off the corner and pipe the mixture into the egg halves. Alternatively, spoon the yolk mixture carefully into the egg halves. Cover loosely with plastic wrap and refrigerate for at least 2 hours.

When ready to serve, top each deviled egg with a garnish of the reserved celery and pickle mixture and sprinkle with paprika. Serve immediately.

CHEF'S TIP ❯ To ensure easy-to-peel and beautiful egg halves, be sure to use eggs that are at least 10 days old, not freshly purchased. Super-fresh eggs tend to have shells that stick when they're hard-cooked. Do not overcook the eggs and place them in an ice bath for 5 minutes prior to peeling.

CHARRED GULF SHRIMP COCKTAIL WITH HORSERADISH CHIMICHURRI

Shrimp cocktail has been a widely popular appetizer on countless restaurant menus for many years. After all, what's not to love about perfectly cooked and chilled Gulf shrimp dipped in a spicy cocktail sauce? I bet some people order the shrimp just so they can eat the sauce. Since shrimp cocktail is always a hit, especially when entertaining guests at home, I created my own spin on this classic appetizer, seasoning and marinating the shrimp before cooking and then grilling them to achieve a charred crust, which gives the shrimp more complexity in flavor and an interesting texture prior to chilling.

I serve the shrimp with Horseradish Chimichurri, which is made by adding prepared horseradish to my Chimichurri recipe (p. 249). In this shrimp cocktail, it's not just about the sauce, but about the shrimp, too. I use either extra-large Gulf or coastal shrimp from Georgia or South Carolina for this recipe; avoid imported shrimp.

SERVES 4 TO 6

FOR THE SHRIMP

2 teaspoons Adobo Rub (p. 245)

1 teaspoon dried oregano (preferably Mexican), crumbled

2 teaspoons minced garlic

1 teaspoon kosher salt

½ teaspoon crushed red pepper flakes

2 tablespoons extra-virgin olive oil, plus more for the grill

1 pound extra-large shrimp (16/20), peeled and deveined

FOR THE HORSERADISH CHIMICHURRI

1 cup Chimichurri (p. 249)

1 to 2 teaspoons prepared horseradish (not cream style), plus more to taste

Lemon wedges, for serving

PREPARE THE SHRIMP

In a medium nonreactive bowl, whisk together the Adobo Rub, oregano, garlic, salt, red pepper flakes, and oil. Add the shrimp, cover, and marinate in the refrigerator for at least 2 hours, but no more than 4 hours, tossing the shrimp one or two times to distribute the marinade.

To grill the shrimp, heat a gas or charcoal grill to high. Oil the grates and place the shrimp on the grill across the grates so they don't fall into the burner. (You can also skewer the shrimp if that will make cooking them on your grill easier.) Cook the shrimp, flipping them every 30 seconds. Flip them three times on each side so that both sides achieve nice char marks. The shrimp will take between 3 and 5 minutes at most to cook. Remove the shrimp from the grill as soon as they're cooked through, then let cool, cover, and refrigerate for several hours.

MAKE THE CHIMICHURRI

In a small bowl, mix together the Chimichurri and 1 teaspoon of horseradish. Taste and add the other teaspoon of horseradish (or more) as desired. Cover and refrigerate until ready to serve.

TO SERVE

Put the shrimp in a serving bowl and place the serving bowl in a bowl of ice, if desired. Garnish with lemon wedges and serve with the Horseradish Chimichurri alongside for dipping. If you'd rather, plate the shrimp and sauce as a first course.

CHEF'S TIP › Wild-caught shrimp that's been raised in its own habitat, either from the Gulf or East Coast, has a sweet and clean natural flavor. The shrimp are less gritty because they're not being fed commercial feeds like farm-raised shrimp. They are also inspected by the U.S. Department of Agriculture before becoming available from your local fishmonger. If you have a choice between purchasing wild-caught and local shrimp over farm-raised foreign shrimp, choose the domestic and naturally harvested option.

SPICY BLACK-EYED PEA HUMMUS

Black-eyed peas have long been a staple in the South and are usually served in side dishes, like Hoppin' John. Eating them on New Year's Day is a Southern tradition, which is supposed to bring good fortune for the coming year.

If they're known to bring good luck, then I think they should be served more often and prepared in a less traditional way, like hummus. When puréed, black-eyed peas have a similar texture to chickpeas, but offer a unique flavor that pairs well with other ingredients like sun-dried tomatoes, toasted pine nuts, or artichokes. However, I prefer this simple version, made with a little spice from a habanero. It's a quick and delicious appetizer for a party. For more heat, add in the seeds of the pepper, but taste and then decide. If you make this dish ahead, it will get spicier the longer it sits. If you can't find a habanero, then a serrano pepper would be the next choice. Pair the dip with either flour tortillas that have been warmed on the grill or homemade pita chips.

MAKES APPROXIMATELY 2¾ CUPS

1 cup black-eyed peas, picked over and soaked overnight in water	1 small habanero pepper (or serrano), trimmed, seeds and membranes removed, roughly chopped
2 bay leaves	¾ teaspoon kosher salt
1 tablespoon kosher salt	½ teaspoon freshly ground black pepper
3 cloves garlic, roughly chopped	¼ cup extra-virgin olive oil
¼ cup tahini	Warm flour tortillas or homemade pita chips, for serving
Juice and finely grated zest of 1 lemon	

Drain the black-eyed peas and place in a medium saucepan. Cover with water by about an inch and add the bay leaves and salt. Bring to a boil and simmer, partially covered, for 30 to 40 minutes, or until very tender. →

Drain the peas, removing and discarding the bay leaves, and transfer to a food processor. Add the rest of ingredients, except for the olive oil and pitas, and purée until almost smooth. While the machine is running, gradually pour in the olive oil in a steady stream, processing until the mixture is very smooth and the desired texture. You can add a little more oil as needed to loosen up the hummus. Taste and adjust seasonings.

Transfer the hummus to a bowl and serve with the warm tortillas or pita chips. For longer storage, cover the surface directly with plastic wrap (so a skin doesn't form) and then a tight-fitting lid. Refrigerate until ready to use, checking for seasonings before serving. Hummus is best served the day it is made.

WATERMELON AGUA FRESCA

Popular in Mexico as well as the border towns in southern California, this drink is another of my early food memories. Served by street vendors, much like the *mariscos* and fruit stands that I visited as a young boy, this icy and fruity beverage made with watermelon, cantaloupe, pineapple, or other fresh fruits, quickly became a favorite. The translation of the Spanish words agua fresca means "fresh water"—the name alone sounds refreshing.

We love this drink in Louisville in the summertime because of our high heat and humidity, and it's the perfect complement to spicier dishes at Seviche. While some recipes call for puréeing the fruit or straining it out, we serve this version stirred with the fruit and well chilled. It's best when it's freshly made, before all the ice has melted. Be sure to serve with an iced-tea spoon so that you can enjoy the fresh fruit once the juice is gone.

Since fruits will be sweeter at different times of the year, adjust the amount of sugar as necessary. Start with less sugar, then taste, adding more if needed. For a spiked twist, add clear or light liquors such as Puerto Rican white or light rum, vodka, or Cachaça, a natural cane liquor distilled in Brazil.

MAKES A LARGE PITCHER (ABOUT 12½ CUPS)

4½ cups ½- to 1-inch dice watermelon flesh, preferably seedless (approximately half of a 4- to 5-pound melon)

3 quarts ice cubes

1½ quarts ice water

½ to ¾ cup granulated sugar

Thin watermelon slices, lime wedges, or sprigs of fresh mint (optional), for garnish

In a large pitcher, combine the watermelon, ice, ice water, and ½ cup of the sugar. Mix well with a long wooden spoon, stirring briskly to dissolve the sugar. Taste and add the remaining ¼ cup sugar if desired.

Serve immediately in iced-tea glasses, garnished as desired.

VARIATIONS › To make Pineapple Agua Fresca, replace the watermelon with 2 pineapples, peeled, cored, and cut into ½- to 1-inch dice. For Cantaloupe Agua Fresca, replace the watermelon with 2 cantaloupes, peeled, seeded, and cut into ½- to 1-inch dice.

GLAZED SWEET TEA—BRINED QUAIL WITH GRILLED PEACHES & ARUGULA

This dish is the perfect merging of Southern and Latin ingredients, textures, and cultures. The time-honored Southern beverage, sweet tea, is used as a brine for the quail. The quail is then grilled and served with the sweetest summertime local peaches that have been grilled and plated with peppery baby arugula. It's then finished with a Kentucky sorghum glaze with a hint of heat from chipotle peppers and topped with crispy Kentucky country ham pieces or prosciutto.

Quail hunting is a Southern tradition, particularly in south Georgia and north Florida. Usually thought of as a game bird, quail is also raised on farms. If you're not familiar with the species, quail are quite small and have darker meat with a flavor stronger than chicken, but less assertive than duck. For this reason, quail can be seasoned more aggressively than chicken or other poultry. I order quail from Manchester Farms, a family producer in South Carolina. I particularly like their semi-boneless quail. Their birds are a little larger than those from other farmers. You can order quail directly from Manchester Farms (see Resources on p. 277) or use other fresh or frozen quail.

SERVES 6 TO 8

FOR THE BRINE
2 quarts water

6 regular-size tea bags

1 tablespoon whole black peppercorns

3 bay leaves

Juice and peeled zest of 1 lemon

Juice and peeled zest of 1 orange

One 2-ounce piece of fresh ginger

1 cup granulated sugar

¼ cup kosher salt

Six to eight 4-ounce semi-boneless quail (ribs removed)

FOR THE GLAZE
1 cup sweet tea brine

½ cup sorghum (or local honey)

3 tablespoons Chipotle in Adobo Purée (p. 114)

½ teaspoon kosher salt

FOR COOKING THE QUAIL
Canola oil

Kosher salt

Freshly ground black pepper

FOR SERVING
3 to 4 peaches, pitted and sliced, and lightly grilled (⅓ to ½ peach per serving)

½ cup diced Kentucky country ham or prosciutto

6 to 8 cups loosely packed baby arugula (about 1 cup per serving)

MAKE THE BRINE

Combine all of the ingredients except the sugar, salt, and quail in a large nonreactive pot and bring to a boil. Once boiling, add the sugar slowly to dissolve. Remove and reserve 1 cup of the brine mixture for the glaze, then add the ¼ cup salt to the pot, stirring to dissolve. Let cool to room temperature and then cover and refrigerate the brine for 4 to 6 hours, or until chilled. The quail and brine should be the same temperature. Add the quail, cover, and refrigerate for at least 6 hours or overnight.

MAKE THE GLAZE

In a small saucepan, bring the reserved 1 cup sweet tea brine to a boil, then add the sorghum, chipotle purée, and salt. Reduce the heat to medium high and cook until the mixture starts to thicken, about 5 minutes. Remove about a quarter of the glaze for basting the quail.

PREPARE THE QUAIL

Heat a gas or charcoal grill on high. (Alternatively, heat an indoor grill or grill pan on high, adjusting the cooking time as necessary.) Oil the grates for the peaches.

Remove the quail from the brine and pat dry. Brush both sides of the quail with canola oil and sprinkle with salt and black pepper.

Grill the quail for 3 minutes on each side, then brush with the reserved glaze (save the rest for serving) and cook for another minute on each side, just until the glaze starts to caramelize. Add the sliced peaches to the grill and cook just until grill marks form and the peaches begin to tenderize, about 1 minute per side.

In a small skillet, cook the country ham or prosciutto pieces over medium heat until brown and crispy. If the prosciutto is very lean, add a little canola oil to the skillet. Remove and drain on paper towels.

TO SERVE

On either a large platter or individual plates, serve the quail on a bed of baby arugula with several slices of grilled peaches and top with the crispy ham or prosciutto. Drizzle the platter or each serving with the remaining glaze.

CHEF'S TIP ❯ Quail can stand up to a bolder wine. Pair the quail with an assertive Pinot Noir (try one from Oregon), a Rioja from Spain, or a stronger red like a Merlot or Barolo. For a white wine, a late-harvest Riesling will go beautifully with the quail.

FIRST
COURSES

SEASONAL SOUPS
& SALADS

THE SALADS and soups in this chapter can be prepared for a family meal, cocktail party, or dinner party. Any of the salad recipes can be beautifully plated for a buffet just as easily as they can be served individually for a more formal sit-down dinner. They can also be doubled for a larger crowd. Get creative with your plating and focus on making the food the star of your table, not just the tablescapes.

I also get creative when serving soup. Any of these soups can be served in 2- to 4-ounce serving cups or glasses that can be passed as appetizers. Garnish them with micro greens and smaller versions of the suggested accompaniments. It's an unexpected and fun way to serve your soup and will surely impress your guests.

However you choose to serve these recipes, be certain to purchase the best ingredients you can find. It does matter in the end result of the dish. Some of the specialty items (like micro-greens) →

Any of the salad recipes can be beautifully plated for a buffet just as easily as they can be plated individually for a more formal sit-down dinner. Get creative with your plating and focus on making the food the star of your table.

are often available only at farmers' markets or local specialty grocers. While visiting these markets you might also find some unique local cheeses, jams, or artisan breads to include with your meal, making the special trip worth the time.

You'll notice that the recipes in this chapter focus on using in-season ingredients for the best flavor and texture. That doesn't mean you can't make these recipes at other times during the year. Simply look for substitute ingredients that are in season; talk to your local sources to see what's available.

Most of the recipes offer tips for preparing some of the components ahead of time to make mealtime and entertaining less stressful. As I mention several times in this book, develop a cooking strategy for preparing your meals. Make a list and get organized. Work backwards from the time you are serving to calculate when different dishes and ingredients need to be added or completed, and always look to those components that can be made ahead to make the plan run more smoothly without overtaxing you, the cook. It will surprise you how much prep work can be done ahead of time and how seamless having guests and entertaining can be. There's nothing more rewarding than hosting a successful party and enjoying yourself at the same time.

CHIPOTLE POTATO—CHEDDAR BISQUE

I don't know anyone who doesn't love this classic comfort food. I like to spice up my version of potato and cheese soup with a bit of Latin heat to offset those cold, and oftentimes, icy winters that Kentucky is known for.

This rich and creamy soup makes a great family meal with a salad and hot crusty bread, or it can be a perfect first course for casual entertaining in the winter months. You can make the bisque ahead and reheat it the next day. If necessary, add a little water to thin it as the potatoes will thicken the bisque overnight. While we use heavy cream when making the soup for serving at Seviche, this recipe is lightened up a bit with a combination of heavy cream and half-and-half. Either way, it's delicious and satisfying and will melt away those winter blues.

MAKES 2½ QUARTS • SERVES 8 TO 10

2 pounds small red-skinned new potatoes, scrubbed and cut in half

3½ teaspoons kosher salt, divided, plus more as needed

1 bay leaf

½ cup sour cream

½ teaspoon ground white pepper

4 tablespoons unsalted butter

1½ cups grated sharp Cheddar cheese, divided

1½ teaspoons canola oil

½ medium onion, roughly chopped (1 cup)

1½ teaspoons minced garlic

3 cups water

2 tablespoons plus 1½ teaspoons Chipotle in Adobo Purée (p. 114)

1 cup heavy cream

1 cup half-and-half

Sour cream, grated sharp Cheddar cheese, crispy bacon pieces (optional), and sliced scallions, for garnish

Put the potatoes in a large pot and cover with water by an inch or two; add 1½ teaspoons salt and the bay leaf and boil until tender, 15 to 20 minutes. Drain the potatoes (discard the bay leaf) and, while they're still warm, mash with the sour cream, white pepper, butter, and ½ cup of the Cheddar. Cover and set aside.

In a large Dutch oven over medium-high heat, heat the oil until shimmering but not smoking. Add the onion and sweat, 2 to 3 minutes. Turn off the heat and then stir in the garlic. Add the water and chipotle purée. Return the pan to the heat and bring to a boil. Add the heavy cream, half-and-half, and 2 teaspoons salt and heat to just about boiling. Add the potatoes and cook over medium-low heat, stirring constantly so the potatoes don't scorch, for about 3 minutes, until the potatoes are warmed through.

Add the remaining 1 cup Cheddar, stirring it in with a wooden spoon, then switch to a whisk and blend until the cheese is completely incorporated. Use an immersion blender or transfer the soup to a high-speed blender and purée until smooth. Adjust the seasonings.

Serve immediately while hot, garnished with a dollop of sour cream and sprinkled with grated Cheddar, crispy bacon pieces (if using), and sliced scallions.

GREEN-CHILE CAESAR SALAD

At one time a very fashionable salad in high-end establishments (particularly steakhouses), Caesar salad was prepared from scratch, tossed, and served tableside. In more recent times, it has become pretty standard fare on restaurant menus. It's still incredibly popular at Seviche. I think Caesar Cardini, who is credited with the invention of Caesar salad, would have enjoyed this Latino-inspired version of his famous salad for his Mexican restaurants. An Italian immigrant, he emigrated to the United States and Mexico and owned several restaurants, which were made famous by his Caesar salad. I add a little heat to the dressing in my version and use Manchego cheese instead of the traditional Parmigiano. My variation also includes toasted tortilla strips and pepitas in place of croutons for the crunch and texture.

The recipe for the dressing makes 1½ cups, and it will hold for several days in the refrigerator. I like to use a combination of romaine and mesclun for the salad, though sometimes I add baby kale, too. Be sure to use just enough lettuce for the number of servings you will need. For an average first course or side salad, you will want about 2 cups lightly packed greens per serving. If you'd like to make this a main-dish meal, add grilled chicken prepared with Adobo Rub (p. 245), marinated grilled salmon, or the Charred Gulf Shrimp (p. 44) for a true south of the border Caesar salad.

SERVES 6

FOR THE DRESSING
4 cloves garlic, smashed
3 large egg yolks
1 anchovy
1 jalapeño, trimmed and sliced (with seeds)
1 teaspoon red-wine vinegar
½ teaspoon Worcestershire sauce
1 teaspoon kosher salt
½ teaspoon freshly ground black pepper
½ teaspoon crushed red pepper flakes
Juice of ½ lemon

¼ cup grated Manchego cheese, plus more for serving
¼ cup chopped fresh cilantro
1 cup extra-virgin olive oil

FOR THE SALAD
8 cups lightly packed romaine lettuce, washed, dried, and torn into bite-size pieces
4 cups mesclun, washed and dried

Crispy tortilla strips, toasted pepitas, and grated Manchego cheese, for garnish

Combine all of the dressing ingredients, except the olive oil, in a high-speed blender (I use my Vitamix). Pulse several times to combine. With the machine running, slowly add the oil until the mixture is emulsified. Taste and adjust seasonings, if necessary. Transfer to a small container, cover, and refrigerate until ready to use.

In a large serving bowl, combine the greens. Drizzle with a little dressing, then toss well and add more if necessary. Taste and adjust seasonings. Transfer to individual plates or leave in the large serving bowl. Top with crispy tortilla strips, toasted pepitas, and grated Manchego. Serve immediately.

CHEF'S TIP ❯ Smashing (or bruising) garlic cloves will release the oils, providing your dish—or the dressing, in this case—with more flavor. To smash garlic, press down on a clove with the side of a large chef's knife (be careful of the blade).

INDIANA SWEET CORN AND COUNTRY HAM CHOWDER

Louisville is a long stone's throw from Indiana. Separated by the Ohio River, this section of the country is known as Kentuckiana for its close proximity and the merger of markets and culture. In southern Indiana you'll find some of the best farmland, and nothing says "the best" more than Indiana sweet corn. While you can use any fresh corn for this recipe, to really achieve an exceptional flavor, only use locally grown, same-day-harvested corn. I use local Kentucky ham from Newsom's for seasoning the chowder (for more about Newsom's, see pp. 104–105), but any good aged country ham will work. I also include Benton's Bacon in the recipe (see Resources on p. 277). This rich, smoky bacon adds another layer of flavor to the soup, as does the addition of fresh lemon juice and zest. Don't forget to top each serving with the suggested garnishes of crispy country ham or bacon and chopped chives or celery leaves.

MAKES 2 QUARTS · SERVES 6 TO 8

1 tablespoon extra-virgin olive oil

3 ounces Kentucky country ham (or other country ham), cut into ¼-inch dice

2 tablespoons ¼-inch diced smoky bacon

6 ears sweet corn, shucked and kernels cut off the cob (keep the cobs, cut in half, and reserve any juice they produce)

1 tablespoon chopped garlic

⅛ Spanish onion, cut into ¼-inch dice (¼ cup)

1 jalapeño, trimmed, seeds and membranes removed, and cut into ¼-inch dice

1 stalk celery, cut into ¼-inch dice

1 russet potato, peeled and cut into ¼-inch dice

2 bay leaves

8 cups organic or homemade chicken stock

1½ teaspoons kosher salt

1 teaspoon ground white pepper

2 cups heavy cream

Juice and finely grated zest of 1 lemon

1 tablespoon roux (p. 118), plus more as needed, for thickening

Cooked country ham or crispy bacon, and chopped chives or celery leaves, for garnish

In a medium Dutch oven over medium-high heat, heat the olive oil until hot but not smoking. Add the ham and bacon and cook until they begin to render their fat, 1 to 2 minutes. Add the corn kernels, garlic, onion, jalapeño, and celery. Stir together and cook for 2 to 3 minutes, or until the vegetables begin to soften but not brown. Add the potato, bay leaves, chicken stock, salt, and white pepper along with the reserved corn cobs and juices (the liquid may not cover them completely); increase the heat and bring to a boil. Once boiling, lower the heat and simmer for 10 minutes, skimming if necessary.

Remove and discard the corn cobs and bay leaves. Stir in the heavy cream, lemon juice, and zest and return to a gentle boil over medium heat. Lower the heat and simmer for 5 minutes.

To thicken the chowder, whisk in the roux, adding more if necessary until the chowder is the desired thickness; bring to a gentle boil and then lower the heat and simmer for another 2 to 3 minutes. Taste and adjust seasonings. Portion the hot chowder into shallow serving bowls, garnish with crispy country ham or bacon and chopped chives or celery leaves, and serve while hot.

KENTUCKY LIMESTONE BIBB, HEIRLOOM TOMATO, AND CUCUMBER SALAD WITH AVOCADO BUTTERMILK DRESSING

This is one of my favorite salads to serve in the summer months. Made with Kentucky Limestone Bibb lettuce from local farmers and beautiful heirloom tomatoes, this salad is quick to prepare, fresh, and delicious. The crunch of the cucumber and bite of the radish pair beautifully with the thick and creamy dressing.

A Latino and Southern spin on the old-fashioned Green Goddess Dressing, the Avocado Buttermilk Dressing is versatile and can be used with green or red leaf lettuces as well. If you can't find Bibb lettuce, substitute an equal amount of butter lettuce for your salad.

SERVES 6 TO 8

FOR THE SALAD	FOR THE AVOCADO BUTTERMILK DRESSING
3 to 4 small heads Bibb lettuce (Limestone or Boston), washed, dried, and torn into pieces, allowing about 2 cups lettuce per serving	½ cup mayonnaise (not low-fat)
	½ ripe avocado, peeled, pit removed
	½ cup buttermilk
3 heirloom tomatoes, cored, any rough spots removed, and cut into wedges	1½ teaspoons kosher salt
	1 teaspoon garlic powder
1 large cucumber, peeled and sliced ¼ inch thick	1 small clove garlic
	1½ teaspoons freshly ground black pepper
¼ red onion, julienned	Juice of 1 lemon
3 radishes, thinly sliced (I prefer organic)	¼ cup chopped scallions (white and light green parts)

MAKE THE SALAD

In a large serving bowl, toss the ingredients together gently. Leave in the bowl or portion among individual serving plates.

MAKE THE DRESSING

Combine all of the ingredients in a high speed blender (like a Vitamix) and purée until smooth. Taste and adjust seasonings. Use immediately or transfer to an airtight container and refrigerate until ready to use.

TO SERVE

Drizzle the salad with dressing and toss lightly. Serve immediately.

CHEF'S TIP > To remove the pit from an avocado, cut the avocado in half lengthwise, around the pit; twist the two halves to release the flesh from the pit. Place the half with the pit on a work surface and quickly but carefully hit the blade of a chef's knife into the pit. Twist slowly and raise the knife to remove the pit. To remove the peel of the avocado, slide a large tablespoon between the avocado flesh and the peel and scoop out the flesh. Cut as desired.

KENTUCKY HEIRLOOM TOMATO GAZPACHO

This soup is best made with local and beautifully ripe heirloom tomatoes. Farmer Brooke Eckmann at Ambrosia Farm in Finchville, Kentucky (read more about Brooke on pp. 182–183), grows over 82 varieties of heirloom tomatoes that taste just like the ones I grew up with as a boy. Her tomatoes are grown with a genuine love of the land, and each variety is unique in its heritage and flavor profile. These tomatoes are the kind you want to source for making this gazpacho. Look for vine-ripened heirloom tomatoes at your local farmers' market or specialty grocery retailer throughout the summer. I like to use a mix of varieties each time I make this soup. If your tomatoes are overly ripe or too juicy, reserve some of the extra juices when you seed the tomatoes and add it, if needed, at the end. Let your taste buds be your guide as you season the soup.

A simple garnish for the gazpacho is a few thinly sliced radishes, halved heirloom cherry tomatoes, micro arugula, or fresh celery leaves (any or all). Served in a chilled glass bowl, the presentation of this seasonal soup is especially attractive. If you want to make it extra special, add grilled fresh local shrimp to the garnish or combine lump crabmeat with watercress and micro celery.

MAKES ABOUT 2 QUARTS • SERVES 8 TO 10

6 large ripe heirloom tomatoes, cored and seeded, bruised spots and blemishes removed, roughly chopped (5½ to 6 pounds before trimming)

1 red bell pepper, trimmed, seeds and membranes removed, and roughly chopped

1 yellow bell pepper, trimmed, seeds and membranes removed, and roughly chopped

1 poblano pepper, trimmed, seeds and membranes removed, and roughly chopped

4 cucumbers, peeled, halved, and seeds removed, sliced thick

⅛ Spanish onion, chopped (¼ cup)

2 cloves garlic, chopped

3 medium jalapeños, trimmed, seeds and membranes removed, and sliced

Juice of 2 limes

Juice of 2 lemons, plus the finely grated zest of 1 lemon

1 small bunch cilantro, stems trimmed

½ cup extra-virgin olive oil

1 cup red-wine vinegar

1 tablespoon kosher salt

1 tablespoon ground white pepper

Thinly sliced radishes, halved heirloom cherry tomatoes, micro arugula, and small celery leaves, for garnish

Combine all of the ingredients except the garnishes in a large nonreactive pot and use an immersion blender to purée to a thick soup-like consistency, leaving some small pieces for color and texture, if desired. (Alternatively, purée the ingredients in a blender; this will have to be done in two or more batches.) If the tomatoes are not very juicy, you may need to add a little bit of water. Do this sparingly so you don't dilute the flavors. Taste and adjust seasonings and then transfer to a plastic or glass container, cover, and refrigerate for at least 2 hours.

To serve, portion into individual serving bowls and garnish with sliced radishes, halved cherry tomatoes, micro arugula, or small celery leaves or any combination of these.

LEMON—ASPARAGUS SOUP WITH FRESH ASPARAGUS SALAD

Central California, where I grew up, is one of the largest producers of asparagus. In addition to the farms that cultivated asparagus, it grew wild on the roadsides in parts of southern California. As a boy, we would sometimes pick the wild asparagus and Mama would use it for a side dish or in soups and salads.

Today, asparagus is available year-round due to transportation from markets in Central and South America. But while beautiful in color and shape, nothing replaces the taste of local asparagus. It is something special to look forward to each spring. Grilled, roasted, steamed, or thinly shaved, asparagus really does seem to ring in the beginning of the new season. This elegant asparagus soup is another way to utilize spring's favorite succulent and tender green vegetable.

Simple fresh asparagus salad served atop the soup, made from a few of the reserved tips and stems, is an impressive garnish that adds texture and crunch and an element of freshness. Each spoonful of the soup is bright with the subtle hint of citrus from the lemon; with just the right amount of cream, the soup has a lovely luscious texture, but it's not too rich. Add the lemon oil a drop at a time to season, until you've achieved the right balance for your taste. Alternatively, you can substitute freshly grated lemon zest.

MAKES 1½ QUARTS · SERVES 6

FOR THE SOUP

1 quart organic or homemade vegetable stock

1 tablespoon plus 1½ teaspoons kosher salt, divided

1 jalapeño, trimmed, sliced thinly with some seeds (or leave all the seeds for a spicier soup)

1 bay leaf

Juice and peeled zest of 1 lemon, divided

½ teaspoon whole black peppercorns

1½ pounds asparagus, bottom stems trimmed and discarded, cut into 2-inch pieces; reserve a few tips and stem pieces for the salad

½ cup heavy cream

2 tablespoons roux (see p. 118)

¼ cup packed shredded Manchego cheese

⅛ teaspoon lemon oil (see Resources on p. 277) or the finely grated zest of ½ lemon

⅛ teaspoon ground white pepper

Pinch of freshly grated nutmeg

FOR THE ASPARAGUS SALAD

Reserved asparagus tips and stem pieces

1 tablespoon extra-virgin olive oil

Pinch of kosher salt

Crumbled fresh goat cheese or grated Manchego cheese, for additional garnish

In a large saucepan or medium Dutch oven, combine the vegetable stock, 1 tablespoon salt, jalapeño, bay leaf, peeled zest, and peppercorns and bring to a boil. Add the asparagus pieces and blanch for 2 to 3 minutes, until tender. Transfer the asparagus to an ice bath to stop the cooking (about 1 minute), then remove them and drain on paper towels; set aside.

Continue cooking the stock for another 10 minutes and then strain through a fine-mesh sieve into a clean saucepan (discard the solids). Stir in the cream and bring just to boiling. Remove from the heat and, working in batches in a high-speed blender, purée equal amounts of the stock and cream mixture and cooked asparagus, placing the puréed mixture in another clean saucepan or medium Dutch oven. Whisk in the roux, a little at a time, until you reach the desired soup thickness. Add the Manchego and stir until melted. Add the lemon juice, lemon oil (a drop at a time) or zest, white pepper, nutmeg, and the remaining 1½ teaspoons salt to taste. Heat through and adjust seasonings.

While the soup is heating through, make the asparagus salad garnish. Place the reserved asparagus in a small bowl, drizzle with the olive oil and salt, and toss gently to coat evenly.

Portion the hot soup in shallow serving bowls, garnish with about 1 teaspoon of the asparagus salad in the center, and top with either a little crumbled fresh goat cheese or grated Manchego.

MEET JUDY SCHAD ❯
CAPRIOLE GOAT CHEESE, GREENVILLE, INDIANA

FROM ANTHONY

Judy was one of the first food artisans I met after I moved to Kentucky. She used to host a party each year and ask local chefs to come out to her farm and cook. I immediately fell in love with her beautiful farm, her goats, and her farmstead cheeses. There is so much care that goes into each and every one of the cheeses she creates. She loves her "girls" and she's a perfectionist—it shows in her farm and in her cheeses.

FROM JUDY

I decided to sell my girls, 500 of them, back in December of 2012. It was the hardest decision I ever made and I actually have only been in the barn a few times since. It's just too sad. I still have a few of the older girls that I can't bear to part with, but I just couldn't care for that many goats any longer.

We sold the entire herd of goats to another farmer who milks them and then brings us the milk, 900 to 1,100 gallons every 3 to 4 days. We had Alpine, Saanen, and Anglo-Nubians. When they were still with us, my husband, who is an attorney, would have to get up in the morning and milk the goats before going to work. It's labor-intensive between the milking and making the cheese. As we got a little older, it just became too much. I really miss the goats, but not the work.

I had goats for over 36 years and have been making cheese for more than 33 years. We now have a team of six trained cheesemakers at Capriole, but

I'm still here to make sure everything runs smoothly and that the products are consistent and what I want to sell to my customers. When you live on the farm, it's hard not to be actively involved. Even if a cheese looks good and ages well, you need to taste the final product to make sure it's what you expect.

We're currently making three aged cheeses, four surface-ripened cheeses, and two fresh cheeses. We started making the O'Banon, a fresh cheese,

in 1988. It's one of my favorites and was inspired by a French cheese called Banon, which is made in the town of Banon in Provence. My O'Banon has won first-place awards eight times in the American Cheese Society competition, and critics have written that it's better than the ones they've tasted in France. We gave it this name in honor of a good friend and the former governor of Indiana who died suddenly years ago. We use a good bourbon to soak the chestnut leaves that the cheese is wrapped in, giving it a decidedly regional feel and a bit of a kick. It's a beautiful cheese and gets better over time, just like a good wine. Every cheese plate should include an O'Banon.

The most exciting thing for me over the years is that I was a part of this whole artisan cheese movement from the beginning, when it was just a handful of women with a couple of goats. All of the things we talked about back then—local, sustainable, and supporting artisans and farmers—has now come to fruition.

LOBSTER AND PUMPKIN BISQUE WITH FRESH GOAT CHEESE

This is a special-occasion soup, perfect when hosting a formal dinner party or sharing a celebratory evening at home with family. It's luscious and rich and has just a hint of heat from habanero powder. Although I think it's perfect with ⅛ teaspoon, feel free to start with a pinch and work your way up.

The best fresh pumpkin to cook with is Sugar Pie or another heirloom variety, like Fairytale. Do not use a carving pumpkin for the recipe. If you'd rather, use the same amount of butternut squash for the pumpkin.

One lobster is enough to make the stock. If you decide to garnish with lobster meat, reserve the meat from the cooked lobster and reheat in a pan with a little butter before plating the soup. If you'd rather garnish with just the crumbled goat cheese, you can use the lobster meat for another recipe.

We use Capriole's fresh goat cheese made in southern Indiana by cheese artisan Judy Schad (for more about Judy, see pp. 62–63). This cheese is mild but provides a unique flavor to the soup. If you can't find fresh goat cheese, use a thin slice of brie.

MAKES 7 TO 8 CUPS · SERVES 6 TO 8

FOR THE STOCK

6 to 7 quarts water (enough to cover the lobster by 1½ to 2 inches)

2 tablespoons kosher salt

2 teaspoons whole black peppercorns

3 stalks celery, roughly chopped

1 carrot, roughly chopped

1½ onions, roughly chopped

Peeled zest from 1 lemon

1 whole live lobster (about 1 to 1½ pounds), killed humanely (see tip on p. 78)

FOR THE BISQUE

1 cup 1-inch diced fresh pumpkin (see the tip on p. 66) or butternut squash

1 cup whole canned tomatoes, crushed

2 tablespoons tomato paste

¾ to 1 teaspoon homemade Sazón (p. 248)

Pinch to ⅛ teaspoon habanero powder

Pinch of freshly grated nutmeg

⅛ teaspoon lemon oil (see Resources on p. 277), or the finely grated zest of ½ lemon

1 cup heavy cream

4 tablespoons roux (see p. 118)

FOR SERVING

Cooked and picked pieces of lobster meat

Dry sherry

Crumbled fresh goat cheese (optional)

MAKE THE STOCK

In a large stockpot, combine all of the ingredients except the lobster and bring to a boil. Add the lobster, bring the liquid back to a boil, and cook for 7 to 8 minutes, just until tender. Remove the lobster and transfer to an ice bath. Drain the lobster, then remove the meat from the tail, claws, and knuckles; refrigerate until ready to use. Remove and discard the intestines from the lobster shell and place the shells back in the pot. Return the stock to a boil and then lower the heat to a simmer and cook for 1 to 1½ hours. Strain the stock through a chinois or fine-mesh sieve into a large, clean stockpot, pushing on the solids to get all the juices. Discard the solids. →

MAKE THE BISQUE

Measure out 1½ quarts of stock and transfer to a large saucepan. (Put the rest in an airtight container and freeze for up to 4 months.) Bring to a boil and add the pumpkin or squash, then reduce the heat to a simmer and cook, partially covered, until the squash is tender, 15 to 20 minutes, skimming the surface of the stock if necessary. When the squash is tender, add the tomatoes, tomato paste, Sazón, pinch of habanero powder, nutmeg, and lemon oil or lemon zest, stirring to combine well; bring the mixture to a boil, lower the heat, and cook uncovered for 10 minutes. Transfer the mixture to a high-speed blender in batches and purée. Transfer the mixture to a large clean saucepan; add the cream, raise the heat to medium high, and bring the mixture just to boiling; reduce the heat and then stir in the roux, a little at a time, cooking over low heat until the soup is the desired consistency. Taste and adjust seasonings.

TO SERVE

If garnishing with lobster meat, place chunks of the meat in a small skillet with about ¼ cup warm water whisked with 1 tablespoon unsalted butter. Baste for a few minutes, just until heated through.

In individual large shallow soup bowls, place pieces of warm lobster meat on the bottom and then pour in the soup. Drizzle with sherry. Alternatively, sprinkle with fresh goat cheese, if using, and serve immediately.

CHEF'S TIP ❯ When working with fresh pumpkin, first carefully cut it into manageable-size pieces with a large sharp knife or cleaver. Put a kitchen towel on the cutting board so the pumpkin won't slip when cutting it. If you're working with a small Sugar Pie pumpkin, cut it in half. If it's larger (like a Fairytale pumpkin), cut it into wedges. Remove and discard the seeds and remove the peel with either a sharp paring knife or vegetable peeler. Then cut the pieces into the desired size for cooking.

BABY KALE AND RADISH SALAD WITH SMOKED BACON, HABANERO CORNBREAD CROUTONS, AND LEMON BUTTERMILK DRESSING

Kale is having a moment. It seems that everyone is talking kale, and I say kale—yeah! This popular and healthy green is easy to prepare and provides a unique take on a traditional green salad. While it's great when sautéed with minimal seasoning or cooked with other Southern greens, I still think it's best served fresh, tossed in a salad with a few crunchy and tasty ingredients, like the Habanero Cornbread Croutons.

Several of my local farmers produce some of the prettiest, most tender baby kale I've ever seen. You can find baby kale at local farmers' markets in season, but if it's not available, use a smaller organic version of red or green leaf kale, which will be less bitter than a larger variety. We use Benton's bacon (see Resources on p. 277) in this salad, which adds a nice smoky flavor, and prepare a quick and easy batch of homemade spicy croutons for a bit of heat. The creamy buttermilk dressing, with its fresh citrus, is the perfect companion to the baby greens, bacon, and croutons. For a variation on the dressing, use 1 teaspoon of crushed pink peppercorns in place of the freshly ground black pepper. It really makes the flavors pop in this salad. The leftover dressing will hold for several days in the refrigerator.

SERVES 4 TO 6

FOR THE DRESSING	FOR THE SALAD
¼ cup mayonnaise (not low-fat)	1 to 2 bunches (12 ounces) fresh baby kale, picked and ribs removed
¼ cup sour cream (not low-fat)	
½ cup buttermilk	4 radishes, thinly sliced (I prefer organic)
Juice and finely grated zest of 1 lemon	4 strips thick, smoky bacon, cooked until crispy, then chopped (I like Benton's)
½ teaspoon onion powder	
½ teaspoon garlic powder	
1½ teaspoons freshly ground black pepper	Habanero Cornbread Croutons (p. 69)
1 teaspoon kosher salt	

MAKE THE DRESSING

In a small bowl, whisk together all the ingredients until well combined. Cover and refrigerate until ready to serve.

PREPARE THE KALE

Tear the kale into bite-size pieces and then rinse well in warm water three times to remove all dirt and grit. (Put the kale in a large bowl of water, swish it around, then lift it out of the water and discard the dirty water; repeat two more times.) Place the rinsed kale in an ice bath in the refrigerator for 30 minutes before serving; this will help keep the greens crisp.

$\rightarrow$

TO SERVE

When ready to serve the salad, remove the kale from the ice bath and dry it in a salad spinner. Pat dry any excess water from the kale on kitchen towels or paper towels. Put the kale in a large salad bowl or on individual plates, then add the radishes, bacon, and croutons (about 5 per serving). Drizzle some of the dressing over the top and toss well. Taste and add more dressing, if desired, or salt and black pepper, as needed. Serve immediately.

HABANERO CORNBREAD CROUTONS

MAKES ABOUT 5 DOZEN

½ cup all-purpose flour	1 large egg, slightly beaten
½ cup cornmeal	½ cup buttermilk
¼ teaspoon baking soda	¼ cup unsalted butter, melted
¼ teaspoon kosher salt	Nonstick cooking spray or canola oil, for the pan
¼ cup granulated sugar	
⅛ teaspoon habanero powder	

Position a rack in the center of a convection oven and heat the oven to 400°F. Grease an 8-inch square pan and set aside. In a medium bowl, whisk the flour, cornmeal, baking soda, salt, sugar, and habanero powder until thoroughly combined. Make a well in the center.

In a small bowl, whisk together the egg, buttermilk, and melted butter. Add the wet ingredients to the dry ingredients, stirring until just combined and large lumps are dissolved. Spread the mixture in the prepared pan and bake for 15 minutes, or just until golden and a toothpick inserted in the center comes out clean. Transfer the pan to a wire rack and let cool.

When ready to make croutons, invert the cornbread from the pan onto a cutting board and cut into 1-inch squares. Heat the oven to 375°F. Grease a cookie sheet with nonstick cooking spray or canola oil, add the croutons, and toast for 8 to 10 minutes, turning once or twice, until lightly browned and crunchy.

CHEF'S TIP > If you'd rather, toast the croutons in a skillet. Melt a little butter in a medium skillet over medium-high heat, add the croutons in batches, and toast, stirring occasionally, until lightly browned.

ROASTED BEETS WITH YOGURT—GOAT CHEESE CREMA

I love to serve this colorful salad in the spring and summer months, when beautiful baby beets are at their best. The good news for a home cook is that so many farmers' markets and supermarkets carry baby beets in season; oftentimes you'll even find special varietals like Chioggia (or candy stripe). If you can't find smaller specialty beets to make this salad, purchase a mix of yellow and red beets and cut them into smaller pieces. They will still make a stunning presentation when plated and will be delicious marinated and served with the Yogurt—Goat Cheese Crema.

The refreshing combination of flavors in the crema is bright and slightly tangy and pairs beautifully with the sweet roasted beets. If you have leftovers, the crema is great to serve on toasted French bread slices as a quick appetizer. Get creative and top with roasted red peppers or sliced baby heirloom tomatoes, prosciutto, and peppery arugula, or sliced fresh figs.

SERVES 6 TO 8

FOR THE BEETS

2 pounds fresh small or baby beets (preferably a mixture of red, yellow, and Chioggia), roasted (see the chef's tip on the facing page)

3 tablespoons Champagne vinegar or white-wine vinegar

1 tablespoon extra-virgin olive oil

1 teaspoon kosher salt

FOR THE YOGURT—GOAT CHEESE CREMA

1 cup crumbled fresh goat cheese

½ cup plain yogurt (regular or Greek, not low-fat)

½ teaspoon Dijon mustard

Pinch of ground cumin

Pinch of ground coriander

Juice and finely grated zest of 1 lemon

1 teaspoon kosher salt

Pinch of ground white pepper

Baby arugula, for serving

Snipped fresh dill, for garnish

PREPARE THE BEETS

Peel and halve the roasted beets or cut larger beets into quarters or 1-inch slices. If using several different colored beets, place each variety into a separate small bowl to avoid bleeding of colors. In another small bowl, whisk together the vinegar, olive oil, and salt until well combined. Divide among the beets evenly and stir, then cover and refrigerate until ready to prepare the salad.

MAKE THE YOGURT—GOAT CHEESE CREMA

In a small bowl, whisk together all the ingredients until well combined and no lumps of goat cheese remain. Taste for seasonings. Refrigerate until ready to use.

TO SERVE

The salad can either be plated on one larger platter or on individual plates. Smear some of the crema on the plates and then arrange the baby arugula, as desired. Stir the beets to distribute the gathered juices, then drain them on paper towels and arrange decoratively on the plates, mixing up the different colors. Garnish with snipped fresh dill. There should be enough of the crema and arugula to enjoy with each bite of the beets.

CHEF'S TIP ❯ Before roasting the beets, wash, dry, and trim them while you heat a convection oven to 400°F. Wrap the beets individually in aluminum foil and place on a baking sheet. Roast for 50 to 60 minutes, checking every 20 minutes for doneness. Smaller beets will cook in less time. They are done when a sharp knife smoothly penetrates the center. Remove from the oven. To peel the beets, cool slightly and then place in a clean kitchen towel. Fold the towel around the beets and rub together to remove the skins.

CEVICHE, CEBICHE, SEVICHE

SIGNATURE SEAFOOD
STARTERS

CEVICHE, CEBICHE, SEVICHE. Any of the three spellings can be used to describe this specialty seafood dish with origins in Central and South America, and in particular, Peru. The traditional preparation for ceviche includes raw fish or shellfish that has been marinated or "cooked" in citrus juice and then seasoned with chile peppers and other ingredients and spices. Onions, corn, and avocado are some of the more common additions to ceviche, but as with any dish, there are countless variations, especially as ceviche has become popular in many countries around the world; each country puts its own spin on the dish.

The recipes I've included here represent the merging of my Latin and West Coast influences, with flavors that are bold and bright. The savory ingredients are colorful and flavorful, and give the texture and crunch that my dishes are known for. Ceviches are beautiful dishes for entertaining. While simple to prepare, they will be unexpected by guests at gatherings and will make you a culinary star. →

Even though you will be "cooking" the fish in citrus and spices, most ceviches are still technically raw fish, so the fish you use needs to be very fresh.

My first experiences eating ceviche were as a young boy, when my family traveled over the Mexican border and we would stop at the *mariscos* (or seafood) stands on the beach. I remember to this day how those ceviches tasted, with their freshly caught fish, bright citrus flavors, and crunch of vegetables like cucumber and jícama. There was a bit of saltiness and heat, too, yet they were so refreshing. Those food memories were so important and such an inspiration to compel me to name my restaurant Seviche.

I was recognized by the local Louisville media as the first chef in Kentucky to introduce ceviche to the state, though I imagine classic Mexican restaurants were already serving ceviches. The ceviches on my menu are some of my signature dishes, like the award-winning Tuna "Old Fashioned," a play on the classic cocktail. Since we have access to some of the freshest fish in the country, with the UPS hub located in Louisville, much of the fish I serve is caught the prior day, so it's incredibly fresh.

In 2011, I was recognized as one of the Sustainable Seafood Ambassadors for the Monterey Bay Aquarium Seafood Watch Program. I partner with this group to spread the word about choosing seafood that's fished or farmed in sustainable ways. In fact, in the summer of 2014, I was the first chef to present a sustainable seafood dinner in partnership with the aquarium at the James Beard House in New York City. It was a great honor to be asked to represent their efforts in seafood sustainability.

I always tell people to refer to the Seafood Watch Program's online guide, or download the app, to know which fish are sustainable and which to avoid. Also, when buying fish, look for the freshest fish that's in season at your local fishmonger and ask what's best for ceviche. Even though you will be "cooking" the fish in citrus and spices, most ceviches are still technically raw fish, so the fish you use needs to be very fresh. While at the seafood counter, have the fishmonger remove the skin and bones so that the fish is ready to slice and prepare.

CRAB CEVICHE

This is a beautiful ceviche that combines a number of summertime's best ingredients, like Indiana sweet corn, baby heirloom tomatoes, and fresh padron or shishito peppers. If you can't source either of those peppers, substitute fresh jalapeños or Fresno chiles. While corn and fresh tomatoes are at their peak of flavor in the summer, fresh crabmeat is often available in the late fall to early spring.

Seasoning each component of the ceviche individually gives it depth and complex layers of flavor. Prepare each of the individual components ahead of time to let the flavors come together and then combine right before serving. Garnish with very thin slices of fresh peppers and colorful heirloom cherry tomatoes for a pop of color, heat, and crunch.

SERVES 6

FOR THE BROTH

Juice of 3 limes, plus the finely grated zest of ½ lime

Juice and finely grated zest of 1 lemon

Juice of 1 orange, plus the finely grated zest of ½ orange

1 tablespoon extra-virgin olive oil

½ teaspoon Tabasco® sauce

1 teaspoon sea salt or kosher salt

FOR THE CORN SALSA

1 ear fresh sweet corn, charred on the grill

¼ cup julienned red onion

Juice of 1 lime

1 tablespoon extra-virgin olive oil

½ teaspoon sea salt or kosher salt

2 tablespoons packed, chopped fresh cilantro

FOR THE TOMATOES

21 heirloom cherry tomatoes, preferably different varieties, shapes, and colors, sliced in half

Juice of 1 small lemon

1 tablespoon extra-virgin olive oil

½ teaspoon sea salt or kosher salt

1 pound lump crabmeat (or whichever style you prefer that's fresh), carefully picked over to remove any shells

3 or 4 fresh padron or shishito peppers, trimmed, seeds and membranes removed, and very thinly sliced in circles (you can substitute Fresno chiles or seeded jalapeños, thinly sliced)

Large pieces of crispy fried homemade tortilla chips, lightly salted (p. 77)

MAKE THE BROTH

In a small bowl, whisk together all the broth ingredients until well combined. Cover and chill until ready to serve.

MAKE THE SALSA

Holding the stem end of the corn cob and placing the pointed tip on the counter or in a bowl, use a knife to cut down the cob, removing the kernels; place in a small bowl. Add the rest of the salsa ingredients, except the cilantro, to the corn. Toss to combine, then cover and refrigerate until ready to serve. →

PREPARE THE TOMATOES

Just before serving, in a medium bowl, toss the tomatoes with the lemon juice, olive oil, and salt; taste for seasonings.

TO SERVE

Whisk the broth to recombine, taste and adjust seasonings, and then add the crabmeat. Toss well to coat the crabmeat. Add the cilantro to the corn salsa, toss to combine well, and then taste and adjust seasonings. Combine the crabmeat mixture with the corn salsa and let sit for a few minutes. Check again for seasonings and adjust if necessary.

On individual plates, evenly portion the crab–corn mixture (scoop it out of the broth), then top each with about 7 thin slices of the pepper and about 7 halves of different colors and varieties of heirloom tomatoes. Add a little crab broth, if desired, and then drizzle each serving with the juices that accumulated from the tomatoes. Garnish with crispy fried tortilla chips and serve immediately.

CHEF'S TIP ❯ If you can't get Maryland blue crab, you can also source stone crab claws from the Gulf of Mexico and all along the Eastern Seaboard to Connecticut. If you're on the West Coast, use Dungeness crabmeat. Fresh crabmeat is often available from October to early spring.

HOMEMADE TORTILLA CHIPS

. . . .

| Canola oil | Kosher salt |
| Large corn tortillas | |

Heat approximately 1 inch of canola oil in a large cast iron skillet to 350°F (clip a candy thermometer to the side of the pan to check). Cut the tortillas into wedges and fry a few at a time, being careful not to crowd the pan, until they're lightly brown and crispy, about 2 minutes. Flip once during frying to ensure both sides are crisped and browned. Remove from the oil with a slotted spoon and drain on paper towels. Sprinkle immediately with the salt. These are best when served just after preparing.

. . . .

—

LOBSTER CEVICHE WITH HEARTS OF PALM, MANGO, JALAPEÑO, AND YUZU

One of the ceviches that most represents my West Coast training and California influence, this elegant starter is perfect for a special occasion or formal dinner party—the combination of fresh mango, citrus, ginger, and a bit of heat is surprising and refreshing. The color of the broth is beautiful when plated with the lobster meat and hearts of palm.

While the recipe calls for cooking and preparing whole lobsters, you could substitute an equal amount of already steamed whole lobsters or tails and then remove the meat from the shells and add the lobster meat to the broth. The meat will, however, miss the flavor added by boiling it with lemongrass and ginger.

SERVES 4 TO 6

FOR THE LOBSTER	FOR THE BROTH
½ onion, diced (1 cup)	Juice of 6 limes
1 carrot, roughly chopped	1 fresh mango, peeled, pit removed, and cut into ½-inch dice
1 stalk celery, roughly chopped	Juice of 2 oranges
1 teaspoon whole black peppercorns	¼ cup yuzu juice (or additional lime juice)
Peeled zest of 1 lemon	2 teaspoons finely chopped fresh ginger
1 stalk lemongrass, cracked	1 tablespoon extra-virgin olive oil
One 1-ounce piece fresh ginger, peeled	1 jalapeño, trimmed, seeds and membranes removed, and cut into ⅛-inch dice
1 tablespoon kosher salt	1 tablespoon sea salt
2 whole live lobsters (1¼ to 1½ pounds each), killed humanely (p. 78)	
	1 cup sliced hearts of palm, for garnish
	Fresh celery leaves, for garnish →

COOK THE LOBSTERS

In a large stockpot, combine all of the ingredients, add enough water to cover the lobsters by at least 1½ inches, and bring to a boil. Cook until the lobsters are just tender and the shells turn red, 7 to 8 minutes. Remove and plunge in an ice water bath. Discard the cooking water. When the lobsters are cool enough to handle, crack the shell and remove the meat from the knuckles, claws, and tail and cut into 1-inch pieces. Place the lobster meat in a medium bowl or shallow glass container and set aside.

MAKE THE BROTH

Place all of the ingredients for the broth in a high-speed blender and purée until smooth. Pour over the lobster meat, cover, and refrigerate for 4 hours.

TO SERVE

Arrange the chilled lobster meat on individual serving plates and serve topped with the hearts of palm slices. Drizzle a little broth over each plate and garnish with the fresh celery leaves. Serve immediately.

CHEF'S TIP ❯ The most humane way to kill a live lobster is by placing it in the freezer for about 15 minutes so it becomes immobile. Remove the lobster from the freezer and place it on its back on a cutting board. Relax the tail by straightening it out. Place the point of a large (8- to 10-inch) chef's knife at the center of the lobster just below the large claws. With the blade facing toward the head, quickly push the point of the knife through to the cutting board and slice forward through the center of the head. This motion kills the lobster instantly. It is not unusual for the lobster to spasm, an involuntary nerve response and not the lobster reacting. The lobster can then be placed into the boiling water.

PICKLED GEORGIA SHRIMP WITH CUMIN—CORIANDER BROTH

Pickled shrimp is a Southern favorite and is usually made with steamed or boiled shrimp that has been pickled with a mix of vinegar, onions, traditional pickling spices or mustard seeds, and garlic. Of course, my version takes the traditional and amps up the flavors and presentation with a bit of heat, spice, citrus, and a fresh vegetable salsa for texture and crunch. Think of it as Southern pickled shrimp meets ceviche.

If you don't have access to Georgia shrimp, then use Gulf shrimp. As a proponent of using only sustainable seafood that is wild or line caught, I do not recommend using farmed or imported shrimp.

You can prepare all of the components for this dish ahead of time and then assemble the ceviche right before serving. The piquant flavor of the cumin—coriander broth is delicious with the perfectly cooked shrimp and fresh vegetable salsa. Elegantly garnished, this is another favorite dish at Seviche. →

SERVES 4 TO 6

FOR THE SHRIMP

2 quarts water

¼ Spanish onion, roughly chopped (½ cup)

Peeled zest from ½ lemon

½ teaspoon whole black peppercorns

1 teaspoon kosher salt

1 jalapeño, trimmed and split

3 bay leaves

1½ pounds extra-large (16/20) fresh Georgia shrimp, peeled and deveined

FOR THE CUMIN–CORIANDER BROTH

1 cup red-wine vinegar

2 cloves garlic, finely minced

1½ teaspoons cumin seeds, toasted

1½ teaspoons coriander seeds, toasted

1 tablespoon kosher salt

1 teaspoon freshly ground black pepper

Juice of 2 lemons

1 tablespoon extra-virgin olive oil

FOR THE SALSA

2 stalks celery, cut into ¼-inch dice

1 cucumber, peeled, sliced, seeds removed, and cut into ¼-inch dice

¼ fennel bulb, cut into julienne

¼ red onion, cut into ¼-inch dice

¼ red bell pepper, cut into ¼-inch dice

¼ yellow bell pepper, cut into ¼-inch dice

1 jalapeño, seeds and membranes removed, and cut into ¼-inch dice

Juice of 1 lemon

Heirloom cherry tomatoes, sliced in half and tossed with extra-virgin olive oil and pinch of sea salt (1½ tomatoes per person); thinly sliced radishes; snipped fennel fronds or micro greens; and sea salt, for garnish

MAKE THE SHRIMP

In a large pot, combine all of the ingredients, except the shrimp, and bring to a boil. Once boiling, add the shrimp and continue to boil for 2 to 3 minutes, just until the shrimp are translucent. Remove the shrimp and plunge into an ice water bath. With a strainer or slotted spoon, remove the shrimp from the ice bath and refrigerate until ready to serve.

MAKE THE BROTH

Combine all of the ingredients except the olive oil in a high-speed blender and process until smooth. With the machine running, slowly add the olive oil until emulsified. Transfer the broth to a small container and refrigerate until ready to use.

MAKE THE SALSA

In a small bowl, toss together the vegetables and lemon juice. Cover and refrigerate until you're ready to assemble the ceviche.

TO ASSEMBLE

Add the salsa ingredients to the cumin–coriander broth and stir to combine. If plating individual servings, evenly portion the shrimp among shallow serving bowls, then spoon a little salsa over the top. If serving on a platter, arrange the shrimp, then spoon a little salsa evenly over them. For either plating option, drizzle broth over the top of the shrimp and salsa, then garnish with cherry tomatoes, radishes, and fennel fronds or micro greens. Sprinkle with a little sea salt to finish.

SOUTHERN CRAWFISH ESCABECHE

The first time I visited Louisiana, I was introduced to a number of dishes made with crawfish, like étoufée, jambalaya, and a crawfish boil. I fell in love with this local shellfish that's widely used in Cajun and Creole cooking. Crawfish, also commonly referred to as crawdads or mudbugs, are similar in appearance to lobsters, only much smaller. The phrase "Eat the Tail and Suck the Head" is heard in Bayou Country when eating steamed crawfish. This essentially means that in order to eat them properly, you pinch the tails to push the meat out of the shell and then in turn, take off the heads and suck the juices, which is considered a delicacy in this region. It takes a bit of getting used to, but these little crustaceans are mighty tasty once you know what to do with them.

SERVES 4 TO 6

FOR THE CRAWFISH
1 pound frozen steamed crawfish tails, thawed, rinsed, and drained
2 tablespoons extra-virgin olive oil
Juice of 2 lemons
Juice of 2 limes
1 tablespoon kosher salt

FOR THE SALAD
½ red onion, cut into julienne
½ red pepper, cut into julienne
½ yellow pepper, cut into julienne
½ small to medium jícama, cut into julienne
1 jalapeño, seeds and membranes removed, cut into julienne

24 pitted whole Spanish olives with no pimento (such as Manzanilla, Arbequina, or Picual)
1 tablespoon extra-virgin olive oil
1 teaspoon kosher salt
½ teaspoon freshly ground black pepper, plus more to taste

Juice of 1 small lemon
1 tablespoon extra-virgin olive oil
15 cherry tomatoes, halved
Sea salt
½ bunch fresh cilantro, chopped

MAKE THE CRAWFISH

In a medium bowl, combine all the ingredients and toss well to combine. Cover and refrigerate for 1 hour.

MAKE THE SALAD

In another medium bowl, combine all of the ingredients and toss well to combine. Cover and marinate in the refrigerator for 1 hour.

TO SERVE

In a large bowl, combine the crawfish and salad mixtures, stirring well to distribute the ingredients evenly. Taste for seasonings and adjust salt and pepper, if necessary.

In a medium bowl, whisk together the lemon juice and olive oil. Add the tomatoes, a sprinkling of sea salt, and the cilantro. Stir together.

Portion the crawfish mixture evenly among serving plates. Garnish each with 5 dressed cherry tomato halves and serve immediately.

YUZU AND GREEN APPLE CEVICHE

We get beautiful local apples during the fall in Kentucky, so I like to use them in savory dishes as well as in desserts. This is an uncommon twist on a traditional ceviche and perfect to serve just as the seasons begin to change and the sights and smell of fall are in the air.

This recipe features a surprising combination of flavors from the spiciness of the Aji Amarillo, bold citrus, and bright taste and crispness from the green apple. I recommend using a sustainable white fish; try golden tilefish, triggerfish, halibut, wild striped bass, grouper, or snapper. Always check with your fishmonger to see what's freshest and let them know it's for ceviche.

For a ceviche that is rare, let the fish marinate for the shorter time suggested in the recipe. If you prefer that your fish is more done, let it marinate for the longer amount of time, checking it throughout the process.

SERVES 6 TO 8

FOR THE BROTH

½ cup yuzu juice (or additional lime juice)

Juice of 4 limes

Juice of 2 oranges

1 ounce fresh ginger, peeled and chopped

1 teaspoon ground toasted cumin seeds

8 ounces Aji Amarillo paste

1 cup water

2 tablespoons kosher salt

½ cup extra-virgin olive oil

FOR THE FISH

2 pounds fresh white fish fillets

FOR THE SALAD

1 Granny Smith apple, peeled, thinly sliced, and cut into ¼-inch dice

1 stalk celery, cut into ¼-inch dice

1 medium cucumber, peeled, seeds removed, and cut into ¼-inch dice

Juice of 2 limes

1 teaspoon kosher salt

Sea salt and micro celery or chopped celery leaves, for garnish

MAKE THE BROTH

Combine all the ingredients, except the olive oil, in a high-speed blender and process. With the machine running, slowly add the olive oil until the mixture is emulsified. Pass through a strainer and discard any remaining pieces. Cover and refrigerate until ready to use.

MAKE THE CEVICHE

Place the fish in the freezer for 30 minutes to make cutting it easier. Cut the fish fillets either into ½-inch squares or into logs and then cut across the grain into 1-inch ribbons. Place the fish pieces in a large nonreactive or glass dish. Measure out 1½ cups of the broth and pour over the fish. Use more if needed to cover completely, but reserve a little for serving. Cover the dish tightly with plastic wrap and refrigerate for 30 minutes to 4 hours, depending on how well you want your fish to be done. Test along the way if you're unsure.

MAKE THE SALAD AND SERVE

Just before serving the ceviche, toss the salad ingredients together and taste and adjust seasonings. On individual serving plates, arrange equal amounts of the prepared fish. Top each serving with a little green apple salad and, if desired, drizzle a little of the reserved broth around the plate. Garnish with a sprinkle of sea salt and either micro celery or chopped celery leaves. Serve immediately.

CHEF'S TIP › Yuzu is a citrus fruit with origins in East Asia that's very popular in Japanese, Chinese, and Korean cuisines. The fruit is about the size of a tangerine and has leaves that resemble those of a kaffir lime. With its tart citrus flavor likened to that of a grapefruit, it is also very aromatic and has notes of mandarin, lemon, and lime. The oils from the zest and peel are particularly fragrant and are used in cooking along with the fruit's juice. Fresh yuzu is usually available only in international or Asian markets, but many Asian markets carry bottles of the juice; you can also order it online. For the recipes in this book, the best substitution for yuzu is fresh lime juice.

MEET FRED & NOBLE HOLDEN ❯
HOLDEN FAMILY FARMS, LOUISVILLE, KENTUCKY

FROM ANTHONY

Fred Holden (or Farmer Fred, as he's known) has been one of my favorite local farmers for many years. He is one of the first farmers who asked me what I wanted him to grow for me, so we came up with a list of things that included radishes, peppers, baby turnips, collards, and baby bok choy. Fred also grows some of the best garlic I've ever seen.

I grew up in central California, where almost 90% of the garlic consumed in this country is produced. I thought I knew garlic until Farmer Fred introduced me to more varieties than I realized existed. Some are sweet, some very pungent, and some spicy. Working with Fred and other artisans, chefs are learning new things every day as we partner with farmers to grow ingredients and varieties that offer a new opportunity to create unique flavors. Farmers care just as much about how their product is being used as chefs care about how it is grown.

While I have known and done business with Fred, the father, for many years, the farm is now being turned over to his son, Noble. At one time, Noble worked for me in the kitchen at Seviche as a sous chef, so he understands what chefs are looking for and how important produce is to turning out exceptional dishes. It's exciting to see a young farmer with so much passion for his craft taking pride in what he produces, and continuing the tradition of farming that began with his father.

FROM NOBLE

My dad purchased this property about 21 years ago. We farm approximately 4 acres of the 31 total acres, since most of the land is heavily wooded. There is also a strip of land about ⅔ mile long that has frontage on the Floyd's Fork of the Salt River—a perfect spot for a future mushroom farm.

Dad started growing small amounts of garlic for himself when he first bought the farm, but then he realized there was a serious demand for really great garlic, so he planted a lot more in addition to the other crops we were growing. Our most popular variety is China White Elephant, but we grow 26 varieties in total. Garlic is a rotational crop, so you can't plant it in the same place every year. In addition to our garlic (we harvest the bulb and scapes), we grow strawberries, radishes, baby turnips, herbs (like cilantro), greens, peppers, spring onions, and a few other things. Some of them are grown specifically for chefs, like Anthony.

Before I came to work with my dad, I was a cook in Louisville. I also worked part-time on the farm, but then Dad was getting older and really needed more help. Physically, he can't work the farm any longer. So when he asked my friends for help and then hired them to work on the farm, I decided it was time to take it on myself and now I live out here and farm full-time.

When I worked with Anthony at Seviche and managed the incoming produce, I realized how important it was for farmers to custom-grow products for chefs. I was really inspired by the local farmers who were producing specialty ingredients for him, including my dad. There's so much to learn about all the fancy stuff that you can source from a seed catalog, but you need to also grow the basics. That's why we grow so many staples like collards, greens, and radishes in addition to some specialty items.

I would have to say that farming chose me. My profession hasn't changed all that much from working in a kitchen. I'm still providing people with food—it's just that now I'm on the front end of that process.

BLOODY MARY OYSTER SHOOTERS

You can make as few or as many of these fun and spicy little appetizers as you want. Think Latin love potion in a shot glass. We serve five per person as an appetizer at Seviche, but you could serve them as passed appetizers at a cocktail party and allow one or two per person. The broth makes a little over a cup, so depending on your shot glass size (1 to 2 ounces), you can prepare the appropriate amount of broth. For this one-bite appetizer, we like smaller oysters like Kumamotos or Miyagi from Washington State, and the Olde Salts from Rappahannock Oyster Co. in Virginia.

The broth is made with one of the Chef Inspired Bloody Mary mixes I helped to create for Master of Mixes. I use the loaded version for this recipe, which has great fresh tomato taste combined with lots of spice. As it says, it's loaded, so it's full of flavor. The addition of a few other ingredients like fresh citrus, horseradish, and Tabasco really pop the flavors. It's so good that you might want to drink it all on its own, without the oysters. Oh, and don't forget the vodka.

MAKES 5 OYSTER SHOOTERS · MAKES 1¼ CUPS BLOODY MARY BROTH

FOR THE BLOODY MARY BROTH
1 cup Chef Inspired Loaded Bloody Mary Mix
Juice of 1 lime
Juice of 1 lemon
1 ounce vodka
2 tablespoons ketchup
1 tablespoon prepared horseradish (not cream style)
1 tablespoon olive juice (from Spanish olives)

½ teaspoon freshly ground black pepper
½ teaspoon kosher salt
½ teaspoon Worcestershire sauce
½ teaspoon Tabasco sauce

Fresh shucked and cleaned oysters (as many as you want per person)
Pico de Gallo, for serving (pp. 240–241)
⅛-inch diced celery, for serving
Micro greens or chopped celery leaves, for serving

In a medium bowl, combine all of the ingredients for the broth and mix well. Cover and refrigerate until ready to use.

When ready to serve, place fresh oysters in the bottom of 2-ounce shot glasses and top with about 1½ ounces Bloody Mary broth.

Combine equal amounts Pico de Gallo and diced celery and top each shooter with about ½ teaspoon of the mixture; sprinkle with micro greens or chopped celery leaves and serve immediately.

TUNA "OLD FASHIONED"

A play on the classic drink by the same name, this award-winning ceviche has been featured on magazine covers and a number of television shows, and it has been served at several food and wine events across the country. It is also one of our signature dishes at Seviche that was created for a Pappy Van Winkle bourbon dinner.

The broth includes two of our favorite local ingredients, Kentucky bourbon and Bourbon Barrel Food's Bluegrass Soy Sauce, which is made in Louisville with non-GMO soybeans. These ingredients, combined with citrus and spice and then layered with beautiful Ahi tuna and pineapple salsa, create a unique and delectable ceviche. We serve it in a highball glass so that you can see all of the colorful ingredients and add an orange twist garnish to resemble an Old Fashioned. Be sure to include a little salsa and broth with each bite for an explosion of flavors in your mouth.

Ahi tuna (sushi grade) is available in many markets. Get to know your fishmonger and ask him to order some for you if he doesn't carry it on a regular basis. Make sure to use sushi grade tuna as well as the freshest fish available since it will be eaten raw. If Ahi (also known as Pacific Yellowtail) is not available, use Albacore tuna, which is the most sustainable alternative.

SERVES 6

FOR THE BROTH

Juice of 1 orange

Juice of 5 limes

1 tablespoon minced fresh ginger

¼ cup soy sauce (I like Bluegrass Soy Sauce from Bourbon Barrel Foods)

¼ cup Kentucky bourbon

1 tablespoon sambal oelek chile paste

1 tablespoon yuzu juice (or additional lime juice)

½ teaspoon sesame oil

FOR THE PINEAPPLE SALSA

½ pineapple, cut into quarters, trimmed, and cut into ¼-inch dice

Juice of 1 lime

2 tablespoons soy sauce (I like Bluegrass Soy Sauce from Bourbon Barrel Foods)

½ teaspoon sesame oil

1½ ounces Pico de Gallo (pp. 240–241)

1 to 2 tablespoons fresh cilantro, roughly chopped

24 ounces Ahi tuna, cut into ¼-inch dice, well chilled

Orange suprêmes (p. 199) and orange twists, black sesame seeds, micro greens or celery leaves, and thinly sliced radishes, for garnish

MAKE THE BROTH

Whisk all the ingredients together in a small bowl and set aside. Refrigerate for longer storage (up to 6 hours).

MAKE THE PINEAPPLE SALSA

Combine all the ingredients, except for the cilantro, and mix well. Cover and refrigerate until ready to serve the ceviche.

TO ASSEMBLE

Have ready 6 highball or rocks glasses. Place about 4 ounces of tuna in the bottom of each glass. Pour approximately 1 ounce of the broth over the tuna (evenly portion it among the glasses). Stir the cilantro into the salsa, then place 2 tablespoons salsa on top of the tuna. Add an orange suprème, place an orange twist on top or on the glass, then sprinkle on micro greens or celery leaves and a thin slice of radish for bite.

CHEF'S TIP › The pineapple salsa is great over grilled chicken, salmon, and fish and will hold in the refrigerator for 1 day. Wait to add the cilantro until right before using since it will lose some of its flavor once added to the rest of the ingredients.

ALL THE FIXINS'

SOUTHERN SIDES
SPICED UP

MANY PEOPLE associate the South with Soul Food, and to find the best Soul Food, most people head to a Meat and Three, a type of restaurant often known for their side dishes. These casual down-home establishments have perfected the fixins' that accompany the meat. This is not to say that a perfectly fried piece of chicken, chicken fried steak and gravy, or a cooked pork chop isn't a good reason to visit a Meat and Three. However, the star dishes at many of these restaurants are the home-cooked sides. Well, those and maybe a biscuit or two.

Many home cooks pride themselves on their side dishes, bringing them to potluck suppers, church dinners, or barbecues to share with others. Everybody likes to think they have the best macaroni and cheese or the tastiest vegetable side dish. I know I do.

This chapter combines some of my restaurant favorites as well as my family's most requested side dishes. There's something for everyone →

Home cooks pride themselves on their side dishes, bringing them to potluck suppers, church dinners, or barbecues to share with others.

peppers (you'll find the recipe on p. 102). Unlike most vegetables where you toss out the cooking liquid and eat the veggies, don't miss one of the best parts about cooking collards, the Potlikker. This seriously tasty broth can be sipped like soup and sopped up with a piece of cornbread.

Every one of the dishes in this chapter is delicious in its own way, and there are many more than those I mentioned, so turn the page and start drooling (and cooking!). And be sure to check out the chapter called Mi Casa es Su Casa (p. 202), which includes several side dishes from my youth and those that my family enjoys when we dine together at home.

here, from a Southern take on Brussels sprouts (mine features Georgia pecans and sorghum; see p. 95) to everybody's favorite, macaroni and cheese. My version on p. 96 spices things up with poblano peppers and pepper Jack cheese. I know the neighbors will have fixin' envy when you

show up with one of these dishes, or the Vidalia Onion Pudding (p. 107).

Of course, no Southern cookbook would be complete without a collard greens recipe; my rendition features these greens seasoned by our local country ham from Newsom's and spiced up with chipotle

JALAPEÑO INDIANA CORN PUDDING

Corn pudding has always been a popular side dish for family gatherings during the holidays, but for me, there's no better time to make this dish than in the middle of summer, when corn is at its sweetest. Ambrosia Farm in Finchville, Kentucky (for more on Ambrosia Farm, see pp. 182–183), grows special non-GMO corn for Seviche. With all the wonderful fresh corn available in Kentuckiana, I go corn crazy all season long and include corn in just about anything else I can think of, including ice cream.

In this recipe, I add my twist to a classic side dish and layer in some additional flavor and spice from jalapeño peppers and a hint of white pepper. They pair nicely with the sweetness of the corn and richness of the cream. This dish is pretty addictive, so you may have to allow for seconds. Be sure to use very fresh corn—never frozen—for this recipe. If you're selecting corn at your local market, be sure the husks are dark to bright green and the silks are soft and creamy in color, not dried out and brown. Corn starts to become starchy from the time it is picked, so the longer it takes to transport and the longer it sits in the store, the more it loses its flavor. Taste your corn before using it in this recipe. If it's not very sweet, add another tablespoon of sugar. If you like your dishes with a little more heat, use three jalapeños.

SERVES 6 TO 8

9 tablespoons unsalted butter, divided	3 large eggs, lightly beaten
¼ cup all-purpose flour	2 cups heavy cream
2 tablespoons granulated sugar	4 ears sweet Indiana corn, kernels removed (see p. 75)
1 tablespoon kosher salt	
½ teaspoon baking powder	2 to 3 jalapeños, trimmed, seeds and membranes removed, and cut into ⅛-inch dice
½ teaspoon ground white pepper	

Position a rack in the center of a convection oven and heat the oven to 350°F. Grease a 4-quart rectangular casserole dish (approximately 11 x 7 inches) with 1 tablespoon of the butter.

Melt the remaining 8 tablespoons butter and set aside. In a large mixing bowl, combine the flour, sugar, salt, baking powder, and white pepper. In a separate medium bowl, whisk together the melted butter, eggs, and heavy cream until combined. Slowly pour the wet ingredients into the dry ingredients, whisking constantly to avoid lumps. Once that mixture is thoroughly combined, stir in the corn kernels and jalapeños.

Pour the mixture into the prepared casserole dish and bake for 45 to 50 minutes, or until lightly browned and set. Let it sit for a few minutes before serving.

SORGHUM-GLAZED BRUSSELS SPROUTS WITH TOASTED PECANS

To say that Brussels sprouts used to be mistreated is an understatement. Boiled in water for far too long, they were mushy and unpleasant in taste and smell.

Thankfully, preparations have changed; this vegetable shines when it's shaved and dressed in salads, roasted as a side dish, and used in main-dish entrées. My family loves this version of Brussels sprouts because they're cooked perfectly, caramelized with butter, topped with toasted pecans, and then finished with a drizzle of pure sorghum. We eat them like candy. If you can't find sorghum, then substitute a local honey or pure cane syrup. While not the same taste as sorghum, it adds sweetness to the dish.

If you haven't prepared Brussels sprouts lately, then give this recipe a try. Add crispy cooked bacon or country ham for another layer of flavor and texture, adding a salty component to the sweetness and just a little more crunch.

SERVES 4

2 teaspoons kosher salt, plus more as needed	1 tablespoon canola oil
3½ tablespoons unsalted butter, divided	½ cup toasted and chopped pecans (I use Georgia pecans)
1 pound Brussels sprouts, washed and ends trimmed, cut in half	2 to 3 tablespoons sorghum or pure maple syrup

In a large saucepan, bring 2 quarts of water to a boil; add 2 teaspoons of the salt and 2 tablespoons of the butter. Add the Brussels sprouts, cook for 3 minutes, and then remove and plunge in an ice water bath. Once they are cool enough to handle, remove and drain on paper towels.

In a large cast iron or regular skillet, heat the oil until hot but not smoking over medium-high heat. Add the Brussels sprouts in a single layer, flat side down; cook without moving until the bottoms are caramelized and seared to a nice brown color, 3 to 5 minutes. Flip the Brussels sprouts over, add the remaining 1½ tablespoons butter, and cook for another few minutes, until the other side is caramelized, adjusting the heat if necessary so the butter doesn't burn. Add salt to taste and the chopped pecans. Stir well to combine and warm through. Remove from the heat and drizzle with the sorghum. Serve immediately.

CHEF'S TIP > To toast nuts, heat a convection oven to 325°F. Spread the nuts in a single layer on a baking sheet. Toast for 5 minutes, then remove from the oven. Shake the pan to redistribute the nuts and then put it back in the oven for another 5 minutes. Check after the additional 5 minutes. The nuts should be lightly brown and smell nutty. If necessary, toast for another 2 or 3 minutes. Remove the pan from the oven.

Alternatively, brown the nuts in a dry skillet over medium heat, just until they give off a nutty aroma and are lightly browned.

POBLANO JACK MAC AND CHEESE

I love the combination of three different cheeses, including pepper Jack, and the roasted poblano peppers give this rich and slightly spicy dish really great flavor. Once you try this version, you'll never want boring mac and cheese again.

SERVES 8 TO 10

3 tablespoons unsalted butter, plus more for the pan

2 cups grated sharp Cheddar cheese

½ cup grated Monterey Jack or Manchego cheese

½ cup grated pepper Jack (I like Cabot)

5 tablespoons all-purpose flour

3 cups heavy cream, divided

2 roasted poblano peppers, trimmed, peeled, seeds and membranes removed, and cut into ¼-inch dice (for roasting, see the tip on the facing page)

2 teaspoons kosher salt

¾ teaspoon freshly ground black pepper

1 pound raw elbow macaroni

½ cup fine, homemade dried breadcrumbs

1 jalapeño, trimmed and sliced, with seeds

Position a rack in the center of a convection oven and heat the oven to 400°F. Grease a 9 x 13 x 2-inch baking dish with butter and set aside. In a medium bowl, combine the cheeses and set aside.

In a medium saucepan, over medium heat, melt the 3 tablespoons butter. Add the flour and whisk until combined. Cook, whisking constantly, until the roux is smooth and thick, 1 to 2 minutes. Slowly pour in 2 cups of the heavy cream, continuing to whisk and cook over medium heat until the sauce begins to thicken; this will take several minutes. Add half of the cheese mixture and stir until smooth. Add the remaining cream, diced poblanos, salt, and black pepper. Keep warm over low heat.

Meanwhile, cook the macaroni in boiling salted water just until al dente (follow the package directions). Drain well. While the pasta is still hot, spread it in the prepared baking dish, then sprinkle half of the remaining cheese mixture over the top. Pour the warm cheese sauce over the pasta, top with the remaining cheese, and then cover evenly with the breadcrumbs.

Bake for 10 minutes, then remove and top with the sliced jalapeño. Bake until the sauce is bubbling and the top is golden brown, another 5 to 10 minutes. Let sit for a few minutes before serving.

VARIATION ❯ Take this mac and cheese to another level by adding fresh black (French Perigord) or white (Alba) truffles. Add some truffles to the cheese sauce before baking and garnish with shaved truffles (from 1 small truffle) once baked. The combination of truffles and cheese is rich, silky, and sensual. Truffles are best when in season, but you can find them out of season preserved in oil or frozen at specialty markets.

CHEF'S TIP > To roast poblanos, place the peppers directly on a gas burner set on high, turning them with tongs as each side blackens. Or roast on a gas grill, directly on the grates, or under a broiler on a foil-lined baking sheet.

Once the peppers are charred and done roasting, put them in a bowl, cover tightly with plastic wrap, and let sit while they steam to loosen the skins. Alternatively, place them in a tightly sealed zip-top bag. When cool enough to handle, peel off the charred skin with a paring knife and discard. Trim both ends, then cut through one side of the pepper so it opens up to lay flat. Remove and discard the seeds and membranes. Cut as indicated for your recipe.

CRANBERRY—SCALLION COUSCOUS

This version of couscous is great when entertaining because it can be prepared ahead of time and served at room temperature. It is very quick and easy, has great flavor, and makes an attractive addition to a plated dish or buffet. We pair the couscous with the Macadamia-Crusted Sea Bass with Passion Fruit–Habanero Sauce (p. 150) at Seviche—the flavor combination works beautifully together. It would be just as delicious served with grilled chicken or pork tenderloin for a quick weeknight meal.

SERVES 4

¼ teaspoon kosher salt	¾ cup couscous
⅛ teaspoon ground white pepper	½ cup dried cranberries
2 teaspoons extra-virgin olive oil	¼ cup chopped scallions (white and light green parts)

In a small saucepan, combine 1 cup water with the salt, white pepper, and olive oil; bring to a boil. Stir and add the couscous; stir again, move off the heat, and cover. Let stand for 5 minutes, then uncover and fluff with a fork. Add the cranberries, cover, and set aside at room temperature (or put the saucepan in the refrigerator if serving later).

When ready to serve, transfer the couscous to a bowl, cover with plastic wrap or a paper towel, and warm in a microwave (about 2 minutes on medium power). Fluff with a fork and add the chopped scallions. Alternatively, add the scallions to the room temperature couscous and serve.

ROASTED SWEET POTATOES WITH SORGHUM AND CHIPOTLE—PECAN BUTTER

An updated and unique version of sweet potato casserole, this side is one of my boys' favorite dishes. It's perfect paired with roast turkey or baked ham during the holidays. You can roast and mash the sweet potatoes ahead and then finish the dish when ready to serve. The Chipotle—Pecan Butter (p. 240) gives the potatoes a surprising flavor and a little heat, while the chopped pecans and sorghum work to offset the heat with a little sweetness and crunch. Add a splash or two of bourbon to the Chipotle—Pecan Butter for an enhanced depth of flavor.

SERVES 4 TO 6

4 sweet potatoes (about 2¼ pounds total)
2 tablespoons extra-virgin olive oil
1 teaspoon kosher salt, plus more as needed
¼ teaspoon ground white pepper

1 tablespoon unsalted butter, plus more for the pan
4 to 6 slices Chipotle—Pecan Butter (p. 240)
¼ cup toasted chopped pecans
¼ to ½ cup sorghum

Position a rack in the center of a convection oven and heat the oven to 350°F. Wash the potatoes and pat dry. Toss the potatoes in the olive oil with a generous pinch of salt and bake on a baking sheet for 1 to 1½ hours, until fork-tender.

When the potatoes are done and cool enough to handle, cut them in half and scoop out the flesh. Discard the skins and mash the flesh. Season the potatoes with the 1 teaspoon salt, the white pepper, and butter. Stir to combine.

Grease a small (3- to 4-cup) casserole dish with butter and spread the sweet potato mixture in the dish into an even layer. Bake until heated through, 10 to 15 minutes. Remove the casserole from the oven and top the potatoes with slices of the Chipotle—Pecan Butter. Heat for another 2 to 3 minutes, or just until the butter begins to melt. Remove from the oven. Sprinkle with the pecans and drizzle with ¼ cup of the sorghum before serving. For sweeter potatoes, use the entire ½ cup sorghum. Serve immediately.

SOUTHERN-STYLE GREEN BEANS

Most chefs will tell you the best way to cook green beans is to cook them for just a few minutes and then shock them in an ice water bath to preserve their beautiful green color and nutrients (this is called blanching). I was taught that early on in my career.

However, when I moved to the South, I was introduced to green beans that were slow-cooked just like collard greens and full of flavor. When prepared this way, they pair perfectly with side dishes like Roasted Sweet Potatoes with Sorghum and Chipotle–Pecan Butter (p. 99) or Vidalia Onion Pudding (p. 107). Serve them with a roasted chicken or grilled pork chops for a casual family meal. They're also great when paired with Nashville-Style Habanero Hot Chicken (p. 140) and a hefty serving of Mama's Potato Salad (p. 216). That combination of hot, salty, and sweet, with a little mayo to calm down the taste buds, is just what I'm talking about.

Give your green beans the same love that you would collards, creating a wonderful potlikker. Reheat and enjoy any leftovers the next day, after the flavors have had time to get to know each other better, and strain the flavorful broth, drinking it as you would a bowl of special soup, not to waste a drop.

SERVES 8

2 pounds green beans, strings removed, ends trimmed, and rinsed

2 strips smoked bacon cut into ½-inch dice (½ cup)

1 large onion, cut into ½-inch dice

2 tablespoons minced garlic

1 teaspoon crushed red pepper flakes

1 tablespoon freshly ground black pepper

4 tablespoons Chipotle in Adobo Purée (p. 114)

¾ cup red-wine vinegar

1 ham hock (about 2 pounds)

5 bay leaves

2 tablespoons kosher salt, plus more as needed

Juice and finely grated zest of 2 lemons

Soak the prepared green beans in ice water until ready to use.

In a large Dutch oven over medium-high heat, sauté the bacon until it renders its fat and begins to brown. Add the onion and garlic and sweat just until the onion is translucent, about 3 minutes. Stir in the red pepper flakes, black pepper, and chipotle purée and cook for 1 minute.

Deglaze the pan with the red-wine vinegar, then add the ham hock, bay leaves, and salt. Remove the green beans from the ice water, add them to the pot, and add enough water to cover. Bring to a boil and then simmer for 1½ to 2 hours, until the beans are tender but still have texture (check after 1½ hours). Remove and discard the bay leaves. Add the lemon juice and zest and salt to taste. Serve hot.

CHEF'S TIP ❯ When checking for seasoning, taste the broth, not the beans, before making any adjustment. The flavors keep getting better the longer the green beans sit, so make them the day before serving and let them sit in the broth overnight.

SPICED-UP SOUTHERN GREENS

Collard greens are probably one of the first foods that come to mind when you think of traditional Southern cooking. (You can add biscuits, fried chicken, and grits to that list.) It was one of the first foods I sampled when I moved to Kentucky, and I fell in love with the tangy, rich liquor that is left over from cooking collards, called the potlikker. Sipping the potlikker is equally as desirable as eating a big batch of slow-cooked collards. Sopped up with a piece of cornbread (or the Latin version of cornbread, a corn tortilla), it's one of life's simple pleasures.

The flavor of the collard liquor is critical to perfectly cooked collards and, when tasting for seasoning, taste the liquor and not the greens to make the adjustment. The same is true when preparing my Southern-Style Green Beans (p. 100).

This recipe makes a large batch, but collards are often served at family gatherings and barbecues, so you will want to have more. The greens are better the next day, after the ingredients have had time to spend the evening together. This recipe can also be prepared with other favorite Southern greens, such as turnip, mustard, and kale.

SERVES 8 TO 10

2 strips smoked bacon, cut into ¼-inch dice (½ cup)

One 1- to 2-ounce piece country ham

1 medium onion, cut into ¼-inch dice (2 cups)

3 cloves garlic, minced

1 teaspoon crushed red pepper flakes

3 bay leaves

1 tablespoon kosher salt

4½ tablespoons Chipotle in Adobo Purée (p. 114)

½ cup red-wine vinegar

2 pounds washed, trimmed, and picked collards (3 large bunches or about 4 to 4½ pounds before trimming), cut into 2-inch pieces

4 cups organic or homemade chicken stock

Freshly ground black pepper

Juice and finely grated zest of 1 lemon

In a large (10-quart) stockpot over medium-high heat, sauté the bacon and ham for 3 minutes, until they render their fat and begin to brown. Add the onion and continue sautéing for another 3 minutes, until the onion is soft and beginning to brown. Stir in the garlic, red pepper flakes, bay leaves, salt, and chipotle purée and cook for 1 minute. Add the red-wine vinegar to deglaze the pan and then pack the greens into the stockpot, pour in the stock, and bring to a boil. Mix well to incorporate the greens and seasonings and reduce the heat to a simmer. Cook for 1 to 1½ hours, stirring occasionally. If you like your greens cooked a little longer, simmer for another 30 minutes (many cooks in the South will cook their collards all day to make them soft and full of flavor). Taste the potlikker and adjust the seasonings if needed.

Just before serving, stir in black pepper to taste and lemon juice and zest. Remove and discard the bay leaves. For a spicier potlikker, add more chipotle purée to taste.

SUMMER SQUASH CASSEROLE

Squash is abundant in the summertime, with every farmers' market and supermarket selling this vegetable. I venture to guess that every home cook has a favorite recipe for squash casserole, with most being slight variations of the same basic version with Cheddar cheese, eggs, and cracker crumbs. I wanted this one to be a little different.

There's a bit of heat from the white pepper, but this dish is not spicy—it's more peppery. Rather than having a heavy custard base, this recipe lets the squash be the star. I slice it lengthwise, so the pieces are larger, and quickly blanch them before adding to the casserole, so they hold their shape and retain their flavor better. This dish also has fresh herbs, Cheddar cheese, a hint of fresh citrus, and buttery breadcrumbs. I think you'll find this version a nice change from your usual recipe.

SERVES 6 TO 8

3 tablespoons unsalted butter, divided, plus more for the pan

3 pounds yellow squash, trimmed and cut lengthwise into ¼-inch-thick slices

1 tablespoon kosher salt, plus more as needed

1 small onion, cut in half and sliced (1 cup)

1 large egg, lightly beaten

½ cup heavy cream

½ teaspoon ground white pepper

¼ teaspoon freshly grated nutmeg

¼ teaspoon ground cayenne

1 teaspoon chopped fresh thyme

½ cup fine homemade breadcrumbs

Juice and finely grated zest of 1 lemon, divided

2 cups grated Cheddar cheese

Position a rack in the center of a convection oven and heat the oven to 350°F. Grease a 10-inch square casserole dish.

Blanch the squash slices in boiling salted water for 3 minutes, until tender. Remove the squash and drain on paper towels. Put the squash in a large bowl and set aside.

In a large skillet over medium heat, melt 2 tablespoons of the butter. When the foaming subsides, add the onion, reduce the heat to medium, and sauté for 2 to 3 minutes, until the onion is almost translucent and the butter has browned slightly. Move the pan off the heat and gently fold in the squash, coating the squash pieces with the butter and onion.

Meanwhile, in a small bowl, whisk the egg, cream, the 1 tablespoon salt, white pepper, nutmeg, cayenne, and thyme. Set the custard mixture aside.

Melt the remaining 1 tablespoon butter in a small bowl in the microwave. Add the breadcrumbs and lemon zest, stir to combine, and set aside.

Line the bottom of the prepared dish with a third of the squash mixture. Pour a third of the custard mixture over the squash, then sprinkle with a third of the grated cheese. Repeat layering twice more with another third squash mixture, third custard, and third cheese. Sprinkle the top with the breadcrumb mixture, then drizzle with lemon juice. Bake for 70 minutes, until the breadcrumbs are lightly browned and the mixture is bubbly.

MEET NANCY NEWSOM >
NEWSOM'S COUNTRY HAMS, PRINCETON, KENTUCKY

FROM ANTHONY

Country ham is another one of those ingredients that I had never heard of until I moved to Kentucky. As with other Southern favorites, like grits and sorghum, it was exciting to create dishes and flavors with this unique local ingredient. When I first tasted country ham, I was intrigued by its complexity and the salty, rich flavor that is very different from traditional ham. It is perfect for cooking and seasoning foods.

While there are several excellent producers of country ham in the South, Col. Bill Newsom's country ham produced in Princeton, Kentucky, was the one I was first introduced to while working as sous chef at The Oak Room in the Seelbach Hotel. Nancy Newsom, the current generation of artisan ham producers and better known as "The Ham Lady," carries on the family tradition of producing one of the most flavorful hams in the country. Her prosciutto is on par with many Italian cuts. When I served it on *A Moveable Feast with Fine Cooking,* host Pete Evans couldn't stop eating it. We had to take it away from him or there would have been none left for the dinner guests!

FROM NANCY

Can you imagine that people tell me they get hungry when they see me? I suppose that's a good thing—I guess it means they like my hams. In fact, people tell me that our aged prosciutto hams are as good as what they have tasted in Spain. I was humbled when I was invited to attend the 5th World Congress of Dry Cured Hams in Aracena, Spain, in May 2009. We were the only ham from the United States to be honored, and our

ham is still on display at the Jamón Museum, where the event took place.

People often ask me if our hams are free-range and from heirloom breed pigs. Free-range pork is very expensive, so while I do age some hams from free-range heirloom pigs, I don't want to prevent regular people from being able to buy a good ham. Because of this, I produce both types—the original aged country ham and the aged free-range hams from heirloom breed pigs. They're both cured, aged, and smoked the same way, although the heirloom breeds take longer to cure since they're fattier.

My grandfather, H. C. Newsom, started this business in 1917. My family landed in Jamestown, Virginia, in 1634 and then moved to Surry, Virginia. They learned the signature old-fashioned method of curing and aging hams while in Virginia and they eventually moved to Kentucky. When I was a child growing up, there really wasn't much of a market for the smoke-cured hams my dad was making. Some people say that it's a lost art, but fortunately, country hams have become very popular recently with chefs bringing our products and Southern foods to the forefront.

We produce just under 3,000 hams a year at Newsom's, all in the ways I learned by watching my father, family

traditions and secrets that have been passed down through generations. The hams are hand rubbed and nitrate-free. We start the curing process in January and take the hams out in April, then they are hung and smoked in stages. I know when they're done if they have the right color and flavor, which can range between 9 and 10 months. Our aged prosciutto is smoked for much longer, up to 2 years. Creating the perfect ham is not a science. You know when they're ready by experience.

I took over the general store in town, Newsom's Old Mill Store, and our ham business in October of 1987. Dad was almost 74 and he was tired. He'd worked his whole life in this business, so it was time for me to step in, run the business, and make my own history.

When people ask me who the next Newsom will be to produce our hams, I tell them I'm not sure. I know the process and my son John knows some of it. My dad taught me a lot of things, but over the years I've learned a lot on my own. Maybe John knows more than I think he does, just by watching me, just like I watched my dad. One of the most important lessons my dad taught me is "never try to fool the public." That's one lesson I'm sure to pass on to John.

SPANISH RICE

A quick and tasty side dish, this rice is perfect for weeknight meals, accompanying grilled chicken or fish. Get creative and add a little browned chorizo, cooked chicken pieces, seasoned and grilled shrimp, and perhaps a few sautéed peppers along with some additional spices for a simple, quick, and satisfying Latin version of a Louisiana Creole favorite, Jambalaya.

SERVES 8

½ cup tomato sauce
1 medium fresh tomato, quartered
3 cloves garlic
1 tablespoon extra-virgin olive oil
1½ cups raw long-grain rice
¼ medium onion, cut into ¼-inch dice (½ cup)

2 stalks celery, cut into ¼-inch dice
1 small carrot, cut into ¼-inch dice
2½ cups organic or homemade chicken stock
2½ teaspoons kosher salt
1 teaspoon freshly ground black pepper
¼ cup fresh or frozen peas

Combine the tomato sauce, tomato pieces, and garlic in a high-speed blender and purée until smooth. Set aside.

In a medium skillet with a tight-fitting lid, heat the oil over medium-high heat until hot but not smoking. Add the rice and toast for 2 to 3 minutes, stirring frequently, just until it becomes translucent and smells nutty; don't brown the rice. Add the onion, celery, and carrot and mix well. Cook, stirring occasionally, for another 1 to 2 minutes, sweating the onion and celery.

Add the chicken stock, salt, black pepper, and tomato purée and bring to a boil. Cook, uncovered, for 5 minutes, then add the peas, stir to combine, cover, and reduce the heat to low. Cook for 10 minutes, until the rice is cooked and the peas are tender. Move the pan off the heat and let sit for 10 minutes without removing the lid. Stir the rice to combine all ingredients and fluff with a fork. Taste and adjust seasonings.

VIDALIA ONION PUDDING

This dish says "love" from the very first bite. In fact, you'll be scraping the pan for any leftovers because the combination of these flavors just melts in your mouth.

Vidalia onions are grown in Georgia, specifically in 13 counties around the town of Vidalia, where the soil and climate produce these wonderfully sweet root vegetables. The season for these onions extends from spring into early fall due to the warm temperatures in the South. I was introduced to them when I moved to Kentucky and love the flavor this onion gives to various dishes, including this pudding.

You could almost eat this pudding as a dessert—it's that good. It's much like an onion tart without the pastry crust. People really go crazy for this dish, and I know you will, too.

SERVES 8

16 tablespoons unsalted butter, plus more for the pan
6 large eggs, beaten
2 cups heavy cream
½ cup all-purpose flour
¼ cup granulated sugar
1 tablespoon kosher salt
1 teaspoon ground white pepper
2 teaspoons baking powder
6 medium Vidalia onions, trimmed and julienned

Position a rack in the center of a convection oven and heat the oven to 325°F. Butter a 9 x 13 x 2-inch baking dish.

In a large bowl, whisk the eggs and cream. In a small bowl, combine the flour, sugar, salt, white pepper, and baking powder. Gradually add the flour mixture to the egg mixture, whisking until smooth. Set aside.

In a large skillet over medium heat, melt the 16 tablespoons butter. When the foaming subsides, add the onions and cook on medium heat, stirring occasionally, until they are caramelized, about 30 minutes. Move the pan off the heat and fold the onions into the egg mixture. Pour the mixture in the prepared baking dish and bake for 30 minutes, or until the pudding is set and the top is slightly brown. (Check with a toothpick inserted in the center of the pudding; if it comes out clean, the pudding is done.) Let sit for a few minutes before serving.

CHEF'S TIP > You can use Spanish onions or Texas Sweets when Vidalias are not in season. The pudding is still delicious, but with a slightly different flavor. Just add a bit more sugar to make up for the lack of sweetness in the onions.

LAMAS-STYLE ELOTE

Sold as a popular street food by vendors in Mexico and southern California, elote is a charred ear of corn that has been cooked over hot coals and is served with the husk still attached and pulled down from the cob. The hot corn is first sprinkled with a spicy chile salt, then slathered with a spicy mayonnaise-based sauce, and then topped with grated salty Cotija cheese. A squeeze of fresh lime juice finishes it off. You eat it off the cob, and the messy ingredients cover your face.

I reinterpreted this rustic dish to serve at my restaurant, and people went crazy for it. It's so addictive that it's been called "corn crack." For the restaurant version, which can be eaten with a little more finesse, the grilled corn kernels are removed in sheets from the cob and layered on top of a smear of the spicy sauce. Freshly squeezed lime juice goes over the top of the corn and then the mixture is sprinkled with serrano chili salt, topped with Cotija cheese, and finished with a little more smoked serrano powder to kick it up a notch. I garnish this with a blistered padron or shishito pepper—playful yet also delicious dipped into the sauce.

SERVES 4

FOR THE SERRANO CHILE SALT
1 tablespoon smoked serrano powder (or chile de arbol)
1 tablespoon kosher salt

FOR THE SAUCE
1 cup prepared or homemade mayonnaise (not low-fat)
Juice of 1 lime
¼ teaspoon smoked serrano powder (or chile de arbol)
½ teaspoon kosher salt

4 ears fresh corn, with husks, charred on the grill
Grated Cotija cheese
Lime wedges (or use ½ squeezed lime per plate if making the refined version)
Smoked serrano powder (or chile de arbol), if making the refined version
Blistered padron or shishito peppers tossed in a little extra-virgin olive oil and kosher salt and micro greens, if making the refined version, for garnish

Mix together the chile salt ingredients; set aside. In a small bowl, whisk the sauce ingredients until well blended; set aside.

FOR THE RUSTIC PREPARATION

Sprinkle each ear of the charred corn with a little serrano chile salt. Using a pastry brush, coat each ear of corn with the sauce. Sprinkle generously with the Cotija cheese and serve immediately with a fresh lime wedge, for squeezing.

FOR THE REFINED PREPARATION

On small individual serving plates, smear about 2 tablespoons of sauce across the plate. Remove the corn kernels from the cob with a knife (see the photo on p. 76), leaving whole rustic chunks of corn together. Sprinkle the corn decoratively onto the plates, piling it up in the middle.

Squeeze the juice of ½ lime over the corn and then sprinkle with the chile salt. Sprinkle Cotija cheese over the top and then sprinkle with a pinch of smoked serrano powder. Garnish each serving with 1 padron or shishito pepper and micro greens. Serve immediately.

BUTTER BEANS WITH COUNTRY HAM AND OREGANO

Butter beans, as they are known in the South, are similar to the better known lima bean, but are smaller than limas and not as green. Southerners love to slow-cook this creamy-textured bean with smoked meats, like country ham or bacon. I also like to use a Greek spice blend in this dish.

I first learned about Greek seasoning when working with the owner of Timothy's, a restaurant in Louisville, in my early years in Kentucky. Later, I started to use Greek seasoning in my own cooking. While Greek spice mixes vary, they typically contain a blend of oregano, salt, and white pepper, also favorites in Latin cooking. I use both dried and ground Mexican oregano as well as the fresh oregano featured in this dish.

SERVES 4

1 pound fresh butter beans, rinsed and picked over	1 teaspoon kosher salt
1 bay leaf	Juice and finely grated zest of 1 lemon
One 1½-ounce piece country ham	1 teaspoon Greek seasoning (I prefer Cavender's)
2 tablespoons unsalted butter	1 teaspoon chopped fresh oregano
1 clove garlic, sliced thin	

Put the beans in a medium saucepan, cover with water, and add the bay leaf and country ham. Bring to a boil, then reduce the heat to low and cook for 25 to 30 minutes, just until tender. Drain (discard the bay leaf and ham) and set aside.

In a medium skillet over medium-low heat, melt the butter. When the foaming subsides, add the garlic and sweat, about 30 seconds, making sure it doesn't brown. Add the drained beans, salt, lemon juice and zest, and Greek seasoning. Stir well to combine and cook for another 1 minute to warm the beans. Stir in the fresh oregano, then check the seasonings. Serve immediately.

CHEF'S TIP ⟩ Rancho Gordo in Napa Valley, California, is a great resource for many of the heirloom varieties of beans originating in both Latin America and Europe (see Resources on p. 277). When fresh butter beans are not in season, try this dish with the company's dried lima beans; cook until tender and creamy, and season following the above recipe. Do not use canned lima beans.

PASTURES, MOUNTAINS & VALLEYS

MEATS & POULTRY FROM THE LAND

I LEARNED AT an early age to appreciate and respect animals; because of that, I know it's important to support local and small farmers.

Growing up on a farm in central California, we raised our own animals for food. When I worked with Future Farmers of America (FFA), I raised and showed steers. I loved my animals and walked them and exercised them daily. Happy animals are the best animals. Our cattle were grass fed and then finished on corn, which produces a marbling of fat and the best tasting meat. Our chickens were free-range and we didn't feed them antibiotics, as larger scale poultry farmers do today. The egg yolks were a deep yellow color and the eggs had a rich flavor.

I often went hunting when we lived on the farm—for birds, wild boar, squirrel, and rabbits. While it was difficult to think about killing an animal or a bird, I was proud that I was contributing to the family meal and would only hunt what we would eat. My first kill was a pheasant; I brought it home and my mama prepared it that day. She →

The time I spent outdoors in my youth played a large role in shaping my career and priorities as a chef. I saw the right way and the wrong way to raise animals, and I know the difference it makes.

didn't waste any part of the bird, using the bones to create a wonderful homemade stock. Her cooking practices taught me to utilize every part of the animal, something I do today at Seviche and at home.

While the practices at home won't be the same as what I do at my restaurant, you can use leftovers in other dishes. Think ahead and strategize to see how you can make more than one meal out of a recipe. And with the price of food, it's important not to waste anything at home. You'll notice in many of my recipes in this chapter that I give ideas for using leftovers.

The time I spent outdoors when I was younger, particularly in central California, ultimately played a large role in shaping my career and priorities as a chef. I saw the right way and the wrong way to raise animals, and I know the difference it makes. That's why I love people like Bob Hancock and Kit Garrett at Wildwood Farm (see pp. 220–221) and Craig Rogers of Border Springs Farm (see pp. 124–125). They're doing things right: treating the animals with dignity and love from the time they are born until the day they are harvested.

It's great to see that we're bringing back our local farmers in the South and all across the country. People are demanding better products and want humanely raised animals and beautiful seasonal produce. I support this movement, both professionally and personally.

CHICKEN TINGA

I love the word Tinga. It sounds Latin and spicy and believe me, it is. Here, I have taken a rustic dish and refined it by layering the flavors to create an elegant yet simple meal. Chicken Tinga is normally prepared with pulled or shredded chicken cooked in a sauce, served on a tostada with garnishes. For this dish, I braise airline-cut chicken breasts (the first joint of the chicken wing is still attached to the breast) so that they're attractive in presentation. (You can use regular bone-in, skin-on chicken breasts, too.) Brining them overnight makes them incredibly tender. Be sure to get a little bit of each ingredient with every bite to truly experience all of the flavors.

If you taste the sauce when making the Tinga, you might think it is too spicy. Okay, a lot too spicy. Actually, it's damn hot. However, trust me on this—when you add it to the rest of the ingredients as a composed dish, it will temper the heat; you will find that the dish is perfectly balanced with just the right amount of heat and spice. For those who are timid, use less of the sauce or cut back on the puréed chipotle chile in adobo, if you must.

While you can purchase premade tostadas, I recommend that you prepare them at home (see the tip on p. 114).

SERVES 4

FOR THE BRINE
8 cups water
½ cup kosher salt
2 tablespoons black peppercorns
3 bay leaves
Peeled zest of 1 lime
⅓ cup chopped onion
⅓ cup chopped carrots
⅓ cup chopped celery

Four 10- to 12-ounce airline-cut chicken breasts, or regular bone-in, skin-on chicken breasts, chilled

FOR THE TINGA
4 tablespoons olive oil, divided
1 medium Spanish onion, cut into julienne

7 cloves garlic, minced
3 tablespoons Chipotle in Adobo Purée (p. 114)
1 quart organic or homemade chicken stock
Juice of 1½ limes, divided
1 teaspoon kosher salt
2 cups whole crushed tomatoes

FOR SERVING
Four 6-inch corn tostadas (fried corn tortillas; see the tip on p. 114)
2 cups hot, prepared long-grain white rice
¾ cup grated Manchego cheese
Chopped fresh cilantro, for garnish

MAKE THE BRINE

Combine all of the brine ingredients together in a nonreactive medium stockpot and bring to a boil, stirring to dissolve the salt. Remove from the heat, let cool, and then refrigerate until chilled. Add the chicken breasts, cover, and refrigerate overnight.

PREPARE THE TINGA

After 24 hours, remove the chicken from the brine (do not rinse) and pat dry with paper towels. →

Position a rack in the center of a convection oven and heat the oven to 350°F. In a large saucepan, heat 1 tablespoon of the olive oil over medium heat until hot but not smoking. Add the onion and sweat for 2 to 3 minutes, then add the garlic, stir, and continue to cook for another minute. You don't want to brown the vegetables, just soften them. Add the chipotle purée, chicken stock, juice of 1 lime, salt, and tomatoes; stir to combine and increase the heat to high. Bring to a boil, then reduce the heat to medium and cook for 30 to 40 minutes, until the sauce is reduced and thickened.

In a large ovenproof sauté pan or cast iron skillet over medium-high heat, heat the remaining 3 tablespoons oil until hot but not smoking. Add the chicken breasts and cook, skin side down, for 4 to 5 minutes, or until the skin has a nice sear. Transfer the skillet to the oven and bake for 10 minutes, then flip the chicken to the other side, return to the oven, and bake for another 8 to 10 minutes, or until the chicken reaches an internal temperature of 165°F (use an instant-read thermometer to check). Remove the pan from the oven and let the chicken rest for 5 minutes.

TO SERVE

Add the remaining lime juice to the sauce and rewarm if necessary. For each serving, place a warm corn tostada in the middle of a serving plate and top with ½ cup hot rice. Sprinkle with several tablespoons of the grated Manchego and then place a chicken breast on top of the rice and cheese. Drizzle about ¼ cup of the sauce, or more to taste, over the chicken. Garnish with chopped cilantro.

CHEF'S TIP ❯ To make tostadas at home, warm a thin layer of canola or vegetable oil in a sauté pan or cast iron skillet. When the oil is hot but not smoking, add a corn tortilla and fry it lightly on both sides until light brown and crispy, about 40 seconds per side. Drain on paper towels. Repeat as needed. Keep the tostadas warm until you're ready to use them.

CHIPOTLE IN ADOBO PURÉE

MANY RECIPES IN *SOUTHERN HEAT* call for puréed chipotle in adobo. Since you will more than likely not use a whole can within a short period of time, I recommend that you purée an entire can, small or large, in a food processor or blender and freeze the unused portion.

Place the entire can of chipotle peppers in adobo sauce in a food processor or blender and process until puréed. Measure out 2 and 3 tablespoon amounts and freeze in either small zip-top plastic bags or ice cube trays. This way, you will have prepared purée in your freezer next time a recipe calls for the ingredient.

The frozen chipotle purée will last for at least 6 months. You may need to thaw the purée before adding it to certain recipes (such as a cold dish or sauce).

CHEF'S TIP ❯ This dish has lots of flavors going on and can pair with several different wines; however, you have to keep in mind all that spice. Pair this dish with an unoaked and low-alcohol white wine such as a dry Reisling or an Albariño from Spain or a Viognier from France. If you like sparkling wines, then a Spanish Cava works well, too.

COUNTRY HAM AND SPINACH—STUFFED CHICKEN BREASTS WITH LEMON—TOMATO BUTTER

This simple yet elegant chicken dish comes together quickly and is perfect for both weeknight meals or special occasions. I use Newsom's thinly sliced country ham or prosciutto, which is a nice companion to the Manchego and Gouda cheeses and rich Lemon–Tomato Butter. While the chicken is cooking, prepare the luscious Lemon–Tomato Butter (p. 231), a beautiful beurre blanc sauce. If you're entertaining, you can prepare the chicken ahead of time and keep covered in the refrigerator until ready to bake.

Pair this dish with your favorite Sauvignon Blanc. If you have never tried a Spanish Sauvignon Blanc, look for one from the Rueda region of Spain. Castelo de Medina is a good choice.

SERVES 4

Nonstick cooking spray or softened butter, for the pan

¼ cup grated Manchego cheese

¼ cup grated Gouda cheese

4 boneless, skinless chicken breasts, pounded flat into cutlets

Kosher salt

Freshly ground black pepper

8 thin slices aged country ham or prosciutto

Fresh baby spinach leaves

2 tablespoons unsalted butter, melted

½ cup fine dry breadcrumbs

Lemon–Tomato Butter (p. 231)

Chopped fresh curly parsley, for garnish

Position a rack in the center of a convection oven and heat the oven to 350°F. Lightly grease a baking sheet. In a small bowl, combine the two cheeses and set aside.

Lightly sprinkle both sides of the chicken with salt and black pepper. Lay 1 to 2 slices of ham over each chicken breast (to cover); sprinkle with a couple of tablespoons of the cheese mixture, and then top with several spinach leaves. Roll up each chicken cutlet, starting with the shorter end, keeping it tight and pulling in the sides. Secure the chicken cutlets with large toothpicks or skewers.

Pour the melted butter in a small dish, just large enough to fit a rolled chicken breast. Spread the breadcrumbs in another small flat dish, for dredging. One at a time, roll the skewered chicken first in the melted butter and then in the breadcrumbs, and arrange on the prepared baking sheet. Bake for 15 to 25 minutes, just until the chicken is cooked through, the cheese has melted, and the breadcrumbs are slightly browned. Remove from the oven and serve immediately, drizzled with Lemon–Tomato Butter and sprinkled with parsley.

KENTUCKY BURGOO WITH CHIPOTLE, LEMON, AND ROSEMARY

I had never heard of Kentucky Burgoo until I moved to Louisville. This stew is usually made with three types of meats and loads of vegetables; it simmers in a large pot and is often served at social events, particularly during Derby Week. Being Latino, I could easily get into the idea of a pot of stew being served at a large gathering. We Latinos like a party, and the idea of inviting family and friends over to share good times and a meal is right up our alley.

In Kentucky, the Burgoo often comes together when each neighbor or friend brings an ingredient to add to the pot. Looking at the ingredient list, you might get the idea you need a lot of friends. I can promise you that after making this, you'll have a lot more friends who will have heard about your Burgoo and they'll all want to stop by for future gatherings.

Make this stew the day before to let the flavors come together, and then reheat before serving. Be sure to check the seasonings, as you may need to add more lemon juice or zest after reheating. If the Burgoo is too thick, add some of the reserved chicken stock until you've reached your desired consistency.

MAKES ABOUT 3½ QUARTS

½ pound pork shoulder, cut into ½-inch dice

½ pound beef stew meat, cut into ½-inch pieces

2 tablespoons kosher salt, plus more as needed

1 small whole chicken

1 tablespoon whole black peppercorns

3 bay leaves

Freshly ground black pepper

3 stalks celery, 2 roughly chopped (for the stock) and 1 cut into ¼-inch dice

2 carrots, peeled and cut into ¼-inch dice, divided

2 Spanish onions, cut into ¼-inch dice, divided

1 tablespoon canola oil, plus more as needed

2 russet potatoes, peeled and cut into ½-inch dice

½ head cabbage, sliced

1 yellow bell pepper, cut into ¼-inch dice

1 tablespoon minced garlic

¼ cup tomato paste

8 tablespoons roux (p. 118)

1 tablespoon chopped fresh rosemary

1 teaspoon crushed red pepper flakes

⅓ cup Chipotle in Adobo Purée (p. 114)

½ pound cooked lima beans (or 2 cups frozen)

1 cup fresh (or frozen) corn kernels

1 cup fresh (or frozen) peas

Juice and finely grated zest of 1 lemon, plus more as needed

Pat dry the pork shoulder and beef stew meat with paper towels and sprinkle with salt and black pepper; set aside.

In a tall 7-quart stockpot, add the whole chicken and cover with water (about 4 quarts). Add the peppercorns, bay leaves, 2 tablespoons salt, the roughly chopped celery, half of the diced carrot, and half of the diced onion. Bring to a boil, then reduce the heat and simmer for 45 minutes, skimming foam as needed. Remove the chicken from the stock and let cool. →

In a separate tall 7-quart stockpot or large Dutch oven over medium-high heat, heat 1 tablespoon of canola oil until hot but not smoking. Add the pork and beef in batches to brown, being careful not to crowd the pan, adding more oil if necessary. Remove each batch when browned. Once all the meat has browned, return it to the pot and add the remaining carrot and onion, and the diced potatoes. Sauté for 1 minute, stirring, and then add the diced celery, cabbage, yellow pepper, garlic, and tomato paste. Sauté until the vegetables are softened, about 5 minutes.

Meanwhile, skim the fat from the surface of the chicken stock, then strain through a fine-mesh sieve into a large pot; discard the solids. Add 3½ quarts of the stock to the stockpot with the meat and vegetables. Reserve the remaining stock. Bring to a boil and add the roux, a little at a time, until the stew is thickened, stirring constantly over medium-high heat. Add the rosemary, red pepper flakes, chipotle purée, lima beans, corn, and peas. Pick the meat from the chicken and add it to the stockpot. Return the stew to a boil, then simmer for 30 minutes, or until the vegetables are tender and the flavors come together. Add the lemon juice and zest. Taste for seasonings and add 2 teaspoons additional salt and freshly ground black pepper, if needed. If you like a little more citrus flavor, then add more zest or lemon juice.

If the stew becomes too thick, add a bit of the reserved chicken stock.

THICKENERS

I USE TWO DIFFERENT METHODS TO thicken sauces and soups or stews in my cooking. One is a cornstarch slurry and the other is a roux. Roux is the base for making classic sauces such as béchamel. Both are very simple to make. By adding a little of either of these thickeners, you can control the consistency of a dish, making it as thin or as thick as you prefer. Of course, the recipes tell you approximately how much to add or what the consistency of the dish should be.

When using a cornstarch slurry, just make up a small amount, use what you need, and discard the rest. A roux, however, can be prepared ahead of time and stored in the refrigerator. Covered tightly, it will last for several weeks.

To make **cornstarch slurry**, mix together equal amounts of cornstarch and water, usually 1 tablespoon of each. Stir well to completely dissolve the cornstarch.

To make **roux**, in a small saucepan, melt 8 tablespoons unsalted butter. Slowly add an equal amount (8 tablespoons) of all-purpose flour to the butter, using a whisk or spoon to stir constantly while cooking over medium heat. Cook for several minutes, just until the flour taste is cooked out; don't let the mixture turn brown. Remove the pan from the heat and use the roux immediately or transfer to a small container, cover, and refrigerate for longer storage. When you want to use a few tablespoons for a recipe, warm the mixture slightly in the microwave to soften.

KENTUCKY HOT BROWN WITH MANCHEGO—JALAPEÑO MORNAY SAUCE

We like our brown water in Kentucky, bourbon that is, and the history of the Kentucky Hot Brown is rooted in late-night revelry at the Brown Hotel in Louisville, and that just might have included a little bourbon. The story goes that at the Brown Hotel, following a late night of drinking and dancing, partygoers at this downtown landmark were hungry and needed something to soak up the evening's alcohol, so the chef went into the kitchen and whipped up a meal with what he had: thick slices of bread, roast turkey, bacon, cheese, cream, and tomatoes. It was such a hit that it went on the hotel's menu; to this day, it is one of the most popular dishes served at The Brown Hotel.

Many restaurants in the Bluegrass State serve their version of the Hot Brown. My recipe adds a little twist in that I use Manchego cheese in the sauce, and spice it up with some jalapeños. You can add more peppers if you like your sauce a little spicier. Don't be shy when topping the Hot Brown with the rich Manchego—Jalapeño Mornay Sauce. That's one of the best parts. After all, I'm your chef, not your cardiologist.

SERVES 6

FOR THE MANCHEGO—JALAPEÑO MORNAY SAUCE	FOR THE HOT BROWNS
4 cups heavy cream	Nonstick cooking spray, for the dishes
¼ teaspoon freshly grated nutmeg	12 slices French bread or Texas Toast, toasted and crusts removed
½ teaspoon ground white pepper	
2 teaspoons kosher salt	1½ pounds roasted and sliced turkey breast
3 tablespoons unsalted butter	
4 tablespoons all-purpose flour	12 strips Benton's bacon or applewood-smoked bacon, cooked
2 jalapeños, seeds and membranes removed, 1 cut into ¼-inch dice and the other sliced, for garnish	12 to 18 slices heirloom tomatoes, lightly salted
2 cups grated Manchego cheese	Grated Manchego cheese, for topping

Position a rack in the center of a convection oven and heat the oven to 450°F.

MAKE THE SAUCE

In a medium saucepan, warm the heavy cream with the nutmeg, white pepper, and salt over medium heat just until the mixture has bubbles around the edges of the pan but it is not boiling. Meanwhile, in another medium saucepan, melt the butter over medium heat and add the flour, stirring or whisking constantly to make a blonde roux; cook for 2 minutes to cook out the flour taste. Slowly add the warm cream to the roux, whisking constantly to prevent lumps and until the mixture is slightly thickened. Add the diced jalapeños and cheese and whisk until the cheese has melted and everything is blended. Adjust the seasonings. Keep warm.

ASSEMBLE THE HOT BROWNS

Each Hot Brown will be assembled and cooked in an individual greased oval casserole dish. Assembling one serving at a time, place 2 slices of toast on the bottom of the dish. Top each with sliced turkey and then ¾ cup Manchego–Jalapeño Mornay Sauce. Place the bacon slices on top, add the tomatoes, and top with grated Manchego. Place the dish in the oven and cook until the sauce is bubbly and the cheese has melted, about 5 minutes.

CHEF'S TIP ❯ You should pair this dish with a wine high in acid or tannins, which will cut through the richness, stripping the fat from your tongue and cleansing your palate. Try a Sauvignon Blanc for a white or a cool-climate Cabernet Sauvignon for a red; if you're really adventurous, think about a little hair of the dog—a Michelada (p. 21).

ROASTED LEG OF LAMB
WITH LEMON—ROSEMARY DEMI-GLACE

I prepare this dish with leg of lamb from Craig Rogers, better known as The Shepherd, of Border Springs Farm in Patrick Springs, Virginia (for more about Border Springs Farm, see pp. 124–125). I also use his ground lamb for my Albóndigas (p. 19). Craig's lamb appears on many menus across the country. He raises a crossbreed of Katahdins (ewes) and Texel (rams) sheep. The meat is mild and lends itself well to the Latin spices and marinades that I use in my cooking.

In this dish, I rub the lamb with my Adobo Rub, which provides a bit of heat and spice. This is balanced by the pan sauce that features more traditional seasonings for lamb: lemon and rosemary. If you have the time, make the luscious pan sauce from a homemade veal demi-glace; if not, look for one of the excellent prepared demi-glace products at your grocery or specialty foods market to simplify the process.

The lamb makes for a beautiful presentation and is perfect to serve for a holiday; serve with simple pan-roasted potatoes. This dish is an elegant pairing that has lots of deep flavors and can stand up to a complex wine. A California Cabernet Sauvignon, a French Châteauneuf-du-Pape, or a Sangiovese will add a rich and a sophisticated complement to this dish.

SERVES 8

FOR THE LAMB
2 tablespoons Adobo Rub (p. 245)
1 tablespoon kosher salt
¼ cup chopped garlic
2 sprigs fresh rosemary, leaves removed
Juice of 2 lemons, rinds reserved
Freshly ground black pepper
One 5½-pound leg of lamb (bone-in), trimmed, fat reserved
2 tablespoons extra-virgin olive oil

FOR THE PAN SAUCE
Scraps of fat trimmed from the leg of lamb
1 stalk celery, roughly chopped

1 carrot, roughly chopped
½ large onion (or 1 whole medium), roughly chopped
3 cloves garlic, chopped
3 sprigs fresh rosemary
Juice and finely grated zest of 2 lemons
1 teaspoon whole black peppercorns
1 cup organic or homemade beef stock
2 cups Country Ham Chipotle Demi-Glace (p. 238)
¼ to ½ teaspoon lemon oil (see Resources on p. 277)
2 teaspoons kosher salt

PREPARE THE LAMB

Mix together the Adobo Rub, salt, garlic, rosemary leaves, lemon juice, and a few grinds of black pepper, and rub all over the lamb. Place the lamb in a nonreactive pan and add the lemon rinds. Cover and refrigerate overnight.

When ready to cook the lamb, heat a convection oven to 375°F. In a large flameproof roasting pan over high heat, heat the olive oil until hot but not smoking. Add the lamb, fat side down, and sear until brown, reducing the heat if necessary so the lamb doesn't burn. Turn the lamb over and sear on the other side to seal in the juices. Transfer the lamb to the oven and cook for 30 minutes. Reduce the heat to 250°F and continue to cook until the lamb reaches 130° to 132°F on an instant-read thermometer. This could take from 30 to 60 minutes; check after 30 minutes. When cooked to the correct temperature, remove from the oven and tent with foil to keep warm.

PREPARE THE PAN SAUCE

Over medium-high heat, render the fat from the reserved lamb fat in a large saucepan, then add the celery, carrot, and onion to the pan. Stir and cook for 4 to 5 minutes, until the onion becomes translucent. Add the garlic, rosemary, lemon juice, zest, and peppercorns, then add the beef stock and deglaze pan, scraping the browned bits from the sides. Add the demi-glace and bring to a boil. Cook over medium heat for 10 to 20 minutes, occasionally scraping down the sides, until the sauce is reduced to the desired consistency. Add the lemon oil, then taste and add salt. The amount of salt needed will depend on the saltiness of the demi-glace and beef stock. For a more rustic sauce, serve as is; or if you prefer, strain it through a fine-mesh sieve or chinois, pressing on the vegetables to get all the juices. For a refined and smooth sauce, just strain but do not press on the vegetables. Keep warm.

TO SERVE

Slice the warm lamb and serve immediately with the pan sauce drizzled over the top.

CALIFORNIA TRI TIP WITH WILD RAMP CHIMICHURRI

Where I grew up in central California, roadside tri tip stands dotted the countryside. We would often leave school at lunchtime to visit the stands and order tri tip sandwiches that were only $1.50. They were delicious and flavorful and at the time, one of the best things I ever ate. I later learned that most butchers, chefs, and restaurants discarded this cut of meat because it was considered inferior to the prime cuts that were in demand at the time.

With the price of beef constantly rising and the focus on utilizing every part of the animal, butchers and restaurants now offer cuts of beef that many people are not familiar with, like Vegas strip steak, teres major, blade steak, and tri tip. The tri tip is cut from the bottom sirloin and it's triangular in shape. If you don't see a tri tip at your local butcher or grocery store, ask if one can be cut for you. An average tri tip weighs about 3 pounds.

These are the flavors I remember from the street vendors. The meat is rubbed and then marinated in seasonings before being cooked on a charcoal grill. Of course, my seasonings include Latin love, and I let the meat marinate for 4 to 6 hours so the flavors become more deeply infused and the meat becomes very tender. Grilled to medium rare and served with Wild Ramp Chimichurri, you'll wonder where this cut of beef has been all of your life.

SERVES 6

¼ cup extra-virgin olive oil
Juice of 1½ limes
2½ tablespoons chopped garlic
1 tablespoon kosher salt
¼ cup red-wine vinegar

Several sprigs of fresh thyme, plus 1 teaspoon fresh thyme leaves
1 whole tri tip (about 3 pounds), cleaned and trimmed
Wild Ramp Chimichurri (p. 241), for serving

In a small bowl, whisk together all of the ingredients, except for the tri tip and chimichurri. Pat dry the tri tip with paper towels and place the meat in a glass dish or large zip-top bag. Add the marinade, rubbing in the seasonings, and turning over to coat. Cover the dish with plastic wrap or close the bag and refrigerate for 4 to 6 hours, turning the meat occasionally to distribute the marinade evenly.

Heat a grill until very hot and oil the grates. Place the tri tip over direct heat and sear for 5 to 8 minutes on one side and then flip and sear the other side, another 5 to 8 minutes. Move the meat to indirect heat, close the lid of the grill, and cook for another 20 minutes, or until the internal temperature in the center of the tri tip reaches 125°F, for medium rare. To test if the meat is cooked properly, press on the top of the tri tip—it should pop back up quickly.

Transfer the tri tip to a plate, cover with foil, and let rest for 15 minutes to allow the juices to reintegrate into the meat. To serve, slice across the grain of the meat and spoon the chimichurri over the top.

CHEF'S TIP ❯ This dish can be sophisticated or casual. For a sophisticated meal, pair with a Cabernet Sauvignon. For a casual affair, try a Bourbon Mojito (p. 24). Leftovers make a great sandwich, served with a beer.

MEET THE DUO BEHIND LAMBS & CLAMS >
TRAVIS CROXTON RAPPAHANNOCK OYSTER CO. & CRAIG ROGERS BORDER SPRINGS FARM

FROM ANTHONY

Wherever I travel for food and wine events or cooking festivals, I am almost certain to find Travis and Craig. Each is a leading food artisan in his own right, but they also get together to showcase their ingredients and feature young chefs as part of their program called Lambs & Clams.

Travis and his cousin Ryan manage their award-winning family oyster business, which has been in operation since 1899. They grow the Chesapeake Bay's only native oyster, the Crassostrea Virginica, and are focused on preserving this regional specialty and the true flavors of the Chesapeake Bay.

Their efforts to raise oysters is instrumental in cleaning the waters of the Chesapeake Bay, as these bivalves are natural water filters. In addition to oyster farming and managing the family business, Travis is also a restaurateur.

Craig, known as The Shepherd by those in the industry, raises beautiful lamb where the pasture grasses flavor the meat, and he is also part of the glue that brings together chefs and artisans and builds community in the culinary world.

FROM TRAVIS

I met Craig in 2009 at an outdoor event. We were at a backyard barbecue at Bryan Voltaggio's house. Craig was roasting a whole lamb on a spit and I was shucking oysters. That's how many people know us and that's how the relationship started. Things haven't changed much since the first time we met.

We struck up a conversation and began talking about the issues of owning a small business and found we had a lot in common. Craig had just started shipping his lamb, which totally changes the game in this industry, so he wanted to bounce some ideas off me. We also found out that we were overlapping in supplying many chefs in the Northeast and Atlantic regions. At one point we were talking every day and my wife even asked, "Are you cheating on me with Craig?" We

had obviously formed a strong bond and friendship over farming and food.

We decided that together we could reach more people than as individuals, so we came up with Lambs & Clams and began sponsoring after-parties at food and wine events. Working together on these projects with Craig brings more awareness to the incredible food scene in the South and the unique products we have to offer. It also helps chefs and other artisans to stay connected and maintain relationships with each other.

My new project is as a restaurateur. My first restaurant with my cousin, Merroir, is what we call a "tasting room" and it's located in Topping, where we raise and harvest our oysters. The restaurant concept started as a way to sell our oysters directly to customers. We have a number of other restaurant projects up and running, and some in the works, and we are still growing. Of course, my number-one focus will always be on our oysters; that's what's near and dear to my heart.

FROM CRAIG

I consider Travis to be a great friend and mentor in this business. After he helped me to establish a relationship with a distributor to sell my lamb, it freed up my time and allows me to be The Shepherd and spend more time visiting with chefs, rather than driving around delivering my

lamb. His guidance was invaluable, even though our products are so different. Where his oysters cost as little as a dollar, some of my cuts of lamb can be as much as $100, but there are similarities in effectively distributing products from small producers.

With our collaboration on Lambs & Clams, Travis and I share the excitement of featuring great chefs who aren't as well known in the community. We showcase their talent at food and wine events. It's been both rewarding and fun, especially as we now see many of them getting recognized by StarChefs and the James Beard Foundation. Since we're older than many of the chefs, we really enjoy the mentoring aspect and giving back to the community.

As a farmer and artisan, reaching customers who appreciate the quality in our products is critical. For me, to produce special lamb requires special pastures and grasses, because that's where it all begins. In 2011, I started Lambstock as a way to introduce chefs and other artisans to my farm, as well as to create an opportunity for these hard-working people of the culinary world to have some time to kick back and relax. Every year, we camp out in the pasture, share stories, work with the sheep and lambs, laugh, cook, and drink together. In the end, we build lasting relationships.

PUERTO RICAN MOFONGO WITH BACON AND MOJO DE AJO

The classic and rustic Puerto Rican dish Mofongo has West African roots. In fact, many Southern and Latin dishes have ties to Africa and the Caribbean.

Mofongo is served in several Latin countries and goes by different names, depending on where it's prepared. No matter what the name, Mofongo starts with either boiled or fried ripe plantains that are mashed and then served with meats, poultry, or seafood. For my version, I use boiled and fried plantains for texture. The roasted pork has a wonderful flavor from an overnight marinade and slow cooking. There's another layer of flavor when served with the Mojo de Ajo (p. 232), a bright, tangy, and citrusy garlic sauce.

The presentation of this dish makes it more elegant than rustic. It's perfect to serve for a fall supper party, especially because every element can be prepared ahead and then pulled together when ready to serve. For an authentic plating that will impress guests, spread a banana leaf on the plate and then compose the dish. While served as a main dish, it is a smaller plate, so you will want to have another course or two with your meal. Serve with an earthy wine like Grenache or Tempranillo or try a Rasteau from France.

The leftover pork is delicious in tacos. Top with Salsa Verde (p. 243) or Salsa Rojo (p. 242) and serve with black beans and rice, with sour cream and chopped scallions on the side.

SERVES 8

FOR THE PORK
Juice of 2 oranges, rinds reserved
Juice of 4 limes, rinds reserved
2 ounces (about 16 cloves) cloves garlic, roughly chopped
1½ tablespoons Homemade Sazón (p. 248)
¼ cup kosher salt
One 4- to 5-pound bone-in pork butt or pork shoulder

FOR THE PLANTAIN MIXTURE
6 ounces thick-sliced smoky bacon, diced (I use Benton's)

½ onion, chopped (1 cup)
1 tablespoon minced garlic
8 ripe (black peels) plantains, peeled and sliced thick (see the tip p. 128)
1 tablespoon kosher salt, divided
Canola oil
8 tablespoons unsalted butter
½ teaspoon ground white pepper

Mojo de Ajo (p. 232) for serving
Chopped fresh cilantro or micro cilantro, for garnish

PREPARE AND COOK THE PORK

In a small bowl, combine the juices, chopped garlic, Sazón, and salt. Rub the mixture all over the pork, then place in a nonreactive dish. Add the orange and lime rinds, cover, and refrigerate overnight.

When ready to cook the pork, position a rack in the center of a convection oven and heat the oven to 500°F. Transfer the marinated pork, fat side up, to a roasting pan and cook for 15 to 20 minutes to brown. Reduce the heat to 250°F, fill the pan about halfway with water, cover with foil, cook for 4 to 5 hours (or longer), until the meat is tender and falls off the bone. Remove and keep warm. →

MAKE THE PLANTAIN MIXTURE

Cook the bacon in a sauté pan or skillet until it renders its fat and begins to brown. If you're using Benton's bacon, which cooks differently than other types, leave it slightly undercooked. Add the onion and sweat for 4 to 5 minutes. Remove the pan from the heat, add the minced garlic, and set aside.

Meanwhile, put the plantains in a large pot, cover with water, and add 2 teaspoons salt. Bring to a boil, reduce the heat, and cook at a rolling simmer for about 8 minutes, or until the plantains are tender. Drain and set aside.

In a medium cast iron skillet or Dutch oven, add enough oil to come up 1½ inches on the side and heat to 350°F. Pat dry about half of the plantains with paper towels, then add them to the oil and fry until brown and crispy, just a couple of minutes, turning once as they begin to brown. Drain on paper towels. Repeat with the remaining plantains.

When ready to serve, heat the bacon and onion mixture and add the remaining 1 teaspoon salt, the butter, and white pepper. When the butter is melted, add the boiled, fried plantains and mash, leaving some whole and some chunks. Keep warm.

TO SERVE

Shred the pork. Put about ½ cup of the plantain mixture in the center of individual serving plates. Top with about 4 ounces pork and drizzle the Mojo de Ajo around the plate. Garnish with the chopped cilantro or micro cilantro.

CHEF'S TIP > A plantain has thicker skin than a banana. When peeling a plantain, cut the tips off both ends and make lengthwise cuts about ½ inch apart through the skin. Peel the strips down to remove the skin.

PAN-SEARED DUCK BREAST WITH BOURBON—COUNTRY HAM CHIPOTLE DEMI-GLACE

The combination of flavors in this dish is sophisticated, yet you will be surprised at how easy the dish is to prepare. When cooking duck, always start with a cold pan because of the high fat content in the skin. You also want to score the skin before cooking. Doing this renders more of the fat and ensures a crispy skin. It is often recommended that duck be cooked to 165° to 170°F but that, in my opinion, dries out the meat. Even cooking duck to 150°F, which is considered medium well, allows very little pink at the center. I prefer cooking the meat to 135° to 140°F and allowing it to rest for 10 minutes. It will continue to cook and produce a beautiful pink center that is flavorful and moist. If you are at all concerned, cook it to medium-well done, but know that it won't have the same flavor or texture.

Make the pan sauce up to a day ahead, as long as you have the skin and fat scraps trimmed from the duck breasts. Once prepared, I strain the sauce through a chinois for an elegant presentation of the glossy and full-bodied sauce. For a more rustic presentation, you can leave the vegetables in the pan and serve the sauce without straining. I serve the duck accompanied by a mixture of Sea Island Red Peas and Carolina Gold Rice that has been tossed with Pernod Citrus Butter (p. 237). It's a spectacular mix of flavors when combined with the beautiful and luscious pan sauce for the duck. Drink a medium-bodied Oregon Pinot Noir with this dish.

SERVES 6

FOR THE DUCK

Four 10- to 12-ounce duck breasts

Finely grated zest of 1 lemon

1 teaspoon kosher salt

Pinch of ground white pepper

Leaves from 3 sprigs fresh thyme

FOR THE BOURBON–COUNTRY HAM CHIPOTLE DEMI-GLACE

Skin and fat scraps trimmed from the duck breasts

1 stalk celery, roughly chopped

1 carrot, roughly chopped

½ onion, roughly chopped

3 cloves garlic, chopped

5 sprigs fresh thyme

1 teaspoon whole black peppercorns

1 cup organic or homemade beef stock

2 teaspoons kosher salt, plus more as needed (depending on the beef stock)

1 cup Kentucky bourbon (I use Woodford Reserve)

2 cups Country Ham Chipotle Demi-Glace (p. 238)

2 cups Classic Carolina Gold Rice (p.131) mixed with 2 cups Sea Island Red Peas (p. 132), for serving

Chopped fresh curly parsley, for garnish →

PREPARE THE DUCK

Trim the excess skin and fat from the duck breasts, leaving a nice even skin for browning on top. (Reserve the scraps.) Score the skin on the diagonal crosswise, making three cuts, and then score three more cuts in the opposite direction, forming a diamond pattern, but not cutting through to the meat. This will help the skin to sear properly and not curl. Place the breasts, skin side up, in a shallow glass pan and sprinkle with the lemon zest, salt, white pepper, and fresh thyme leaves. Cover and refrigerate for 2 hours.

When ready to cook the duck breasts, position a rack in the center of a convection oven and heat the oven to 350°F. Place the duck breasts skin side down in a cold cast

iron skillet or other ovenproof skillet, then cook over medium-high heat to render fat, just a few minutes. Once quite a bit of fat has been rendered and the fat starts to sizzle, tilt the pan and remove the excess fat. Reduce the heat to low, cover the pan, and cook over low heat for about 10 minutes. Check to make sure the skin is nicely seared. Remove from the heat, flip the breasts over, and place the skillet in the oven. Cook for 5 to 7 minutes, or until the duck reaches the desired temperature (see the headnote on p. 129). Cover with foil and let the meat rest before slicing; the duck will continue to cook.

MAKE THE DEMI-GLACE

Meanwhile, put the skin and fat scraps in a separate cold skillet, place over medium-high heat, and cook until they render fat, several minutes. Add the celery, carrots, onion, and garlic, lower the heat to medium, and cook to soften the vegetables, 3 to 5 minutes. Add the thyme, peppercorns, beef stock, and salt. Bring to a boil, reduce the heat, and cook over medium until the mixture is reduced by half, about 5 minutes. Add the bourbon to deglaze the pan and cook for 4 to 5 minutes over medium heat to burn off the alcohol. Add the demi-glace, return to a boil, then reduce the heat to medium and cook until the mixture is thick, shiny, and smooth, 10 to 15 minutes. If you like, strain the sauce through a chinois and into a clean pan. If desired, you can reduce the sauce further. Keep warm or refrigerate for later use.

TO SERVE

Slice the duck. On individual serving plates, place a serving of the Classic Carolina Gold Rice–Sea Island Red Pea mixture and lay several slices of duck over the top. Drizzle with the demi-glace and garnish with parsley.

CLASSIC CAROLINA GOLD RICE

· ·

MAKES 3¼ CUPS · SERVES 6

1 tablespoon kosher salt	1 cup raw Carolina Gold Rice
2 tablespoons unsalted butter	1 teaspoon canola oil

Bring 2 quarts of water, the salt, and butter to a boil. Add the rice and make sure there is 4 to 6 inches of water above it; if not, add more. Return to a boil and boil for 1 minute while stirring constantly. Turn the heat to low, cook uncovered for about 12 minutes, stirring occasionally, just until the rice is fully cooked. Drain and quickly rinse with cold water to stop the cooking. Transfer to a baking sheet, drizzle with the oil, and toss to distribute (the oil will keep the rice fluffy), then spread out the rice and let it dry until ready to use.

If not using right away, transfer to an airtight container, cover, and refrigerate for up to 2 days. To warm, spread on a baking sheet and place in a 250°F convection oven for a few minutes.

· ·

SEA ISLAND RED PEAS

MAKES 4 CUPS · SERVES 8 TO 10

1 cup Sea Island Red Peas, soaked overnight in water to cover, then rinsed	2 quarts water
3 bay leaves	1 tablespoon kosher salt, divided
One 3-ounce piece country ham	2 tablespoons Pernod Citrus Butter (p. 237; optional)

In a large saucepan, combine the peas, bay leaves, ham, water, and 2 teaspoons of salt and bring to a boil over high heat. Reduce the heat and simmer for about 45 minutes, or until the peas are very tender. Once the peas have been cooking for about 20 minutes, taste the broth and add another 1 teaspoon salt if needed. Check from time to time to see if additional water is needed.

Drain the peas, add the Pernod Citrus Butter, if using, and combine well.

CHEF'S TIP ❯ To finish and serve with the Pan-Seared Duck Breast, stir together 2 cups cooked Sea Island Red Peas, 2 cups Classic Carolina Gold Rice (p. 131), and 2 tablespoons (or more, to taste) melted Pernod Citrus Butter (p. 237). Season with salt and pepper. Refrigerate and reheat any leftovers.

CHEF'S TIP ❯ Many of us have old cast iron skillets that our mothers or grandmothers used in their kitchens and that have been passed down through several generations. These pans get better with age—they build up a "seasoning" on the surface from years of use. When treated properly, they will last forever.

To properly season a cast iron skillet, wipe it down and coat with a thin layer of canola oil. Turn upside down and place in a hot 500°F oven for 3 to 4 hours. Place a pan under it to catch the drippings from the oil. Remove from the oven and let cool. Use a paper towel to remove any excess oil. The best way to clean cast iron pans is to wipe them clean with a paper towel after use and then scrub them with a brush, kosher salt, and a little oil. You can periodically re-season the pans. The more you use the pans, the more stick-resistant they become.

PORK LOIN WITH CHIPOTLE—ORANGE BOURBON GLAZE

This recipe is an updated version of an award-winning dish I made for a statewide cooking challenge sponsored by Woodford Reserve in Versailles, Kentucky. It was a proud moment for me to win a recipe contest in the Bluegrass State, combining my traditional Latin flavors with Southern ingredients, especially Kentucky bourbon. Probably one of the best-known bourbons, Woodford Reserve is the perfect culinary bourbon. It's full-bodied, with a balance of flavors ranging from caramel, butter, and spice to apple and orange notes; these flavors blend beautifully with the smokiness and heat in my dishes.

Be sure to make the dish when you can fire up the grill, the preferred method to get a nice char on the meat. You'll bring it indoors to finish in the oven.

Serve this dish with Champagne or an Alsatian white wine. For a red wine, choose something with a little earthiness for the pork and fruit to offset the bourbon glaze, such as a Côte du Rhône like a Gigondas or Rasteau.

SERVES 6

5 cloves garlic, roughly chopped

2 tablespoons Chipotle in Adobo Purée (p. 114)

Juice of 1 orange, rinds reserved

Juice of 2 limes, rinds reserved

1 tablespoon kosher salt

2 tablespoons Homemade Sazón (p. 248)

¼ cup olive oil

One 2¼- to 2½-pound pork loin

Chipotle Orange–Bourbon Glaze (p. 135)

Cheddar Poblano Grits (p. 160), for serving

Charred Corn Salsa (p. 235), for serving

Combine the first seven ingredients in a small bowl and whisk well to combine.

Pat dry the pork with paper towels and place in a nonreactive dish. With bare hands or food-safe gloves, rub the marinade all over the pork, working it in well. Add the reserved rinds. Cover the meat with plastic wrap and refrigerate for 24 hours.

Heat a grill to high. Grill the pork until you get a nice sear on all sides, Alternatively, sear the pork in a very hot cast iron pan or skillet with a little olive oil.

Position a rack in the center of a convection oven and heat the oven to 350°F. Once the meat has a nice sear, transfer from the grill or skillet to a small roasting pan, along with the reserved rinds, put the pan in the oven and cook for 20 to

30 minutes, until the internal temperature is between 150° and 155°F. Remove from the oven, tent with foil, and let rest before slicing.

Slice the pork into serving-size pieces and drizzle with the Chipotle Orange–Bourbon Glaze. Serve with Cheddar Poblano Grits and Charred Corn Salsa on the side.

CHIPOTLE ORANGE–BOURBON GLAZE

MAKES ABOUT 3 CUPS

1 teaspoon canola oil	1 teaspoon onion powder
½ onion, cut into ¼-inch dice	1 teaspoon garlic powder
One 15-ounce can diced tomatoes	¾ cup Kentucky bourbon (I like Woodford Reserve), divided
1 teaspoon Worcestershire sauce	
1 tablespoon Chipotle in Adobo Purée (p. 114), plus more as needed	1 teaspoon kosher salt
	1 teaspoon freshly ground black pepper
2 cups ketchup	1 bay leaf
1 cup orange juice	Juice of 1 lemon
1 tablespoon minced garlic	3 drops orange oil (see Resources on p. 277), or finely grated zest of 1 orange

In a medium saucepan, heat the canola oil until hot but not smoking. Add the onion and sweat for 2 to 3 minutes. Add the rest of the ingredients including ½ cup bourbon. Stir well and bring to a rolling boil. Continue to boil, stirring frequently, for 3 minutes. Lower the heat and simmer until the mixture is reduced and thickened, about 30 minutes. Let cool slightly and remove and discard the bay leaf. Blend the mixture with an immersion blender or in a high-speed blender, then add the remaining ¼ cup bourbon, if desired, for a more pronounced bourbon flavor. Transfer to an airtight container and store in the refrigerator until ready to reheat and use.

The sauce can be reduced further and used as a barbecue sauce for grilled pork chops and chicken.

CHEF'S TIP ❯ There is a big debate about thermometers—analog versus digital. Traditional analog thermometers are placed in the meat while in the oven and remain there, allowing you to watch the temperature during cooking. Digital thermometers are slow and many seem to be inaccurate. I have been through many digital thermometers and have never been pleased with the quality and accuracy of these until I found the Thermapen®. This digital thermometer reads the temperature quickly and is very accurate. You'll never have to purchase another digital thermometer again.

RED CHILE—CORIANDER RIB-EYE STEAKS

If you love steak as much as I do, then you probably enjoy a great rib-eye prepared outdoors on the grill every now and then. This cut of beef, along with the tri tip (see the recipe on p. 123), is another one of my favorites. It's well marbled, so it has great flavor and is incredibly tender. While some cuts of beef are leaner, they tend to be chewy or don't have much flavor.

Give these steaks a little extra love and seasoning with a quick and easy marinade and then add a bit of heat and a subtle smoky flavor with the Red Chile—Coriander Rub. If you can't find dried habaneros, then just skip that ingredient. Store the remaining rub in an airtight container and use on grilled hamburgers and other cuts of beef prepared on the grill.

This dish calls for a big, robust, spicy wine, so open a bottle of Syrah, Cabernet Sauvignon, or a Zinfandel to complement the rub.

SERVES 4

Four 12- to 14-ounce rib-eye steaks

FOR THE MARINADE
1 tablespoon kosher salt
¼ cup extra-virgin olive oil
Juice and finely grated zest of 2 lemons
Leaves from 5 sprigs fresh thyme
1 clove garlic, minced
1 tablespoon red-wine vinegar
1 tablespoon freshly ground black pepper

FOR THE RED CHILE—CORIANDER RUB
5 dried habaneros (½ ounce) (omit if not available)
5 dried pasilla or ancho chile peppers (2 ounces)
10 dried guajillo chile peppers (2 ounces)
1 tablespoon crushed red pepper flakes
2 tablespoons smoked Spanish paprika (pimentón)
1 tablespoon cumin seeds
1 tablespoon coriander seeds
2 tablespoons whole peppercorns
4 tablespoons kosher salt

PREPARE THE STEAKS

In a small bowl, combine all of the ingredients for the marinade and whisk together to blend. Rub the steaks with the marinade and place in a plastic zip-top bag or nonreactive dish and refrigerate overnight.

MAKE THE RUB

Place the dried peppers in a hot dry skillet and lightly toast over a low flame. Let cool and then remove the stems and seeds. Roughly chop the peppers. Put the peppers and the remaining ingredients in a small blender and process until the mixture is medium to finely chopped. If whole seeds or peppercorns remain, mash them by hand with a mortar and pestle and then add to the mixture.

COOK THE STEAKS

When ready to grill the steaks, heat a charcoal or gas grill on high. Remove the steaks from the bag or dish and lightly sprinkle both sides with the rub. Cook over a hot grill,

searing on one side and then flipping once. Cook to the desired temperature, preferably medium rare, 130° to 135°F on a digital thermometer. Let sit for a few minutes before serving.

CHEF'S TIP ❯ The rub recipe makes more than you will need for the steaks. Store the remaining rub in an airtight container. It will keep for about 6 months.

SPICED-UP CINCINNATI-STYLE CHILI

I had never heard of Cincinnati chili until I moved to Kentucky. Now it's one of my guilty pleasures. The story behind Cincinnati chili is that it was originally sold as a Greek pasta sauce and that didn't have much success, so the family began to market it as chili and it suddenly took off. In addition to its unique flavor and texture of the meat, Cincinnati chili is served over spaghetti and has various toppings, like onions, beans, and cheese. On my off hours, I like to grab some chili at Skyline Chili, one of the largest Cincinnati chile restaurants.

The meat in this chili is pulsed to a fine texture, so it's probably different from what you might recognize as traditional chili. It's rarely served by itself and should be thought of as a sauce or gravy. Most people either love it or hate it, and if you love it, like I do, you're really particular about how you eat it. I like mine served 4-way—that's with spaghetti, chili poured over the top, and then sprinkled with a whole lot of grated Cheddar cheese and minced onions.

The recipe is a family secret and while there are many copycat recipes out there, none are exactly like the original at Skyline Chili. Of course, I had to create my own version of this dish for the book. The flavors are unusual and there's even a hint of chocolate in the spice mix.

You can make this the same day you serve it or let it sit overnight to let the flavors come together.

Personally, I think nothing goes better with chili than a beer and I use a regional amber, Abita®, made in New Orleans, in the recipe. You can also pair Abita with the prepared chili. If you want to add some international flair to this meal, try a lighter beer such as Presidente from the Dominican Republic or traditional Mexican beer, Tecate or Dos Equis Amber Lager. Any way you pair it, this chili is the bomb.

SERVES 6 TO 8

1 tablespoon canola oil

2 pounds lean ground beef

2 yellow onions, cut into ¼-inch dice

6 cloves garlic, finely minced

¼ cup chili powder

1 tablespoon ground cumin

1 teaspoon ground cinnamon

1 teaspoon ground cayenne

1 teaspoon ground coriander

¾ teaspoon unsweetened cocoa powder

¼ teaspoon ground cloves

1½ tablespoons kosher salt, divided

1 quart organic or homemade beef stock

1 bottle (12 ounces) dark amber beer or stout (I like Abita)

2 cups canned crushed tomatoes

3 bay leaves

Cooked spaghetti, grated Cheddar cheese, rinsed kidney beans, and chopped onion, for serving

In a large Dutch oven over medium-high heat, heat the canola oil until hot but not smoking. Add the ground beef, breaking it up into pieces with the back of a spoon. Stir and cook for a few minutes just until the meat begins to brown, then add the onion, garlic, chili powder, cumin, cinnamon, cayenne, coriander, cocoa powder, cloves, and 1 tablespoon of salt; stir and cook for a few minutes until the meat is cooked through and the mixture is aromatic. →

Add the beef stock, beer, and tomatoes; stir well. With an immersion blender, pulse the mixture until the meat is in small pieces. Add the bay leaves and bring to a boil. Boil for 2 minutes, stirring constantly and scraping down any browned bits on the side of the pot. Lower the heat, partially cover, and simmer for 2 to 3 hours (longer is better), stirring frequently. If necessary, add a little water during cooking if the mixture becomes too thick.

Remove the bay leaves; taste and adjust seasonings and add the remaining 1½ teaspoons salt if needed. Skim the fat from the surface (or refrigerate overnight to make it easier to remove fat the next day). Serve hot over spaghetti and top with grated Cheddar, kidney beans, and chopped onion, as desired.

CHEF'S TIP > If you're going to prepare Cincinnati chili, you need to get the proper lingo down. Chili 3-way is spaghetti, chili, and cheese. If you want to serve this 4-way, that will mean adding chopped onion to the spaghetti, chili, and cheese. A 4-way with beans substitutes kidney beans for the onion, and 5-way is spaghetti, chili, cheese, onion, and kidney beans. Another favorite way to serve it is over hot dogs, or Coney dogs as they are called, that are dressed with chili, grated Cheddar, and a little mustard.

NASHVILLE-STYLE HABANERO HOT CHICKEN

Nashville is known for country music, a full-size reproduction of the Greek Parthenon, the Tomato Art Festival, and hot chicken. Gwen, Roger, and I went to a famous hot chicken shack in Nashville for lunch after a late night of celebrating that included just a little bit of bourbon. Spicy food was just the thing we needed. While I can eat hot foods, this stuff was just too hot and we found that it really didn't have any flavor, just heat. With that in mind, I was determined to create a hot chicken that was really moist, with just the right amount of heat and a complexity of flavor throughout.

Each bite is more than just hot—it is packed with flavor. The brine creates the moistness, with seasonings that penetrate the meat. The crispy skin is achieved by double dipping in flour with spices and using a buttermilk base. Papa's Famous Hot Sauce adds another layer of flavor and complexity of heat with a little sweetness. Papa is a member of my culinary team at Seviche and more like family after working with me in the industry for over 15 years. We developed this recipe for hot sauce several years ago and it has been one of our "secret sauces" in several dishes. When you're not sure what the spice is, it just might be Papa's Famous Hot Sauce.

While the chicken is best prepared after 24 hours in the brine, you can leave it for as long as 48 hours for an even hotter version, and you can brush on more of Papa's Famous Hot Sauce before baking to achieve a "burn your shorts off" version. For details on how to achieve different levels of heat and spice, see the tip on p. 143.

One 3½- to 4-pound whole chicken,
cut into 8 pieces

FOR THE BRINE
2 quarts water
½ cup granulated sugar
¾ cup kosher salt
4 habaneros, cut in half, with seeds
¼ cup Papa's Famous Hot Sauce (p. 143)

FOR THE COATING
3 cups all-purpose flour
4 tablespoons kosher salt
2 tablespoons smoked
Spanish paprika (pimentón)
1 tablespoon ground habanero
1½ teaspoons ground cayenne

1 tablespoon Homemade Sazón (p. 248)
1 tablespoon freshly ground black pepper
1 tablespoon onion powder
1 tablespoon garlic powder
1 teaspoon ground sage
1 teaspoon ground oregano
1 teaspoon celery salt

FOR THE BUTTERMILK DREDGE
1 quart low fat buttermilk
1 tablespoon habanero powder
1½ teaspoons ground cayenne

Canola oil
Papa's Famous Hot Sauce (p. 143)
White bread and sliced homemade or
store-bought sour pickles, for garnish

MAKE THE BRINE

Combine all of the ingredients in a nonreactive pot and bring to a boil, stirring to dissolve the sugar and salt. Remove from the heat and let cool to room temperature, then cover and refrigerate until cold, 4 to 6 hours. Once the brine is cold (the chicken and brine should be the same temperature), add the chicken pieces, cover, and refrigerate for 24 hours.

PREPARE THE CHICKEN

Position a rack in the center of a convection oven and heat the oven to 350°F. In a medium bowl, mix together the flour and spices for the coating, then transfer the mixture to a large plastic zip-top bag for dredging. In a shallow glass dish, combine the buttermilk with the spices for the dredge and whisk to blend well.

When ready to cook the chicken, remove it from the brine and pat dry with paper towels. Put a couple of pieces at a time in the bag with the coating mixture and shake to coat well. Remove the chicken, shaking off excess, and set aside on a plate while you coat the remaining chicken pieces.

Add the chicken, one piece at a time, to the buttermilk mixture. Coat well and then return it to the plastic bag with the flour. Coat well, shake off the excess, and set aside on a wire rack. Continue until all chicken pieces are dredged.

Place a clean ovenproof wire rack on a baking sheet and set aside. In a large cast iron skillet or large Dutch oven, add enough canola oil to come about 1½ inches up the side (just to cover the chicken pieces) and heat to 325°F on a candy or deep-frying thermometer. Place the chicken, skin side down, in the pan, frying in batches to avoid crowding the pan, until golden brown, turning once, for a total of 5 minutes. Adjust the heat as needed to keep the temperature at a constant 325°F. →

Transfer the chicken to the clean rack. If desired, use a pastry brush to mop each piece of chicken with Papa's Famous Hot Sauce (see the tip below for how much to add based on your desired heat level), lightly covering the crispy skin on top. Place the chicken in the oven for 10 to 15 minutes, or until the internal temperature in a breast reaches 165°F.

Serve the chicken with slices of white bread and garnish with pickles. For a little more kick for any heat level, serve with Papa's Famous Hot Sauce on the side.

PAPA'S FAMOUS HOT SAUCE

MAKES 1½ TO 1¾ CUPS

3 whole habaneros (1½ ounces)
½ cup organic or homemade vegetable stock
½ onion, roughly chopped (1 cup)
4½ tablespoons tomato paste
½ cup white vinegar
½ cup canola oil

½ teaspoon onion powder
¼ teaspoon garlic powder
1 tablespoon kosher salt
2 tablespoons plus 1 teaspoon light brown sugar
1 teaspoon freshly ground black pepper
1 tablespoon minced garlic

Place the ingredients in a small saucepan and bring to a boil. Stir well and reduce the heat, but keep the mixture at a rolling simmer for 30 minutes (or longer), until it's thick and syrupy, stirring often. Do not put your face near the pot and use good ventilation. The habaneros should be very soft. Cool the mixture and then purée in a high-speed blender. Transfer to an air-tight container and refrigerate. The sauce will hold for several weeks.

CHEF'S TIP ❯ Make the dish as hot as you want by following these guidelines: **Medium:** Brine the chicken for 24 hours and do not brush Papa's Famous Hot Sauce on the chicken before baking. ❯ **Hot:** Brine the chicken for 36 hours and use Papa's Famous Hot Sauce for light dipping or mop on after finishing in the oven (don't brush the sauce on the chicken prior to baking). ❯ **Burn-your-shorts-off hot:** Brine the chicken for 48 hours and brush Papa's Famous Hot Sauce over the chicken prior to baking. Serve with white bread and mayonnaise or a mayonnaise-based side dish (like Mama's Potato Salad on p. 216), as the fat will reduce the burn from the hot chicken.

RIVERS, OCEANS & STREAMS

FISH & SEAFOOD
FROM COAST TO COAST

MY FIRST EXPERIENCES with tasting fresh seafood from the ocean were as a young boy when my family traveled to the beaches of southern California and over the border into Mexico, where we went to the *mariscos* stands that sold beautiful ceviches with fresh octopus and fish. When we visited (and ultimately moved to) the mountain and lake region of central California, fishing was one of my favorite pastimes and a way to provide food for my family. It was here that I learned to fish at Bass Lake and I remember catching my first fish, a crappie; we cooked it on the grill that evening for dinner. Looking back, I have always loved fresh fish caught from the rivers and streams as well as the ocean. Fresh fish has such a mild and delicate flavor that easily takes on added spices and rubs. Fish that is not fresh can ruin a meal.

When I returned home to central California and to Bass Lake in the →

145

Fish that are free to roam in their natural habitat and harvested humanely are better tasting than farm-raised fish.

summer of 2014 to film an episode of *Moveable Feast with Fine Cooking*, it brought back those memories; I even found an old photograph of me eating the crappie that I caught in the lake as a young boy. It also reminded me of the times when my cousin Mando would come and stay with us in central California; we would swim in the river and hike up into the mountains. It was an adventure, traveling to what seemed so far away at that time and getting lost for hours.

I learned to appreciate exceptionally fresh fish and seafood early on and, fortunately for me, I was exposed to so much of it during my training at Coronado Bay Resort. Now, as a chef and owner of a restaurant, I insist on using and serving only the freshest and best fish and shellfish that is available. I am lucky to live in Louisville, where the largest UPS hub in the United States is located. I can call any coastal provider and order fish for the next evening that was swimming the day before. It doesn't get much fresher than that.

As a Sustainable Seafood Ambassador for the Monterey Bay Aquarium, it is also very important to me to use only sustainable fish at my restaurant. Check out the online Seafood Watch Program guide to see which fish are sustainable and to look for those varieties when purchasing fresh fish. Get to know your fishmonger as well as know where your fish comes from and be sure that it's wild or line-caught. In general, avoid most farm-raised fish (there are a few exceptions) and seafood imported from Asia and much of South America. Fish that are free to roam in their natural habitat and are harvested humanely are much better tasting. The muscles are better developed and the natural food source produces a healthier and better quality fish.

If you are a sportsman and enjoy fishing, please fish responsibly. We must preserve the dwindling numbers of fish in our rivers, oceans, and streams. Fish for what's sustainable and think about what other species of fish you can substitute in your dishes. If you're accustomed to using black grouper, consider snapper, sustainable sea bass, or wreckfish from South Carolina as an alternate.

While farmed salmon is generally best to avoid (as I mentioned), there is one farming operation that I do support. Verlasso Salmon in Patagonia, Chile, is a sustainable seafood operation approved by the Monterey Bay Aquarium, and their aquaculture practices are unique. Raised and harvested in the cold waters of southern Patagonia, their methods for aquaculture produce a quality product.

While I prefer wild, line-caught and sustainably raised fish, I realize that our oceans are overfished and that the cost of seafood is becoming incredibly expensive. It's inevitable that we will have to move to more farm-raised products, and that's why I support operations that are doing a good job of managing the environment, the feed, and the health of the fish. It's important to become educated about the process of fish farming.

Remember, if you're serving seafood to guests, be sure to ask them about shellfish allergies.

BAJA-STYLE FISH TACOS

Some of my greatest early food memories as a kid were of trips to Baja, Encinada, or Rosarito Beach in southern California to eat fish tacos, a Mexican's answer to the American fried sandwich. The first restaurant to make these tacos famous in the United States is a place called Rubio's in San Diego. The owner, Ralph Rubio, traveled to San Felipe, Mexico, and returned to create his own version of the fish taco in the early 1980s.

I was the first chef to bring fish tacos to Louisville, and people fell in love with them. I can't take the dish off my menu because many people come to the restaurant just for that. My version of fish tacos is lighter than the original from Rubio's. I grill the fish rather than fry it. Alternatively, you can pan sauté the fish. We serve mahi-mahi tacos at Seviche, since the texture of this fish holds up well, but you can use grouper, snapper, or triggerfish, which are similar to mahi-mahi, or a flakier fish like halibut, which provides a more delicate flavor. This recipe uses halibut, but ask your fishmonger which fish is freshest and go with that.

When serving tacos, we do it the traditional way, which is to double up the corn tortillas. It gives you a sturdier taco to hold all the fillings and toppings. You can easily double this recipe for a larger crowd. When entertaining at a casual dinner party, serve the tacos and garnishes buffet style and let guests assemble the tacos themselves. If you're entertaining in the summer, pair ice-cold Micheladas (p. 21) with these tacos.   →

When shopping for fresh fish, you can often buy the remnant or smaller pieces of fillets from your fishmonger at a better price. Those work fine for these tacos, so be sure to ask before buying whole fillets.

SERVES 4 (2 TACOS PER SERVING)

FOR THE FISH	FOR THE TACOS
Four 6-ounce portions halibut fillets, skin removed	16 warm corn tortillas (2 per taco)
Kosher salt	Cumin–Lime Aïoli (p. 232)
Freshly ground black pepper	Shredded cabbage
Extra-virgin olive oil	Fresh lime wedges
Juice of 1 lemon	Pico de Gallo (pp. 240–241)
	Sea salt
	Yellow rice (p. 227), for serving (optional)

PREPARE THE FISH

Pat dry the fish with paper towels and place in a glass baking dish. Sprinkle one side with salt and black pepper. Drizzle with olive oil and a little lemon juice. Flip the fish over and repeat on the other side. Cover and refrigerate for ½ to 1 hour.

When ready to serve, heat a grill on high and oil the grates well. Place the marinated fish directly on the grates (non-skin side down first), close the lid, and grill without moving until you have achieved some char marks. This will take just a minute or two. Flip and cook on the other side for just a few minutes, until the fish flakes easily with a fork.

TO SERVE

Warm the corn tortillas quickly on the grill, flipping them over to heat both sides. Let them get a little char on the edges for color. Layer two together, doubling up the tortillas for each taco. Add a smear of Cumin–Lime Aïoli and top each with 3 ounces of fish. Top with a handful of shredded cabbage, a squeeze of a lime, a spoonful of Pico de Gallo, and a sprinkle of sea salt. Serve immediately with Yellow Rice on the side, if desired.

CHEF'S TIP ❯ If you want to finish the fillets indoors, grill them just until they have char marks and before they're cooked all the way through; transfer to an oiled baking sheet and place in a 300°F convection oven until ready to serve. This way you can get the char marks on the fish, but then hold them in the oven until every-thing else is prepared and set up to serve the tacos.

CHORIZO AND GEORGIA SHRIMP DIRTY RICE

Several years ago, I traveled to the great city of New Orleans. That trip provided the inspiration for this recipe as well as my Southern Crawfish Escabeche (p. 81). I love the flavors in Cajun and Creole dishes, many of which take long hours to prepare, especially when they involve a dark roux. Dirty rice is a favorite Cajun dish, but its preparation is much quicker than many other traditional Cajun dishes. It uses chicken livers or gizzards to impart the "dirty" color and earthy flavor to the rice.

In my Latino-meets-Cajun version of dirty rice, I use Mexican chorizo and sofrito to achieve the wonderful and complex flavors and colors in this dish. The sofrito is made with red peppers, tomatoes, onions, and a blend of seasonings, which marry well with the spicy chorizo. Three types of peppers are combined with a Southern favorite, okra, for a vibrant and festive dish.

Use coastal Georgia or Gulf Coast shrimp and either Carolina Gold, long-grain, or homemade yellow rice (p. 227) for a quick and incredibly flavorful dish that merges several cuisines and cultures. This is great to serve at a large gathering, so feel free to double the recipe as needed.

SERVES 4 TO 5

1 pound ground Mexican chorizo

1 red bell pepper, cut into julienne

1 yellow bell pepper, cut into julienne

1 poblano pepper, seeds and membranes removed, cut into julienne

1 tablespoon minced garlic

6 fresh okra, blanched in salted water for 5 minutes then sliced

1 pound extra-large (16/20) shrimp, peeled and deveined, each shrimp cut into 3 pieces

2 cups cooked Carolina Gold, long-grain, or yellow rice (p. 131)

1¼ cups Sofrito (p. 244)

Kosher salt

Freshly ground black pepper

Juice of ½ lime

Sliced scallions and chopped fresh cilantro or cilantro sprouts, for garnish

In a large skillet over medium-high heat, cook the chorizo, breaking it up with a wooden spoon. Cook until the meat is lightly browned and renders some fat, then add all of the peppers. Cook, stirring occasionally, for 5 minutes, or until the peppers begin to soften. Add the garlic and cook for 1 minute, until aromatic, then add the okra and shrimp. Cook for another minute or two, just until the shrimp are translucent. Add the rice,

Sofrito, a pinch of salt, and a few grinds of black pepper, stirring to mix well, and continue to cook until everything is hot. Taste and adjust seasonings. Squeeze the juice of ½ lime over the pan before serving.

Serve immediately, garnished with scallions and chopped cilantro or cilantro sprouts.

CHEF'S TIP > Pair this dish with a low-alcohol, low-tannin dry white wine like Chenin Blanc or Viognier. Of course, a cold beer brewed in New Orleans, like Abita, works well too.

MACADAMIA-CRUSTED SEA BASS WITH PASSION FRUIT–HABANERO SAUCE

I have made this dish everywhere I've been a chef in Louisville, and it has become one of the recipes I am known for. Susan Riegler, the food critic for the *Louisville Courier-Journal*, mentioned this dish in one of her columns after I had just moved to Louisville and started cooking at Picasso. She said just as you would want to follow the yellow brick road in the *Wizard of Oz*, you might want to follow this dish to follow my career and see where I land. I was obviously flattered, and people have taken her suggestion to heart, following me throughout the city and requesting this specific dish.

While this recipe calls for sustainable sea bass, you can use any firm and mild white fish for the dish, including halibut, triggerfish, tilefish, or grouper. The flavors of the dish are tantalizing, with a mix of slightly sweet, salty, and heat, finished off with a tropical touch. While there are a few components, everything can be prepared ahead of time, except for the fish. Make the couscous earlier in the day and then reheat it slightly, adding the chopped scallions right before serving. You can also prepare the Passion Fruit–Habanero Sauce and refrigerate until ready to use. Serve the sauce at room temperature or warm it gently over a double boiler.

SERVES 4

Four 6-ounce portions sustainable sea bass fillets, skin removed	1 cup chopped and toasted macadamia nuts
Kosher salt	Cranberry–Scallion Couscous (p. 97), for serving
Freshly ground black pepper	Passion Fruit–Habanero Sauce (p. 152)
1 to 2 tablespoons extra-virgin olive oil	

Position a rack in the center of a convection oven and heat the oven to 350°F. Place the sea bass fillets on a platter and sprinkle both sides with salt and black pepper. Let sit for a few minutes. In a nonstick ovenproof skillet over medium-high heat, heat

1 tablespoon of the oil until hot but not smoking. Place the fish top side (non-skin side) down in the pan, cooking in batches, if necessary, to avoid crowding the pan. Add more oil as needed so the fish doesn't burn. Sear for 1 to 2 minutes, or until nicely browned. Carefully flip and cook for another minute, depending on the thickness of the fish.

Move the skillet to the oven and cook for 3 minutes, until the fish is almost cooked through. Remove the skillet, top the fish evenly with the chopped macadamia nuts, lightly patting them onto the fish, and return the pan to the oven; cook for another 3 to 5 minutes, until the fish is fork-tender and perfectly flaky.

Serve immediately on individual plates, placing a halibut fillet on top of the warm Cranberry–Scallion Couscous. Drizzle the pan juices and nuts over the top and then drizzle Passion Fruit–Habanero Sauce around the plate. →

PASSION FRUIT—HABANERO SAUCE

MAKES 2 CUPS

½ cup passion fruit purée (pure purée, no sugar added; I use The Perfect Purée of Napa Valley, see Resources on p. 277)

¾ cup heavy cream

¾ cup granulated sugar (or less if you use purée with sugar added)

Pinch of habanero powder

Pinch of kosher salt

In a medium bowl, combine all of the ingredients and whisk together until the sugar is dissolved. Taste and adjust seasonings. Cover and refrigerate until ready to use. Serve slightly chilled or at room temperature.

CHEF'S TIP ❯ Serve this dish with a mild, fruity white wine, like Pinot Grigio. Be sure not to confuse Pinot Gris with Pinot Grigio. Made from the same grape, they are very different in style—Pinot Gris is usually more full-bodied, richer, and spicier than Pinot Grigio.

CRAB CAKES

It's all about the crab in this spiced-up version of a traditional crab cake. For this classic dish, I use jumbo lump crabmeat. When forming crab cakes, be sure to use a light hand, shaping them as little as possible. I like to prepare and serve them more freeform rather than making them perfectly round. You can prepare these ahead, cover, and refrigerate until ready to serve. They're delicious when served with either Cumin–Lime Aïoli or Latino Butter.

Crab cakes can be the highlight of a menu at a dinner party or served as an elegant appetizer or first course. Pair them with a soft, smooth Chardonnay to impress your dinner guests.

MAKES SIX 4-OUNCE CRAB CAKES

Nonstick cooking spray

2 large eggs, lightly beaten

4 tablespoons mayonnaise (not low-fat)

1 tablespoon Dijon mustard

1 tablespoon kosher salt

1 teaspoon freshly ground black pepper

2 tablespoons chopped fresh curly parsley

2 tablespoons ⅛-inch diced red onion

1 stalk celery, cut into ⅛-inch dice

1 Fresno chile or sweet red jalapeño, trimmed, seeds and membranes removed, and cut into ⅛-inch dice

1 jalapeño, trimmed, seeds and membranes removed, and cut into ⅛-inch dice

1 pound jumbo lump crabmeat, picked over

¼ cup fine dried breadcrumbs

Extra-virgin olive oil, for the pan

Cumin–Lime Aïoli (p. 232) or Latino Butter (p. 236), for serving (optional)

Line a baking sheet with parchment and lightly spray with cooking spray. Set aside.

Mix together all the ingredients except for the crab and breadcrumbs. Stir until well combined. Gently add the crabmeat and breadcrumbs; folding together to bind the mixture without breaking up the crab.

Using your hands, freely form the crab cakes, patting them gently so they hold together. Place them on the prepared baking sheet. If you aren't cooking immediately, cover tightly and refrigerate for up to 6 hours.

Heat a convection oven to 350°F. In a large nonstick skillet, heat enough oil to lightly coat the bottom of the pan over medium high until hot but not smoking. Add the crab cakes to the pan so they aren't crowded (cook in batches if needed) and cook until lightly browned, 1 to 2 minutes. Gently flip and repeat on the other side, adding more oil as needed so that the pan doesn't dry out. If you add more oil bring it back up to temperature before cooking the crab cakes.

After all the cakes are browned, return them to the parchment-lined baking sheet and bake for 15 minutes. Serve immediately with the Cumin–Lime Aïoli or Latino Butter, if desired.

MOQUECA A LA LAMAS (FOR TWO)

When I was at Picasso, a restaurant where I trained early on in Louisville, I worked with a Brazilian woman who taught me how to make several traditional Brazilian dishes, including Moqueca. A classic seafood soup that is prepared with many types of fresh fish, shellfish, and coconut milk, the flavors in my version are also inspired by my training at Coronado Bay Resort on the West Coast, when Pacific Rim dishes were all the rage.

The rich coconut milk in this broth pairs perfectly with our local Bluegrass Soy Sauce. Made here in Louisville by Bourbon Barrel Foods, this is the only soy sauce produced in the United States with traditional Japanese methods. Bourbon Barrel uses only non-GMO soybeans and then ages the sauce in old Woodford Reserve bourbon barrels. There's a subtle hint of bourbon notes in the soy sauce that harmonizes beautifully with the other flavors in this dish.

This is a special dish, so I recommend making it for you and one very lucky partner or guest. Cooking the seafood can take a few minutes to get each individual piece prepared just right, but be sure you don't overcook the fish, as it will cook a little more in the broth. The broth can be made ahead and then added to the seafood to heat everything through at the last minute. You'll end up with a bit of broth leftover, but it will keep in the refrigerator for several days.

Serve this flavorful seafood soup in a large bowl with a side of macadamia rice (see the tip on the facing page) and garnished with fresh cilantro and chopped scallions. The rice is delicious in the broth and the crunch of the nuts and scallions adds a surprising texture to the dish.

SERVES 2 TO 3

FOR THE BROTH
Two 13.5-ounce cans coconut milk, shaken well

2 tablespoons finely minced fresh ginger

⅓ cup Bluegrasss Soy Sauce (see Resources on p. 277)

⅓ cup sambal oelek chile paste

1 teaspoon pure sesame oil

Juice of 1½ to 2 limes

FOR THE SEAFOOD
2 diver scallops or other large scallops, preferably dry packed

Four 2-ounce pieces fresh fish, skin removed (combination of grouper, bass, salmon, or whatever is in season and freshest)

4 extra-large (16/20) shrimp, peeled and deveined

6 mussels

Kosher salt

Freshly ground black pepper

1 to 2 tablespoons canola oil

Two 2-ounce pieces sushi-grade Ahi tuna

Macadamia rice (see the tip on the facing page), for serving

Chopped fresh cilantro and chopped scallions, for garnish

MAKE THE BROTH

In a large bowl or plastic container, combine all of the ingredients and whisk to mix well. Cover and refrigerate until ready to prepare the fish and shellfish for serving.

PREPARE THE SEAFOOD

Season the fish and shellfish with a little salt and black pepper. Heat 1 tablespoon of the oil in a large nonstick skillet over medium-high heat until hot but not smoking. Add the scallops first and cook until they begin to take on a nice sear. Add the fish fillets, non-skin side down, and sauté until the first side starts to lightly brown, then add the mussels. They will begin to open their shells as they cook.

Flip the scallops and fish fillets over and cook on the other side, adding more oil if necessary. Add the shrimp and sauté, flipping them two or three times on each side to cook properly. You want the scallops to have a nice sear but remain translucent in the middle and the shrimp to turn pink, but not rubbery, and maintain a translucent center down the back. The fish should have a nice sear on the top side.

Meanwhile, heat a grill or medium skillet until hot, then add a little oil and quickly sear the tuna on two sides. You want it rare, so sear gently. Remove from the grill or pan and keep warm. Keep the tuna separate from the other fish, as it will top the Moqueca and not cook in the broth.

FINISH THE DISH AND SERVE

When ready to serve, stir the broth well, then add 2½ to 2¾ cups to the pan with the fish and shellfish. Increase the heat and bring to a boil. Once the mixture comes to a boil, lower the heat and cook for about 3 minutes. Turn off the heat and let the stew sit for 2 minutes.

Remove the seafood from the broth. Using large, deep serving bowls, place 1 scallop and 2 pieces of fish in the bottom of each bowl; top with 2 shrimp and 3 mussels each. Divide the broth evenly between the bowls. Slice the tuna into several pieces and place on top of the broth. Garnish each serving with a pinch of cilantro and sprinkling of scallions. Serve with macadamia rice on the side or place in the bottom of the bowl before adding the seafood.

CHEF'S TIP ❯ Macadamia rice is simple to prepare and adds a nice textural element to whatever else you're serving. The flavor and crunch will surprise your guests. For a more aromatic rice, use either jasmine or basmati rice.

Prepare the desired amount of jasmine, basmati, or long-grain rice according to the package directions or prepare Classic Carolina Gold Rice (p. 131). Top each serving of rice with chopped toasted macadamia nuts. You can also make pepita rice by substituting toasted, salted pepitas for the macadamia nuts.

CHEF'S TIP ❯ This beautiful Brazilian fish stew pairs well with native South American liquors like rum and Cachaça. Try it paired with Caipirinhas (pp. 24–25) or if you prefer wine, serve a crisp white like Sauvignon Blanc or a French Chardonnay.

MOUNTAIN TROUT WITH COUNTRY HAM AND LEMON—TOMATO BUTTER

This flavorful and easy-to-prepare trout dish is beautiful, making it perfect when entertaining, especially in the warmer months when you can grill outdoors. Use whole fresh trout that have had the heads, tails, and bones removed by your fishmonger. The simple filling and quick marinade give the trout a wonderful flavor. If you're using a charcoal grill, that will add a nice smoky flavor to the fish as well.

We use thinly sliced local Newsom's country ham to season this dish, much as we do in the chicken recipe on p. 116. It imparts a bit of saltiness and hint of smokiness.

Grilling is my favorite method for cooking the trout, but I give an alternative for cooking on the stovetop and finishing in the oven. In either case, serve the trout with Classic Carolina Gold Rice (p. 131) and Lemon—Tomato Butter (p. 231), an elegant beurre blanc that highlights the flavors of this impressive fish dish.

SERVES 4

4 whole trout (12 ounces each), cleaned, trimmed of heads and tails, and deboned

Thin slices country ham, cut like prosciutto, enough to cover the bottom side of the fish

Several sprigs fresh thyme, leaves removed

2 to 3 padron peppers or serrano chiles, seeds and membranes removed, thinly sliced

Extra-virgin olive oil

Kosher salt

Freshly ground black pepper

1 cup all-purpose flour

Classic Carolina Gold Rice (p. 131), for serving

Lemon—Tomato Butter (p. 231), for serving

Place one whole trout on a cutting board and lay it open like a book to expose the flesh. On one side of the fish, layer enough country ham slices to cover that side (or half) of the fish, then sprinkle the country ham with fresh thyme leaves. Top with several slices of the peppers, drizzle with olive oil, and sprinkle with salt and black pepper. Bring the sides of the trout together and tie around the outside in three or four places with kitchen twine. Repeat with the other 3 trout.

Heat a charcoal or gas grill on high. When it's hot, oil the grates well so the fish doesn't stick.

Combine the flour with a generous pinch of salt and a few grinds of black pepper.

Lightly dust the trout with the seasoned flour. Place the trout directly on the grates and cook for 6 to 7 minutes on the first side, until browned. Flip the fish over carefully, using two spatulas, and cook on the other side for another 5 to 6 minutes. Check the inside flesh of the fish by nudging in between the twine with the tip of a knife to make sure it's cooked through, flaky, and opaque. Remove immediately from the grill. (Alternatively, sear the trout in a hot ovenproof skillet lightly coated with olive oil for about 2 minutes, and then finish cooking in a 350°F convection oven for 6 to 7 minutes, until the fish is cooked through. If desired, baste with a little melted unsalted butter before placing in the oven.)

Before serving, remove the twine. On individual serving plates, lay 1 trout across a bed of Classic Carolina Gold Rice and drizzle with Lemon–Tomato Butter.

CHEF'S TIP ❯ This dish should be paired with a wine that will complement the saltiness of the country ham without overpowering the delicate trout. A dry Reisling or Viognier will do just that. Don't use a late-harvest Reisling, though, because it's too sweet and is best as a dessert wine.

NUEVO LATINO SHRIMP AND GRITS WITH BOURBON RED-EYE GRAVY

It would be hard to have a restaurant in Kentucky and not pay homage in some way to one of the South's most quintessential dishes, Shrimp and Grits. I start with local Weisenberger grits (see Resources on p. 277) that have been seasoned with grated Manchego cheese and roasted poblano peppers and top it with my take on Red-Eye Gravy, which is made with Kentucky bourbon.

This signature dish was the one I prepared on *Beat Bobby Flay* that aired on Food Network. One of the judges said my poblano pepper garnish made the dish too hot, so, I didn't win. But look for the rematch. I'm coming for you, Bobby! While poblanos aren't typically hot, many peppers can be unpredictable (for more on this, see p. 12).

Very popular in the South, red-eye gravy is made by cooking slices of country ham in water to release the flavors from the fat and then adding a few other ingredients, like coffee, butter, or even beef broth. It's the drippings from this incredibly flavorful country ham that give the gravy its unique flavor and mouth-feel.

I use local Kentucky freshwater prawns or shrimp from Georgia or the Gulf Coast for this dish. The shrimp are marinated to give them great flavor and then sautéed quickly, so they're not overcooked. Alternatively, you can grill them for a perfect sear and char, as shown in the photo on p. 158. While the shrimp may appear to be the star of the show, it's the different layers of flavor when taken together in one bite that will have your taste buds tingling.   →

SERVES 4 TO 5

FOR THE SHRIMP

1 pound extra-large (16/20) Georgia or Gulf Coast shrimp, peeled and deveined

Juice of ½ lemon

3 tablespoons olive oil

2 cloves garlic, minced

1 tablespoon chopped fresh oregano

1 teaspoon ground achiote

½ teaspoon kosher salt

2 teaspoons Chipotle in Adobo Purée (p. 114)

FOR THE BOURBON RED-EYE GRAVY

9 tablespoons unsalted butter, divided

1½ ounces country ham with some fat, cut into ¼-inch dice

¼ onion, cut into ¼-inch dice

¼ teaspoon minced garlic

1 teaspoon chopped fresh thyme

¼ cup brewed coffee, at room temperature

½ cup Woodford Reserve (or your favorite Kentucky bourbon)

¼ teaspoon whole black peppercorns

1 teaspoon kosher salt (this will depend on the saltiness of your country ham)

Juice and peeled zest of 1 lemon

¼ cup heavy cream

1 tablespoon cornstarch slurry (p. 118), as needed

Roasted Poblano and Manchego Weisenberger Grits (p. 160), for serving

Chopped fresh curly parsley, micro celery, or micro greens, for garnish

MAKE THE SHRIMP

Put the shrimp in a medium nonreactive bowl. In a small bowl, mix the lemon juice, oil, garlic, oregano, achiote, salt, and chipotle purée. Stir well to combine then pour over the shrimp. Cover and refrigerate for 2 to 4 hours, stirring occasionally to distribute the marinade.

MAKE THE BOURBON RED-EYE GRAVY

In a medium skillet over medium-high heat, melt 1 tablespoon of the butter and then add the diced country ham. Cook until it renders some fat and just begins to brown, 2 to 3 minutes, reducing the heat if necessary. Add the onion, garlic, and thyme and sweat the onion and garlic until aromatic, 2 to 3 minutes. Add the coffee to deglaze the pan, scraping up any browned bits. Take the pan off the heat, pour in the bourbon, and light it to burn off the alcohol. Return the pan to the heat and then add the peppercorns, salt, lemon juice, lemon zest, and heavy cream. Bring to a boil, then reduce the heat to medium and cook until slightly reduced, just a few minutes. Thicken with a little of the cornstarch slurry (½ teaspoon to start); whisking to combine well. The sauce should be the consistency of buttermilk.

Reduce the heat to low and add the remaining 8 tablespoons butter, 1 tablespoon at a time, whisking well after each addition. Remove the pan from the heat once the butter is fully incorporated. Taste and adjust seasonings. Keep the sauce warm over a double boiler until ready to serve.

COOK THE SHRIMP

Remove the shrimp from the marinade (discard the marinade). Add a little olive oil to a large skillet and heat over medium until the oil is hot but not smoking. Add the shrimp in batches if necessary to avoid crowding the pan, and cook just until they turn pink, 2 to 3 minutes per side. Remove immediately and keep the shrimp warm until ready to plate.

TO SERVE

Strain the gravy through a fine-mesh sieve or chinois. In individual shallow serving bowls, evenly divide the Roasted Poblano and Manchego Weisenberger Grits. Top with some of the strained Bourbon Red-Eye Gravy, followed by 4 or 5 cooked shrimp. Garnish each bowl with the chopped parsley, celery leaves, or micro celery.

CHEF'S TIP ❯ Shrimp and grits can be a challenge to pair with wine or spirits since there's a lot of different flavors and heat going on. However, I like to support our regional artisans, and the wines of Virginia are some of the finest in the world. Try a Viognier from Barboursville Vineyards, where our friend Luca Paschina is producing some of the best wines around.

ROASTED POBLANO AND MANCHEGO WEISENBERGER GRITS

SERVES 4 TO 5

2 cups water	1 large or 2 small poblano peppers, roasted (see p. 97), peeled; seeds, stems, and membranes removed; and roughly chopped by hand or in a food processor, or one 8-ounce can chopped and drained green chiles
1 teaspoon kosher salt	
½ cup white stone-ground grits (I use local Weisenberger grits)	
2 ounces heavy cream	
4 tablespoons unsalted butter	1 cup grated Manchego cheese
	Freshly ground black pepper

In a medium saucepan, combine the water and salt and bring to a boil. Slowly stir in the dry grits, pouring them in a thin stream and stirring constantly so lumps won't form. Cook over high heat, stirring constantly, until the grits start to thicken a little, then reduce the heat to low and cook uncovered, stirring frequently to ensure they don't scorch. Adjust the heat as necessary. Cook for 20 to 25 minutes, until the grits are done, like a thick cooked farina.

Stir the heavy cream, butter, roasted poblanos, and Manchego into the hot grits, seasoning to taste with freshly ground black pepper.

VARIATION ❯ To make Cheddar and Chipotle Weisenberger Grits, substitute grated Cheddar for the Manchego and use 2 tablespoons Chipotle in Adobo Purée (p. 114) instead of the roasted poblanos.

MEET PHILIP WEISENBERGER ➤
WEISENBERGER MILLS, MIDWAY, KENTUCKY

FROM ANTHONY

Not far from Louisville, in the tiny town of Midway, Kentucky, is a small producer of stone-ground grits and other milled products, Weisenberger Mills. Visiting the historic old mill located in South Elkhorn Creek is a step back in time. We use stone-ground Weisenberger Grits at Seviche and are proud to feature their locally grown products on our menu. Just as with our local farmers, we appreciate the care that goes into every package Weisenberger sells.

FROM PHILIP

Things haven't changed much here since my ancestors first started the business in 1865. August Weisenberger emigrated from Baden, Germany, to Midway in 1862 and purchased the mill three years later. I'm the sixth generation of Weisenbergers to be involved with the mill, and we still grind corn and grain much as we always did, by twin turbines in the waters of South Elkhorn Creek. Of course, today everything is electric, but the mill has always relied on water to power the machines.

The original mill developed a large crack in the side and was unsafe, so it was torn down and rebuilt in 1913. The "new" mill is made of concrete from the ground-up stones of the original mill. We're one of the few old-fashioned mills still remaining in the United States and the oldest continuously operating mill in Kentucky. We're also on the National Register of Historic Places.

Weisenberger Mill is a small operation with just six employees. We buy local Kentucky-grown corn and wheat and are now able to source both white and yellow non-GMO corn. We've had relationships with some of the same farmers for generations and will often label the packages with the farm name where the original product was sourced. We source ingredients up to about 100 miles away. In addition to our grits, we produce cornmeal, flour, and a number of other whole-grain products (like wheat berries), and have created our own complete package mixes, such as fish batter and a biscuit and pancake mix. We actually sell about 70 different products. There was a demand for these baking products, so we developed the recipes.

Cornmeal and flour are the main products we produce at the mill, with about 50,000 pounds of cornmeal and 25,000 pounds of flour ground per week. Making grits is one of the longer processes since the dried corn is divided into three components: grits, cornmeal, and bran. The bran is used for bulk feed.

It's interesting that grits used to be a side dish, something served with just butter. Now stone-ground grits are the star of the show, acting as the foundation for many different dishes. They're nothing like instant grits; they have their own unique flavor and texture and they hold up well to other flavors. We're just glad to be a small part of this interest in local and Southern foods.

PAN-SEARED HALIBUT WITH RED-CHILE BLUEGRASS SOY BUTTER

The seasons for Pacific halibut run from late spring to mid-summer and from early to mid-fall. This mild-flavored and firm white fish lends itself beautifully to lots of flavors, so check with your fishmonger to see when it will be available in your local stores and then prepare this dish or the Macadamia-Crusted Sea Bass on pp. 150–152. Ask your fishmonger to remove the skin so that you won't have that chore once you get home.

The Red-Chile Bluegrass Soy Butter is a luscious beurre blanc that uses our local Bluegrass Soy Sauce and pairs perfectly with the fish. At Seviche, I serve it with macadamia rice (see the tip on p. 155). As I've said before, the salty, sweet, and crunchy texture of this rice makes a beautiful accompaniment to many dishes, including this one, and your family and guests will love it. I promise.

Remember to start with a really hot pan to properly sear the fish and seal in the juices. Make sure it is perfectly seared and caramelized before flipping the fillet over to finish in the oven.

SERVES 4

Four 6-ounce portions halibut fillets, skin removed	1 to 2 tablespoons extra-virgin olive oil
Kosher salt	Red-Chile Bluegrass Soy Butter (see the facing page)
Freshly ground black pepper	Macadamia rice (p. 155), for serving

Position a rack in the center of a convection oven and heat the oven to 350°F. Lay the halibut fillets on a platter and sprinkle both sides with salt and black pepper. Let sit for a few minutes. In a nonstick ovenproof skillet over medium-high heat, heat 1 tablespoon of the oil until hot but not smoking. Place the fillets non-skin side down in the pan, cooking in batches if necessary to avoid crowding the pan. Add more oil as needed so the fillets don't burn. Bring the oil back to temperature before adding more fish. Sear for 1 to 2 minutes, or until nicely seared. Carefully flip and cook for another minute, depending on the thickness of the fish.

Transfer the skillet to the oven and cook for 6 to 8 minutes, until the fish is fork-tender and perfectly flaky.

Serve immediately over a bed of macadamia rice and drizzle with Red-Chile Bluegrass Soy Butter.

CHEF'S TIP ❯ Pair this dish with a Spanish Cava. The bubbles cut the spice of the Red-Chile Bluegrass Soy Butter without overpowering the delicate fish.

RED-CHILE BLUEGRASS SOY BUTTER

MAKES 1½ CUPS

½ cup dry white wine

1 shallot, thinly sliced

Juice and peeled zest of 1 lemon, divided

1 teaspoon chopped fresh ginger

¼ cup heavy cream

¼ cup Bluegrass Soy Sauce (see Resources on p. 277)

2 teaspoons cornstarch slurry (p. 118), as needed

8 tablespoons unsalted butter, sliced

¼ cup sambal oelek chile paste

In a medium saucepan over high heat, combine the wine, shallot, lemon zest, and ginger. Bring to a boil and reduce the mixture by about half, 2 to 3 minutes. Lower the heat to medium, add the cream and soy sauce, and mix well. Cook until the sauce is reduced, smooth, and semi-thick, 2 to 3 minutes. Reduce the heat to low, pour in the lemon juice, and then slowly add the cornstarch slurry, a little at a time, whisking constantly, until the sauce returns to a nice, smooth consistency. Whisk in the butter, 1 tablespoon at a time, until it is fully incorporated. Strain the mixture through a fine-mesh sieve or chinois, then add the chile paste and mix well. Taste and adjust for seasonings. Keep warm over a double boiler until ready to serve.

SEARED SCALLOPS WITH FAVA BEAN AND INDIANA CORN SUCCOTASH AND LEMON–JALAPEÑO BUTTER

This composed dish of succulent, beautifully seared diver scallops and summer's fresh corn and fava beans is an impressive dish to serve for a special occasion. Use only the freshest and sweetest scallops you can find and preferably those that are dry packed. Before cooking, thoroughly pat them dry and season the scallops with salt and black pepper.

In the South, lima beans, when in season, are traditionally paired with fresh corn and then tossed with a little butter, salt, and pepper for a classic succotash. For this version, we use Kentucky country ham and butter to season the succotash and then give a little Latin love to the mix by substituting fava beans for the lima beans. Favas have a smoother, richer, and sweeter flavor than lima beans. Favas need to be shelled twice, so see the tip on p. 168 on how to do just that.

The addition of one of my favorite beurre blancs, Lemon–Jalapeño Butter (p. 168), really makes this dish stand out. The sweetness of the seared scallop with the luscious and bright sauce is pure heaven. Combined with the

fava beans and corn that have been cooked with the country ham, you will impress yourself, and your guests, with this gorgeous dish.

Don't forget the wine. Get creative and try something different like a white wine from Friuli, Italy, such as Vespa Bianco by Bastianich Vineyards or a Sancerre from France.

SERVES 4

FOR THE FAVA BEAN AND INDIANA CORN SUCCOTASH

1 tablespoon unsalted butter

¼ cup diced country ham

¼ Spanish onion, cut into ¼-inch dice

1 teaspoon minced garlic

3 ears Indiana Silver Queen corn, kernels cut from cobs (p. 75)

¼ cup organic or homemade chicken stock

1 pound fresh fava beans, shelled and outer coating removed (see the tip on p. 168)

1 teaspoon kosher salt

Freshly ground black pepper

FOR THE SCALLOPS

1 to 1½ pounds large or diver scallops, preferably dry packed

Kosher salt

Freshly ground black pepper

2 to 3 tablespoons canola oil

1 tablespoon unsalted butter

Lemon–Jalapeño Butter (p. 168), for serving

MAKE THE FAVA BEAN AND INDIANA CORN SUCCOTASH

In a large skillet over medium-high heat, melt the butter until the foam subsides, then add the country ham. Cook until the ham is just slightly brown and beginning to get crispy, 2 to 3 minutes, reducing the heat if necessary so that the ham doesn't brown too quickly. Add the onion, stir, and sweat it for 2 minutes. Add the garlic and cook for another 30 seconds, then add the corn kernels and chicken stock. Reduce the heat to medium and stir to combine well. Cook the mixture for 1 to 2 minutes, stirring occasionally, so the corn remains crunchy. Stir in the fava beans and season with the salt and a few grinds of black pepper. Continue cooking until the fava beans are tender, 5 to 7 minutes, stirring several times to incorporate the ingredients. Taste and adjust seasonings. Set aside.

MAKE THE SCALLOPS

Position a rack in the center of a convection oven and heat the oven to 325°F. Pat dry the scallops with paper towels and then sprinkle both sides with salt and black pepper. In a large cast iron skillet over very high heat, heat 2 tablespoons of the canola oil until hot but not smoking. Add the scallops, cooking in batches if necessary to avoid crowding the pan; add the remaining 1 tablespoon oil if needed, bringing back to temperature. Sear the first side for 4 to 5 minutes. Once the scallops are nicely seared, flip them and transfer the skillet to the oven; cook the scallops for 4 to 5 minutes, just until translucent. Remove the skillet from the oven and add the butter to the hot pan. Once melted, quickly baste the scallops with the butter. Remove and serve immediately.

TO SERVE

Portion the succotash among serving plates, then arrange the seared scallops on top (3 to 4 scallops per serving). Drizzle the Lemon–Jalapeño Butter around the plate and serve immediately.

LEMON—JALAPEÑO BUTTER

MAKES ABOUT 1 CUP

½ cup dry white wine

1 shallot, thinly sliced

1 jalapeño, trimmed and sliced (with seeds)

Juice and peeled zest of 1 lemon, divided

1 teaspoon kosher salt

½ teaspoon whole black peppercorns

½ cup heavy cream

1½ teaspoons cornstarch slurry (p. 118), as needed

8 tablespoons unsalted butter, sliced

In a medium saucepan over high heat, combine the wine, shallot, jalapeño, lemon zest, salt, and peppercorns. Bring to a boil and reduce the mixture by half, 3 to 4 minutes. Lower the heat to medium, add the cream, and stir; cook until the sauce is reduced and semi-thick, 2 to 3 minutes. Add the cornstarch slurry, a little at a time, whisking constantly, until the sauce is thickened. Reduce the heat to low and add the lemon juice. Whisk in the butter, 1 tablespoon at a time, until it's fully incorporated. Strain the mixture through a fine-mesh sieve or chinois. Keep warm until ready to serve.

CHEF'S TIP ❯ To prepare fava beans, first remove the beans from the pod by either opening it up on one end and popping the beans out with your finger or breaking open the pod in the middle and then removing the beans. Bring a pot of water to boiling. Add the beans and blanch for 1 minute. Remove the beans and plunge into an ice water bath for 2 to 3 minutes to stop further cooking. Drain the beans and find the slight opening on one side of the bean. With your nail, pry it open and remove the skin of the bean to reveal a smaller bright green bean on the inside.

WILD ALASKAN SALMON WITH WHITE BEANS, COUNTRY HAM, AND SPINACH WITH LEMON–ROSEMARY BUTTER

I always say that the only time we should be eating wild-caught salmon is when the bears are enjoying it in Alaska, which is late May to early October. Wild salmon from the Pacific, known as Chinook, is sometimes sold as either coho or king salmon. This fatty fish is rich in health benefits and flavor, so don't miss the opportunity to prepare this recipe during wild salmon season. For a very special treat, watch for Copper River salmon starting in May. A prized catch for its texture and fat, you have to act fast, as the season only lasts three weeks.

The subtle flavors of the white beans and spinach are wonderful in this recipe, and the Lemon–Rosemary Butter, a simple-to-prepare compound butter, adds a brightness and luscious mouth-feel. While rustic enough to serve for a family meal, you can also plate this dish for an elegant dinner with friends. Garnish the composed dish with sliced heirloom cherry tomatoes and squeeze some fresh lemon juice over the plate to finish with a bit of brightness. If desired, add a pat of the Lemon–Rosemary Butter (p. 171) at the end for some more buttery rich goodness.

SERVES 4

FOR THE FISH

1 whole side wild Alaskan salmon (1½-pound fillet), cut into four 6-ounce portions

Extra-virgin olive oil

Kosher salt

Freshly ground black pepper

Finely grated zest of 1 lemon

2 tablespoons Lemon–Rosemary Butter (p. 171), plus more for serving

FOR THE WHITE BEANS AND SPINACH

½ pound dry white beans, rinsed and soaked overnight

One 2-ounce piece Kentucky country ham (or other good-quality country ham)

2 bay leaves

2 to 3 teaspoons kosher salt, depending on the saltiness of the ham, divided

Extra-virgin olive oil

3 to 4 tablespoons Lemon–Rosemary Butter (p. 171)

2 cloves garlic, minced

4 cups packed fresh baby spinach leaves

Freshly ground black pepper

A squeeze of fresh lemon juice and halved heirloom cherry tomatoes, for garnish

PREPARE THE SALMON

Carefully remove the skin and fatty belly parts (dark flesh) from the fillets with a sharp knife. Also remove any remaining pin bones. Pat the fish dry with paper towels and place on a large plate. Drizzle each fillet with olive oil and then sprinkle both sides with salt, black pepper, and lemon zest. Rub the fillets well and place them flat in a gallon-size zip-top bag. Remove the air and seal, then place the bag in a large dish, keeping the fillets in a single layer, and refrigerate for at least 4 hours or overnight.

MAKE THE WHITE BEANS

Drain the beans that have been soaked overnight and put them in a medium saucepan. Cover with water by about 2 inches and add the country ham, bay leaves, and 2 teaspoons salt. Bring to a boil, then reduce the heat and simmer for 50 to 60 minutes (this length of time gives the beans a nice creaminess).

→

When the beans are at the desired texture, drain and rinse with cold water. Remove and discard the bay leaves and then season with a pinch of salt and a teaspoon of olive oil. Stir to combine and then either cover and set aside or refrigerate for longer storage. (This process keeps the beans from sticking together so that you can prepare them ahead before plating the rest of the dish.)

If serving right away, melt 3 tablespoons of the Lemon–Rosemary Butter in a large skillet over medium heat. Add the garlic, stir, and cook for 20 to 30 seconds, or until fragrant. Add the white beans. Stir and cook until warmed through, just a few minutes. Add the spinach and cook until wilted, just another minute or two, basting with the butter. Add the remaining 1 tablespoon Lemon–Rosemary Butter if you want a bit more sauce. Taste and adjust seasonings. Keep warm.

COOK THE SALMON

Heat a grill on high and oil the grates. Remove the salmon from the marinade (discard the marinade) and arrange the salmon directly on the grates, non-skin side down. Cook for about 5 minutes, until the fish is nicely seared, then carefully flip the fillets over with a large spatula (or two) and cook for another 4 minutes on the side where the skin was removed. (Alternatively, heat a large ovenproof nonstick skillet over medium-high heat with a thin layer of extra-virgin olive oil. When the oil is hot but not smoking, add the salmon fillets non-skin side down and cook until they're nicely seared, about 4 minutes. Flip the fillets over and cook on the other side, about another 5 minutes, lowering the heat to medium if needed. Or finish cooking the salmon in a 350°F convection oven for 5 to 7 minutes. Add 2 tablespoons Lemon–Rosemary Butter to the pan, melt the butter, and baste the fillets during final cooking.) The flesh should be opaque for medium to medium-well done.

TO SERVE

Evenly distribute the white bean mixture among individual serving plates or spread on a large serving platter. Arrange the cooked salmon fillets on top. If desired, add another pat of Lemon–Rosemary Butter to each piece of salmon. Squeeze fresh lemon juice over the fish and garnish with the cherry tomatoes.

LEMON—ROSEMARY BUTTER

MAKES A 1-POUND LOG

1 pound unsalted butter, softened	1 teaspoon kosher salt
2 sprigs fresh rosemary, diced fine (like powder)	1 teaspoon freshly ground black pepper
	1 teaspoon Pernod
Juice and finely grated zest of 2 lemons	¼ teaspoon lemon oil (optional; see Resources on p. 277)

In a medium bowl, using your hands or an electric hand-held mixer fitted with wire beaters, gently combine all of the ingredients until well blended. Lay a large piece of parchment on the counter. Use a spatula to scrape the mixture onto the center of the paper and shape the butter mixture into a log. Wrap and tighten the ends, twisting to seal tightly. Wrap the butter in parchment in a piece of plastic wrap to keep it airtight. Refrigerate for at least 2 hours to firm before using. The butter will hold in the refrigerator for a few weeks, or place in a zip-top plastic bag and freeze for up to 2 months. Alternatively, you can store the butter in an airtight container.

CHEF'S TIP ❯ This dish pairs nicely with a Spanish Rioja Crianza (pronounced cree AHN tha), a value-priced young and juicy red wine with just a little hint of oak. Red wine with fish? When you have such a beautiful salmon, this red wine is the perfect match and worth finding.

FIELDS,
GARDENS &
PRESERVING THE
HARVEST

PLANT-BASED
DISHES FOR EVERY
SEASON

I LOVE TO WATCH the seasons change throughout the year. When I would see lemons and limes in the citrus groves in central California, I knew what season it was and anticipated the ingredients that my mama would use in her cooking. The same is true with me today. When I begin to feel the first nip of fall in the air and watch the leaves start to change in the Bluegrass State, I know that the fresh Indiana corn and heirloom tomatoes will soon be replaced by hearty winter greens, winter squashes, and pumpkins, but that's what makes cooking exciting. We're always changing the ingredients and how we prepare them.

I learned cooking and eating seasonally as a way of life long before the term "farm to table" became trendy. When I was young, harvesting and using products that were in season was the way we ate.

With the recent focus on meatless dishes and many chefs moving away from meat-centric menus to more plant-based dishes, eating within the seasons is more important than →

I hope these recipes will inspire you to add more plant-based dishes to your rotation of meals at home and to shop the farmers' markets in season and preserve the bounty of the harvest.

ever. It's exciting to get creative with vegetable-centric dishes, especially because I work with so many incredible local farmers growing spectacular produce.

Several of them grow specific products for me. Last year I told a farmer that I would take all the peppers she could grow. She took me quite seriously, showing up with hundreds of pounds of peppers, so I decided I better get to canning and preserving the harvest. A few years ago I received my state certification to serve and sell the canned products in the restaurant; now Seviche is the only state- and FDA-certified restaurant in the state of Kentucky for canning.

One local ingredient that I love to preserve in late sum-

mer is pawpaws. I had never heard of this unique fruit until I moved to Kentucky, but I immediately fell in love with it. The taste is like a cross between a banana, mango, and pineapple. One farmer brings me everything his pawpaw trees produce—almost 400 pounds! I've used pawpaws to create a flan (see p. 259), a spicy beurre blanc sauce, and preserves; I also add them to ice cream.

Years ago when I was working my apprenticeship at Coronado Bay Resort, a guest requested that the chef prepare her something that was not on the regular menu, a dish that was lighter and vegetarian. I created a beautiful grilled vegetable plate with some unique flavors and textures.

Some time after the plate had gone out, I was told that this guest wanted to see me. When I went over, it was none other than Oprah Winfrey. She wanted to tell me how much she enjoyed my dish. I have never forgotten that moment. It was also an inspiration for me to create a gorgeous and delicious plate of food without any meat or seafood.

This chapter offers a combination of vegetarian dishes as well as some of my best-loved canning recipes. I hope these recipes will inspire you to add more plant-based dishes to your rotation of meals at home and to shop the farmers' markets in season and preserve the bounty of the harvest to use in your kitchen throughout the year.

VEGETABLE CAZUELA

Full of flavor and traditionally cooked in a clay pot (*cazuela* in Spanish), this hearty stew usually consists of chicken or beef combined with vegetables like corn, potatoes, butternut squash, beans or peas, and a well-seasoned stock. *Cazuelas* can be served with rice and topped with cilantro and other accompaniments.

Think of my version of *cazuela* as a vegetable-based Posole. I like the combination of textures and flavors in this recipe, but feel free to get creative and add whatever vegetables or ingredients you have in your garden, refrigerator, or pantry. For a particularly rustic version, cut the corn cobs in half and add them to the stew.

This recipe makes a large batch, so you can feed a crowd and then still have leftovers. When you reheat it, change it up by adding some extras like garbanzo beans or fresh seasonal vegetables, or both.

SERVES 10 TO 12

1 tablespoon extra-virgin olive oil

1 medium butternut squash (1¾ pounds), peeled, seeded, and cut into 1-inch pieces

2 russet potatoes, peeled and cut into 1-inch pieces

¼ head cabbage, sliced

1 medium onion, cut into ¼-inch dice

3 stalks celery, cut into ¼-inch dice

5 cloves garlic, roughly chopped

1 red bell pepper, cut into julienne

1 yellow bell pepper, cut into julienne

3 tablespoons kosher salt, divided

2 teaspoons freshly ground black pepper

2 teaspoons chopped fresh thyme

2 quarts organic or homemade vegetable stock

1 cup crushed tomatoes

2 yellow summer squash, ends trimmed, halved, and cut into ½-inch slices

3 zucchini, ends trimmed, halved, and cut into ½-inch slices

3 ears fresh sweet corn, kernels removed from the cobs (p. 75)

3 medium carrots, peeled and cut into ¼-inch slices

1 cup fresh (or frozen) lima beans

½ teaspoon ground turmeric

¼ teaspoon ground cayenne

1 teaspoon pure lemon oil (see Resources on p. 277), or the finely grated zest of 1 lemon

Juice of 1 lemon

Chopped fresh cilantro, for garnish

Fresh lime wedges and warm tortillas or cornbread, for serving

In a large stockpot over medium-high heat, heat the oil until hot but not smoking. Add the butternut squash, potatoes, cabbage, onion, and celery. Stir well and sweat the vegetables for about 5 minutes, reducing the heat if necessary so they don't burn. Add the garlic, stir, and cook for 1 to 2 minutes more. Add the bell peppers, 1½ tablespoons of salt, the black pepper, and the thyme. Stir well and reduce the heat. Cook for 20 minutes, stirring frequently to distribute the natural juices from the vegetables.

Add the vegetable stock, tomatoes, yellow squash, zucchini, corn, carrots, lima beans, turmeric, and cayenne and season with the lemon oil (or zest) and lemon juice. Bring to a boil, reduce the heat, and simmer for 20 to 30 minutes, until the vegetables are tender. Taste and adjust seasonings. You might need to add as much as 1½ tablespoons additional salt.

Serve hot in individual *cazuelas* or bowls, garnished with fresh cilantro, with lime wedges and warm tortillas or cornbread on the side.

FIDEO WITH ASPARAGUS, ARTICHOKES, GOAT CHEESE, AND JALAPEÑO—BASIL PESTO

This beautiful vegetarian pasta features the best of spring, with fresh asparagus, artichoke hearts, and a spicy Jalapeño–Basil Pesto. As with many of these recipes, you can prepare a number of things ahead to make it easier to pull dinner together in the evening, especially if you're entertaining.

Cook the pasta ahead, shock it in ice water, drain, and then season it with a little salt and extra-virgin olive oil and keep covered in the refrigerator until you're ready to prepare the rest of the dish. You also can cook the vegetables ahead and refrigerate until ready to serve. You can even cook the vegetables first and then cook the pasta in the same water, saving an extra pot on the stovetop. It also infuses the flavor of the vegetables into your pasta. The pesto can be made beforehand, too.

This recipe uses only the hearts of the artichokes, so prepare and steam the whole artichoke, reserve the hearts, and nibble on the outer leaves while prepping the rest of dinner. Dip the leaves in melted butter or a sauce made of mayonnaise, lemon juice, and garlic. They are delicious!

SERVES 4

¾ pound thin spaghetti

1 pound fresh asparagus, trimmed, cut on the diagonal into 2-inch pieces

1 to 2 tablespoons extra-virgin olive oil, or enough to coat the pan

2 cloves garlic, minced

¾ cup dry white wine

2 large artichoke hearts, steamed, and quartered (see the tip on p. 178), or use frozen artichoke hearts, not canned

1 to 1½ cups Jalapeño–Basil Pesto (p. 178)

2 tablespoons unsalted butter

1 teaspoon kosher salt, plus more as needed

½ teaspoon freshly ground black pepper, plus more as needed

FOR GARNISHES

4 ounces fresh goat cheese, crumbled

Halved fresh heirloom cherry tomatoes

Toasted pine nuts

Finely grated lemon zest

Cook the pasta according to the package directions, then transfer to an ice water bath to shock it. Drain.

To blanch the asparagus, either use the pasta water or bring a medium pot of salted water to a boil. Add the asparagus pieces and cook for about 2 minutes, until not quite tender. Remove and transfer to an ice water bath to shock the pieces. Drain and set aside.

Heat the olive oil in a large skillet over medium-high heat until hot but not smoking. Add the garlic and stir, cooking just until fragrant, about 20 seconds. Add the wine and cook for a few minutes to burn off the alcohol. Add the pasta, stir, and then add the asparagus and artichoke hearts, using tongs to mix well. Leave on the heat for a few minutes to warm everything through.   →

Add 1 cup or more of pesto, to taste, the butter, salt, and black pepper. Toss everything together, warming the pasta, sauce, and vegetables. Taste and adjust seasonings.

Portion the pasta among four serving bowls or plate in a large pasta bowl. Garnish with the goat cheese, tomato halves, pine nuts, and lemon zest. Serve immediately.

JALAPEÑO–BASIL PESTO

MAKES 2 CUPS

½ pound fresh basil, trimmed of large stems
½ cup pine nuts, toasted
5 large cloves garlic
2 jalapeños, trimmed and sliced (seeds and membranes removed for less heat)

½ cup grated Parmigiano-Reggiano cheese
1½ to 2 teaspoons kosher salt, plus more as needed
1 cup extra-virgin olive oil

Place all of the ingredients, except for the olive oil, into a high-speed blender (I use my Vitamix). Pulse several times to combine the ingredients. With the machine running, add the olive oil slowly in a steady steam through the feeder tube until the pesto is smooth and emulsified. You may need to stop the machine a few times to scrape the sides. Transfer the pesto to a container. If not using immediately, cover the pesto with a thin layer of olive oil, cover with plastic wrap pressed directly on the surface, and refrigerate for up to 2 days. Freeze any leftover pesto and use as a base for flatbreads (pp. 191–192).

CHEF'S TIP ❯ To prepare the artichokes for steaming, trim the tops by ¾ inch, trim the tops of the leaves to remove the points, pull off smaller leaves from the base, and remove any excess stem, leaving about an inch. Insert a steaming basket into a large pot, fill with water to the base of the basket, add the artichokes, and bring the water to a boil. Cover the pot and reduce the heat to a simmer. Cook, covered, for 25 to 45 minutes, until the outer leaves can easily be pulled off. Cooking time will depend on the size of the artichoke. To get to the heart, remove all the leaves en masse to expose the artichoke heart. With a knife, scrape and discard the choke (the fuzzy part), leaving the heart.

GWEN'S HEIRLOOM TOMATO PIE

Gwen was inspired to make this stunning pie after she first tasted heirloom tomatoes from Brooke Eckmann's Ambrosia Farm in Finchville, Kentucky (for more on Brooke, see pp. 102 183). Gwen's version of this popular recipe adds a little heat in the crust, making it taste almost like a cheese straw, a Southern favorite. The filling includes a Vidalia onion, giving the pie a hint of sweetness, along with a nice blend of cheeses including salty Manchego and the mild Mexican melting cheese, Chihuahua®. She also gives the pie a unique fresh taste and texture by adding additional slices of heirloom tomatoes toward the end of the cooking process.

While there are a few steps involved in making this recipe, it is a very special dish that can only be made during a short window in the summertime, when heirloom tomatoes are at their sweetest and best. When guests come back for second helpings (and they will) that will be the best reward and compliment you could get for your efforts.

Be sure to use colorful varieties and different types of heirloom tomatoes with different sizes and shapes, which adds to the beauty of the dish.

MAKES ONE 9-INCH DEEP-DISH PIE

FOR THE CRUST

1 cup all-purpose flour

¾ cup yellow stone-ground cornmeal

¾ teaspoon kosher salt

⅛ teaspoon habanero powder

8 tablespoons unsalted butter, chilled and cut into ½-inch pieces

¼ cup grated Manchego cheese

3 to 5 tablespoons ice water

FOR THE FILLING

3¼ pounds mixed colors and varieties of heirloom tomatoes

1¾ teaspoons kosher salt, divided

2 tablespoons plus 1 teaspoon extra-virgin olive oil, divided

1 large Vidalia onion, cut in half and thinly sliced

¼ cup mayonnaise (not low-fat)

¾ cup grated Manchego cheese

¾ cup grated Chihuahua cheese

3 tablespoons fine breadcrumbs

1 tablespoon chopped fresh flat-leaf parsley

1 tablespoon chopped fresh chives

1 teaspoon chopped fresh thyme

½ teaspoon chopped fresh oregano

½ teaspoon freshly ground black pepper, divided

Snipped fresh dill, for garnish

MAKE THE CRUST

In the bowl of a food processor, combine the flour, cornmeal, salt, and habanero powder and pulse several times. Add the butter, several pieces at a time with the processor running, and the

Manchego and pulse until the mixture is crumbly and forms pea-sized pieces. With the processor running, add ice water 1 tablespoon at a time, pulsing just until the dough comes together. You might not need all of the water. Remove the dough from the food processor and form into a disk, approximately 5 inches in diameter. Wrap tightly in plastic and refrigerate for 1 hour.

Remove the dough from the refrigerator, unwrap, and place between two sheets of parchment. Roll out the dough into a 13-inch round (turn and flip the dough as you roll to ensure it's an equal thickness). Remove the top sheet of parchment, slide your hand under the bottom sheet of parchment so the dough is centered on the palm of your hand, and in one motion, flip the dough into a 9-inch deep-dish pie plate. Remove the parchment and press the dough into the pan, folding under any excess on the

edge of the plate; crimp the edges, as desired. Pierce the bottom of the crust all over with a fork. Cover lightly with plastic wrap and refrigerate for 30 minutes.

Position a rack in the center of a convection oven and heat the oven to 350°F. Line the crust with foil and fill with pie weights or dried beans. Bake until the edges of the crust are golden brown, about 20 minutes. Remove from the oven, remove the foil and weights or beans, and bake for another 10 to 15 minutes, or until the crust is golden all over. Let cool on a wire rack. Leave the oven on and increase the temperature to 375°F.

MAKE THE FILLING AND BAKE

Reserve about 1 pound of tomatoes of various colors and shapes to top the pie toward the end of cooking. Cut the remaining 2¼ pounds of tomatoes into ¼-inch slices and sprinkle with 1 teaspoon of salt. Place in a colander and let their juices drain for about ½ hour. Toss them carefully several times during this process. Remove the tomatoes and place on paper towels to further dry them.

While the tomatoes are draining, in a large skillet, heat 1 tablespoon of the oil over medium heat until hot but not smoking. Add the onion and cook until lightly caramelized, 10 to 15 minutes, stirring occasionally and adjusting the heat if necessary so the onion doesn't brown too quickly. Remove the pan from the heat and cool.

In a medium bowl, combine the mayonnaise, Manchego, Chihuahua, breadcrumbs, parsley, chives, thyme, oregano, and ¼ teaspoon each salt and black pepper. Add the sautéed onion and stir to combine well. Spread the mixture evenly in the bottom of the crust. Arrange the drained tomatoes on top, alternating colors and sizes. Drizzle with 1 tablespoon olive oil and season with the remaining ¼ teaspoon black pepper. Bake until the tomatoes are lightly caramelized, about 45 minutes.

While the pie is cooking, cut the remaining tomatoes into slices and sprinkle with ½ teaspoon salt. Place in a colander and let the juices drain for about ½ hour, tossing them carefully several times during the process. Remove the tomatoes and place on paper towels.

Remove the pie from the oven. Place the additional tomato slices on top of the pie, arranging decoratively. Lightly drizzle with the remaining 1 teaspoon olive oil. Return to the oven and bake for another 5 to 10 minutes, until the tomatoes are lightly browned, or quickly broil the top of the pie just until the tomatoes are wilted and slightly caramelized. Let the pie sit for a few minutes, then garnish with snipped fresh dill and serve immediately.

CHEF'S TIP ❯ Heirloom tomatoes are very watery, so they need to be salted and to drain a while to release some of the juices before putting them into the pie. To ensure the tomatoes are fully drained, place them first in a colander and then on paper towels, which will absorb any remaining water. After the pie bakes, the height of the pie is reduced because the tomatoes cook down, so the additional fresh tomatoes on the top will not only raise the height of the pie but also add a different texture and taste since those tomatoes are just barely cooked, creating more layers of flavor.

MEET BROOKE ECKMANN >
AMBROSIA FARM, FINCHVILLE, KENTUCKY

FROM ANTHONY

I don't even know where to begin when I talk about this woman other than to say, I love her. She grows beautiful produce, especially tomatoes, at Ambrosia Farm. Brooke inspires me with everything she delivers to our back door at Seviche. When she came into the restaurant in 2012 and asked me to come out to her farm to see her heirloom tomatoes, I said sure, having no idea what I would find. Well, when I saw the farm and what she was growing, I was blown away.

Brooke and I have become great friends over the years and my wife and boys love her, too. We'll drive out to the farm just to visit and gather fresh produce to take home. Just as I did as a child, my boys will pick fresh tomatoes from the vines and eat them like apples. I have never tasted tomatoes quite like hers; they're truly spectacular and one of the many reasons she was named a Local Food Hero in 2014, one of only three people in Kentucky to earn that recognition.

FROM BROOKE

I left teaching to become a farmer and have never looked back. Although I loved teaching, I felt as though there was something missing in my life. When I first bought the farm in 2011, my plan was to grow herbs and teach people how to cook with them, but then I started to take things as they came my way and it all changed. The farm is 178 acres, so I had plenty of land to work with. I learned about growing heirloom tomatoes and planted as many varieties I could the first year, along with some other produce. It developed from there. I feel so blessed every day that I am able to grow these beautiful products for Anthony, one of the best chefs in the country.

When I first brought baby squashes to Seviche and introduced myself to Anthony, I told him I was growing tomatoes and wanted him to come out to the farm for a visit. I know he was thinking that I was just some girl growing tomatoes. He came out about a week later and was amazed at the 65 varieties of tomatoes I was growing at that time. The colors, sizes, shapes, textures, and flavors were beyond anything he had ever seen or tasted.

Today, I grow 82 varieties of heirloom tomatoes. I also grow heirloom and special varieties of radishes, kale, beans, cucumbers, squash, pumpkins, turnips, peppers, and herbs, to name the largest groups. I have ½ acre of non-GMO corn. In addition, I grow some unique items like Chinese long beans, popping sorghum, red cotton, and many varieties of heirloom beans for drying such as Calypso, Christmas Lima, Dragon Tongue, Good Mother Stallard, Hidasta Shield, Jacobs Cattle, Lina Sisco's Bird Egg, and Painted Lady Painted Pony.

Some of my produce is grown just for Anthony, but I sell to other chefs and at farmers' markets, too. I also open a portion of the farm to the public as a "pick your own." It's exciting for people, especially children, to see where their food comes from and how it's grown. They rarely have that opportunity and are amazed at the variety they have to choose from here.

Our working farm is approximately 15 acres now. I have a young fig and fruit orchard with about 70 trees. One of the most exciting projects is our new truffle orchard with 500 hazelnut trees and 49 white oak trees. It's a long process to grow truffles, taking more than seven years to cultivate. I can't wait to uncover that first piece of culinary gold.

Farming can be frustrating, especially between late May and early June, when you're waiting for the results. The season is fluid and you have to see what works, how it grows, and what people like. There is also a learning curve when growing for a chef to see how much he actually needs at his restaurant, but it's encouraging to have Anthony's support and to try growing different things for him. To have Anthony and his talented team using my ingredients is inspirational.

Farming is a finicky business, so to bring in new revenue, I converted and renovated the barn to be a special-events venue. We host Heirloom Tomato Tastings and will be using the facility for chef dinners and other special events, like weddings. The farm is a beautiful place and people who come to visit feel a return to something natural and calming.

I'm often asked why I named my farm Ambrosia. In Greek, the word means fruit or food of the gods. Ambrosia was believed to bestow immortality on whoever consumed it. Thanks to my relationship with Anthony, I am even more confident of the name choice.

BLACK BEAN TORTILLA LASAGNA WITH TOMATO SALSA

Many of us prepare vegetarian lasagna when we're entertaining friends who don't eat meat. Think how many times those folks have probably been served pasta noodles, veggies, and cheese. This hearty and flavorful lasagna will be a welcome surprise and a new twist on that one-dish favorite.

The colors of the lasagna are bold, making an impressive and attractive dish when you cut it into squares and serve it with Yellow Rice (p. 227), Salsa Verde (p. 243), sour cream, and sliced scallions. That's the way we serve it at Seviche, and it has become a very popular dish, even for non-vegetarians.

Leftovers will hold for a couple of days in the fridge and reheat nicely for lunch or the next day's dinner.

SERVES 8 TO 10

FOR THE LASAGNA
1 pound dried black beans, rinsed, picked over, and soaked overnight
1 tablespoon kosher salt
3 bay leaves
1 tablespoon Adobo Rub (p. 245)
1 large Spanish onion, divided, one half cut into ¼-inch dice and the other half cut into julienne
2 poblano peppers, cut into julienne
1 red bell pepper, cut into julienne
1 yellow bell pepper, cut into julienne
½ bunch fresh cilantro, trimmed and roughly chopped

2 cups grated sharp Cheddar cheese
2 cups grated Chihuahua cheese
Nonstick cooking spray or olive oil, for the pan
24 corn tortillas

FOR THE TOMATO SALSA
3 cups canned whole tomatoes, with a little of their juice
½ onion, chopped (1 cup)
3 cloves garlic, smashed
1 tablespoon kosher salt

Yellow Rice (p. 227), Salsa Verde (p. 243), sour cream, and sliced scallions, for serving

Drain the black beans and place in a large Dutch oven or stockpot. Cover with 2 quarts of water and add the salt, bay leaves, Adobo Rub, and diced onion. Bring to a boil, then reduce the heat to medium and cook for 45 to 60 minutes, or until the beans are tender. Drain, remove and discard the bay leaves, and set aside.

Meanwhile make the tomato salsa. Put all of the ingredients in a high-speed blender and pulse until chunky. Add to the cooked black beans and mix well.

In a large bowl, combine the julienned onion, poblano peppers, bell peppers, and cilantro, and mix well. Reserve 1 cup of the vegetable mixture for the top layer and portion the rest into thirds.

Combine the two cheeses in a separate bowl. Reserve 1 cup for the topping and portion the rest into thirds.

Grease a 9 x 13 x 3-inch casserole or lasagna dish with olive oil or cooking spray. Layer 6 tortillas evenly on the bottom. They will overlap. Add about 2 cups of the black bean mixture, distributing it evenly across the tortillas. Divide the rest of the black bean mixture in half for the remaining layers. Sprinkle a third of the vegetable mixture over the top of the bean mixture in the pan, covering evenly. Top with one-third of the cheese mixture. Repeat the process two more times with 6 tortillas, beans, veggie mixture, and cheese, ending with the remaining 6 tortillas. Top with the reserved 1 cup vegetable mixture and 1 cup cheese.

Position a rack in the center of a convection oven and heat the oven to 350°F. Cover the pan with foil and bake for 45 minutes. Remove the foil and bake for another 15 to 20 minutes to brown the top. Let sit for a few minutes before cutting.

Serve with hot yellow rice, Salsa Verde, sour cream, and sliced scallions.

CHEF'S TIP ❯ A sharp knife is a safe knife—most accidents happen when knives are dull. I love Korin® knives—they fit into my hand nicely and have a razor sharp blade. Invest in a few knives that you think will be most useful in your kitchen and see how much easier, safer, and enjoyable chopping and slicing in the kitchen will become.

VEGETABLE CHIMICHANGA WITH BUTTERNUT SQUASH SAUCE

We serve this entrée regularly at Seviche, and it's popular with vegetarians and non-vegetarians alike. At the restaurant, we quickly deep-fry the chimichangas, but we've simplified it here so that home cooks can bake them in the oven. The butternut squash sauce is almost like a soup—silky, rich, creamy, and aromatic. It has wonderful spice and a bit of heat. We use a Vitamix to achieve the incredibly smooth texture of this sauce.

You can sauté the vegetables and cook the butternut squash ahead of time. Reheat the butternut squash mixture before puréeing it in the blender. I like to prepare the sauce just before serving to achieve that beautiful consistency that really makes the dish. Taste the sauce before serving. If you want it a little spicier, then add a dash more ground habanero or cayenne.

We use Gouda from Kenny's Farmhouse Cheese in Kentucky, a local cheesemaker (see Resources on p. 277). Their cheeses are made with a vegetable-based rennet, but you can use any good Gouda. A medium or aged Gouda will add more flavor.

SERVES 6

FOR THE SAUTÉED VEGETABLES
1 large zucchini, ends trimmed and cut into ¼-inch julienne

1 large yellow summer squash, ends trimmed and cut into ¼-inch julienne

1 red bell pepper, ends trimmed and cut into ¼-inch julienne

1 yellow bell pepper, ends trimmed and cut into ¼-inch julienne

1 chayote squash, peeled, ends trimmed, and cut into ¼-inch julienne

1 medium red onion, cut into julienne

1 teaspoon ground white pepper

1 tablespoon kosher salt

1 teaspoon dried Mexican oregano (rubbed between your fingers to make the leaves finer)

5 tablespoons olive oil, divided

6 cloves garlic, smashed and minced

FOR THE BUTTERNUT SQUASH SAUCE
1 butternut squash (about 1½ pounds), peeled, seeded, and cut into small cubes

1 tablespoon chopped yellow or Spanish onion

¼ teaspoon freshly grated nutmeg

¼ teaspoon ground cinnamon

⅛ teaspoon habanero powder or ground cayenne, plus more as needed

1 teaspoon granulated sugar

1 teaspoon kosher salt

1 bay leaf

½ cup heavy cream

FOR ASSEMBLING
Olive oil

Six 12-inch flour tortillas

About 12 slices Gouda cheese (about ⅛ inch thick)

Pepita rice (see the tip on p. 155), for serving

Sliced scallions, for garnish

MAKE THE SAUTÉED VEGETABLES

Cut all of the julienne vegetables about 3 inches long. In a large bowl, mix them together with the white pepper, salt, and Mexican oregano. Drizzle with 4 tablespoons of the oil and combine well to coat the vegetables.

In a large skillet, heat the remaining 1 tablespoon oil over medium-high heat until the oil is shimmering but not smoking. Stir the vegetables—they will have released some of their juices—and drain; add to the pan and stir. Cook for 3 to 4 minutes; add the garlic, stir, and continue to cook for 1 to 2 minutes, just until the vegetables begin to soften but still have some crunch, reducing the heat if necessary to avoid scorching. You want a firmer texture since they will continue to cook when baked.

Set a large colander over a large clean bowl and place the cooked vegetables in the colander. Once the vegetables have cooled slightly, cover and place the colander and bowl in the refrigerator, allowing the juices to drain into the bowl.

MAKE THE BUTTERNUT SQUASH SAUCE

Put the butternut squash in a medium saucepan and add enough water to just cover the squash. Add the rest of the ingredients, except for the heavy cream, and bring to a boil. Reduce the heat to low and cook until the squash is fork-tender, about 15 minutes. (You can prepare up to this point and then set aside or cover and refrigerate for several hours.)

$\rightarrow$

Add the heavy cream, increase the heat, and bring almost to a boil, just until small bubbles form around the edge of the pan. Reduce the heat and cook, stirring frequently, until the mixture starts to thicken (it will thinly coat the back of a spoon), 20 to 25 minutes. Remove and discard the bay leaf.

Transfer the squash mixture to a high-speed blender. Add the juices from the drained vegetables and process until silky smooth, being careful to hold the lid down with a kitchen towel since the mixture is hot. Keep warm.

ASSEMBLE THE CHIMICHANGAS

Heat a convection oven to 425°F. Oil a rimmed baking sheet and set aside.

Soften the tortillas by holding them with kitchen tongs over a gas flame for just a few seconds on each side. Alternatively, cover several tortillas at a time with a damp towel and microwave for 30 seconds, or until warm. Slightly warming the tortillas makes them easier to fill and roll.

Place the tortillas on a flat surface. Position 2 slices of Gouda in the center of each tortilla, leaving space at the top and bottom to tuck and roll, about 1 inch on each side. For each chimichanga, place 1 to 1½ cups of the cooked vegetables on top of the cheese. Roll them up like a burrito, tucking in the bottom and top of each tortilla and then rolling to seal. Use a toothpick or 4-inch skewer to secure the rolls, if desired, and then brush with olive oil until glistening. Place the burritos seam side down on the prepared baking sheet and bake for about 7 minutes on one side, or until lightly browned. Flip the chimichangas over and bake for another 5 minutes, or until lightly browned. If necessary, brush the chimichangas with a little more olive oil to brown. Remove immediately.

TO SERVE

Place a mound of Pepita Rice in the middle of each plate. Slice each chimichanga on the diagonal and lay one half down, on its side, on the plate and the other half standing up with the vegetables showing, leaning onto the other half. Drizzle the sauce around the plate, garnish with sliced scallions, and serve immediately.

CHEF'S TIP > If you own a mandoline, use it to cut the vegetables. For the squashes, remove and discard the middle section with the seeds. As an alternative, you can julienne the vegetables by hand. Be sure to cut them into equal sizes, which makes for a more attractive presentation. You can also julienne the chayote squash. Peel it first and discard the seeds and the tougher part in the middle.

SWEET POTATO GNOCCHI WITH BROWN BUTTER, MANCHEGO, PINE NUTS, AND LEMON

It's particularly important with vegetarian recipes to layer in the ingredients to create bold, bright, and complex flavors that will be delicious, nourishing, and satisfying. I think you will find this gnocchi recipe achieves all of those goals.

The gnocchi is made with a combination of sweet and russet potatoes. The starch from the russet potato gives the gnocchi the proper texture since sweet potatoes alone are very moist. The little potato dumplings are simply flavored with grated Manchego, a bit of nutmeg, and a touch of heat from white pepper. It's the nice combination of flavors in the recipe that makes the finished dish so tasty.

If you'd like to boost the flavor of your gnocchi while cooking them, you can add some celery, carrots, onions, and a bay leaf to the salted water, similar to preparing a stock. Also, be sure not to overcook the sweet potatoes when roasting them in the oven, as they will become too watery. You want them cooked, but not overly soft.

For a heartier dish, add roasted cauliflower or sautéed seasonal wild mushrooms.

SERVES 4

1 large russet potato (about 12 ounces)	1¼ cups all-purpose flour, plus more for rolling
1 pound large sweet potatoes (2 potatoes)	8 tablespoons unsalted butter
Extra-virgin olive oil	½ cup grated Manchego, plus more for garnish
Kosher salt	
1 large egg, lightly beaten	¼ cup toasted pine nuts, plus more for garnish
¼ cup grated Manchego	
2 teaspoons kosher salt	Finely grated zest of 1 lemon
¼ teaspoon ground white pepper	Chopped fresh flat-leaf parsley
½ teaspoon freshly grated nutmeg	

MAKE THE GNOCCHI

Position a rack in the center of a convection oven and heat the oven to 400°F. Rub the potatoes with olive oil and sprinkle with a little kosher salt. Put the russet potato in the oven first and set a timer for 15 minutes. Then add the sweet potatoes and cook for another 50 to 60 minutes, or until the potatoes are done. If a knife can be inserted easily through the sweet potatoes, then they are done. (If your sweet potatoes are smaller, then check for doneness sooner.) Once the potatoes are cooked through, remove from the oven and let cool until they can be handled.

Cut the potatoes in half lengthwise, scoop out the flesh, and put it in a large bowl. Using a ricer or food mill, rice all of the potatoes. Alternatively, you can mash the potatoes with a masher. Add the egg, cheese, and seasonings and stir to combine. Mix in 1 cup of the flour, ½ cup at a time, until a soft dough forms. Add more flour sparingly, if necessary. Do not overwork the dough.   →

Line a baking sheet with parchment and set aside. Turn the dough out onto a floured surface and portion into 6 equal pieces. Working with one piece at a time, roll it between your palms and then on the floured work surface to make a rope about 1 inch in diameter. Sprinkle with flour if the dough becomes sticky. Cut each rope into 1-inch pieces. If desired, roll each piece over a fork to make indentations. Place the gnocchi on the prepared baking sheet.

When ready to cook, add 1 tablespoon kosher salt to a large pot of water and bring to a boil. Working in batches, boil the gnocchi until they are tender and rise to the surface, about 5 minutes. With a large slotted spoon, transfer the gnocchi to a clean baking sheet. Tent lightly with foil and keep warm while preparing the sauce.

FINISH AND SERVE

In a large skillet over medium-high heat, melt the butter and cook, swirling the pan occasionally, for about 5 minutes, until the foaming subsides and the solids begin to brown, adjusting the heat to ensure the butter doesn't burn. Once the butter is light brown and has developed a nutty aroma, add the gnocchi to the pan, stirring to combine and basting the gnocchi with the butter to warm through.

When ready to serve, sprinkle the gnocchi with the grated Manchego and toasted pine nuts. Toss together and taste and adjust seasonings. Portion the gnocchi among individual serving bowls and sprinkle with the lemon zest and chopped parsley. Serve hot, with more grated Manchego and toasted pine nuts at the table.

CHEF'S TIP ❯ If you are making the gnocchi ahead of time, before cooking, place them on parchment-lined baking sheets, dust lightly with flour, cover lightly with plastic wrap, and store in the refrigerator for up to several hours. If you want to prepare them ahead and then freeze them, do not cover them. Just place the baking sheets in the freezer. Once the gnocchi are frozen, transfer to freezer-safe zip-top plastic bags. They will hold for about a month in the freezer.

COCAS (FLATBREADS) WITH JALAPEÑO—BASIL PESTO, HEIRLOOM TOMATOES, AND GOAT CHEESE

This quick-to-prepare recipe is the Latino's version of Italian flatbread or pizza. Once you make the dough, you can get really creative and top the flatbreads with any combination of ingredients. In this version, we use a spicy basil pesto that we also serve with our Fideo with Asparagus and Artichokes (pp. 176–178), and then add sliced heirloom tomatoes and fresh goat cheese. We top the flatbreads with goat cheese from Capriole Farms in Greenville, Indiana (for more about Capriole Farms, see pp. 62–63), but you can use any good fresh goat cheese that you can source locally.

I like to add chopped fresh herbs to my dough to give it additional layers of flavor; they also make the flatbreads more interesting. Choose herbs that would complement the topping, such as fresh basil and oregano with tomatoes and mozzarella. When making the dough, as with any yeast bread, don't overwork it and do not add more flour than necessary, which will make the dough tough. It should be pliable and soft.

For a fun way to entertain, par-bake the flatbreads for a few minutes, set up your table with a selection of ingredients, and let your guests choose their toppings. Finish them in the oven.

MAKES 8 SMALL OR 6 LARGE COCAS

1 cup warm water (100° to 110°F)

2½ teaspoons active dry yeast

½ teaspoon honey

½ teaspoon granulated sugar

2 cups all-purpose flour, plus more for kneading

1 teaspoon kosher salt

1 tablespoon chopped fresh herbs of your choice (optional)

Extra-virgin olive oil

Jalapeño–Basil Pesto (p. 178)

4 to 6 heirloom tomatoes, sliced ¼ inch thick

Fresh goat cheese, crumbled

Sea salt

In a small bowl, combine the warm water, yeast, honey, and sugar. Stir to mix and then let sit until the yeast mixture is frothy, about 5 minutes. In a large bowl, combine the flour, salt, and chopped herbs, if using. Make a well in the center of the flour and slowly add the yeast mixture. Combine with your hands to mix well until thoroughly blended.

Turn the dough out onto a wooden board that has been lightly dusted with flour. Knead the dough until it becomes smooth, 5 to 7 minutes. Shape into a ball and place in a large oiled bowl. Cover with a clean kitchen towel and place in a warm spot for 1 hour, or until the dough has doubled in size.

Position a rack in the center of a convection oven and heat the oven to 500°F; lightly oil two or three baking sheets. Turn out the dough onto your work surface and punch it down. Cut the dough into 6 or 8 pieces, depending on how many you're serving. Roll out the dough into free-form ovals, about ⅛ inch thick, and carefully transfer to the oiled baking sheets. (At this point, if desired, you can par-bake the *cocas* for a few minutes, then let fully cool, store in plastic zip-top bags, and top and finish baking later when ready to serve.)

Brush the *cocas* lightly with olive oil. Spread a thin layer of Jalapeño–Basil Pesto over each *coca,* leaving about ½ inch uncovered around the edges. Arrange the sliced tomatoes on top of the pesto and then sprinkle with the goat cheese. Bake for 7 to 10 minutes, until the *cocas* are hot and browned. (If they have been par-baked, adjust the cooking time.) Remove from the oven, drizzle with a little olive oil, sprinkle lightly with sea salt, and serve immediately.

VARIATIONS ❯ Try one of these variations, which aren't all vegetarian. Before topping the flatbreads, brush them with a little olive oil and sprinkle with kosher salt and freshly ground black pepper. ❯ Crumbled feta, topped with a Greek salad (sans lettuce) of chopped peeled cucumbers, chunks of tomato, chopped red onion, and sliced Greek olives tossed in a light dressing of extra-virgin olive oil and red-wine vinegar with a little kosher salt and black pepper to taste. ❯ Grated Manchego cheese, diced country ham (or prosciutto), and arugula. ❯ Instead of brushing on olive oil, spread fig preserves on top of the dough, then sprinkle with duck confit and arugula. ❯ Crumbled cooked Mexican chorizo, cooked diced potatoes, and sliced roasted poblanos.

BOURBON CHERRIES

Most recipes for Bourbon Cherries call for adding cherries to a mixture of simple syrup with a little bourbon added in for flavor. Here in Kentucky, it's all about the bourbon, and we want our cherries to taste like Bourbon Cherries, not cherries with bourbon. The only way to do this is to add more bourbon! For this recipe, I make bourbon syrup from a full liter of bourbon and boil it down to make a syrup. I use a less expensive wheat bourbon like Old Forester®. If you like a little spice, then use a rye bourbon like Old Overholt®.

Since we are bringing this mixture to just above the boiling point at 215°F, you need to keep your eye on the pot and continue stirring as soon as the mixture starts to boil; beware—it will boil over quickly. Just as when making caramel, you need to be certain the mixture does not begin to form crystals on the sides of the pan as it boils since that will leave a layer of crystals in the bottom of your jars. You can brush down the sides of the pan with a wet pastry brush if this begins to happen.

These cherries are perfect for making cocktails such as the Perfect Pineapple–Cherry Manhattan (p. 37) or to serve over homemade vanilla ice cream. Better yet, just eat them right out of the jar.

MAKES SIX 8-OUNCE JARS (½ PINTS)

1½ pounds fresh sweet (Bing) cherries, stems removed (if desired) and pitted	1 liter bourbon 4 cups granulated sugar

Sterilize six ½-pint jars following the instructions for sterilizing from the National Center for Home Food Preservation (http://nchfp.uga.edu/publications/publications_usda.html). Evenly distribute the cherries among the jars. They should be packed—about 12 to 16 cherries each.

In a large saucepan or medium stockpot with tall sides, combine the bourbon and sugar and bring to a low boil over medium-high heat, stirring thoroughly to dissolve the sugar before the mixture boils. If the alcohol begins to flame, remove the pan from the heat and cover with a lid. If crystals begin to form on the side of the pot, remove them with a wet pastry brush. Bring the temperature of the liquid to 215°F, measuring with a thermometer and stirring the entire time. This can take 30 minutes or more. Once the bourbon syrup is thickened, remove from the heat immediately and pour into the jars packed with cherries, leaving a ½-inch headspace.

Remove air from the jar by inserting a silicone spatula, wooden chopstick, plastic knife, or canning tool made especially for this task down the sides of the jar and around the cherries. Wipe the rims clean with a damp warm cloth. Seal the jars with sterilized lids and rims. Process in a water bath canner for 10 minutes (follow the manufacturer's instructions as well as processing time if you are at a higher altitude). Remove the jars from the canner and allow them to sit untouched for 24 hours. Check to make sure the lids have "popped" and are sealed. Store in a cool, dark place. Bourbon cherries should last for 1 year unopened.

CHEF'S TIP ❯ You can remove the pit from the cherry by hand or with a sharp paring knife, but that is a messy process and will also cause the cherries to lose their nice shape. Instead, use a cherry pitter. You'll find hand-held models as well as ones that suction to the counter.

CACTUS CHOW CHOW

Chow chow is a popular condiment in the South and is used to top anything from grilled hot dogs and burgers to bean dishes. You can also use chow chow as you would a sweet relish, adding it to tuna salad, chicken salad, macaroni salad, deviled eggs, or tartar sauce. There are many versions of this pickled relish, and most are made with a combination of cabbage, tomatoes, onions, and peppers, but this recipe just might be the first time you've seen it made with nopales.

Nopales are the "thorny" pads from the prickly pear cactus. They are a staple in Mexican cuisine and used raw in salads or pico de gallo. They can also be grilled or cooked for use in tacos, scrambled eggs, and other dishes. Nopales are rich in antioxidants, so they are now part of the superfood revolution. The texture of the cactus leaves makes them perfect for chow chow, and I think this traditional Latin favorite marries rather well to this Southern pickle dish.

This recipe makes four half-pints. Since it's a quick pickle, the chow chow needs to be stored in the refrigerator and should be used within 2 weeks. Chow chow makes a great gift for neighbors and friends when showing some of that famous Southern hospitality.

MAKES FOUR 8-OUNCE JARS (½ PINTS)

5 medium nopales (prickly pear cactus pads), spines scraped and edges trimmed, cut into strips (see the tip below)

1 whole small yellow onion, peeled and trimmed

5 cloves garlic, 3 left whole and 2 minced

1 bunch fresh cilantro, trimmed

2 tablespoons kosher salt, divided

½ cup apple cider vinegar

1 teaspoon mustard seeds

Juice of 2 lemons

1 tablespoon olive oil

1 medium red onion, cut into ⅛-inch dice

1 red bell pepper, trimmed, seeded, and cut into ¼-inch dice

2 jalapeños, trimmed, seeds and membranes removed, and cut into ⅛-inch dice

1 tablespoon granulated sugar

In a medium stockpot, combine the cactus strips, onion, whole garlic cloves, cilantro, 1 tablespoon of salt, and just enough water to cover (about 6 cups). Bring to boil, then reduce the heat and simmer for 15 minutes. Strain in a fine-mesh strainer; remove and discard the onion, garlic, and cilantro. Remove and reserve the cactus strips.

Cut the cactus strips into small dice (about ¼ inch) and transfer to a clean medium saucepan. Add the remaining ingredients and mix well, bring to a boil, and cook for 5 minutes, skimming any foam from the surface. Ladle the chow chow into airtight containers and refrigerate for up to 2 weeks, or ladle into sterilized canning jars and process for longer storage (follow the instructions for sterilizing and processing from the National Center for Home Food Preservation at http://nchfp.uga.edu/publications/publications_usda.html).

CHEF'S TIP ❯ When preparing nopales, use a vegetable peeler to remove the spines, then cut off the two ends to make them more even to cut into strips. You can also lightly peel any skin with brown spots; otherwise, it's okay to cook nopales with the skin.

PEACH—HABANERO PRESERVES

We make many batches of these delectable preserves in the summertime, when we get bushels of gorgeous Indiana peaches. These preserves have a nice balance of sweetness with just a hint of heat and are perfect to serve with a cheese plate appetizer. They are particularly delicious as an accompaniment to the Georgia Pecan–Encrusted Brie (pp. 33–34). These preserves are great to pull out and serve around the holidays when entertaining family and friends. A jar also makes a wonderful gift—it's special to share a labor of love and food with someone you care about.

Gwen will tell you that South Carolina peaches are the best (even though she lives in Georgia), but I must say that I'm partial to the peaches from Kentuckiana. Whichever peaches you choose, just make sure they're in season, preferably local, and ripe but still a little firm. Peaches shipped in from far away tend to be mealy and not sweet. Vine-ripened, local peaches will make the best preserves.

Unlike jams, where the fruit is mashed, preserves leave the fruit in large chunks. These nuggets of goodness will give you the opportunity to relive summer's best and sweetest peaches all over again.

MAKES NINE 8-OUNCE JARS (½ PINTS)

4 pounds peaches, peeled and sliced	Pinch of kosher salt
1 habanero, finely minced (membranes and seeds removed for less heat)	6 tablespoons RealFruit™ Classic Pectin
Juice of 2 lemons	6 cups granulated sugar

In a medium stockpot with tall sides, combine all of the ingredients, except the sugar, and bring to a boil over high heat. Add the sugar, stirring constantly until dissolved. Bring to a rolling boil and cook, stirring constantly, for 1 minute. Reduce the heat to where the mixture is still a slow boil and continue to cook, stirring frequently, for another 4 to 5 minutes, until the peaches are softened and the mixture is syrupy. Skim the foam, if necessary.

Ladle the preserves into sterilized ½-pint glass jars (follow the instructions from the National Center for Home Food Preservation (http://nchfp.uga.edu/publications/publications_usda.html), leaving a ¼-inch headspace. Remove air from the jar by inserting a silicone spatula, wooden chopstick, plastic knife, or canning tool made especially for this task down the sides of the jar and around the fruit. Wipe the rims clean with a damp warm cloth. Seal the jars with sterilized lids and rims. Process in a water bath canner for 10 minutes (follow the manufacturer's instructions as well as processing time if you are at a higher altitude). Remove the jars from the canner and allow them to sit untouched for 24 hours. Check to make sure the lids have "popped" and are sealed. Store in a cool, dark place. The preserves should last for 1 year unopened.

KUMQUAT—HABANERO MARMALADE

Kumquats look like miniature oranges and taste like a clementine with a little sour bite. A popular Asian fruit, this tiny citrus is grown in Texas and Florida and along the East Coast to parts of South Carolina.

During the fruit's winter growing season, from November to March, you will find kumquats in some grocery stores, but especially at farmers' markets and specialty grocers. When you're able to source this fruit, buy a bag (or several containers) and make this marmalade.

Sweet and delectable, you will love the combination of kumquats, orange, and lemon with just a hint of heat from the habanero. I find the balance of heat, sweet, and sour to be perfect, but if you are cautious with spice and heat, try one habanero and then add a second one as the mixture cooks. If you want an even hotter marmalade, you can add the seeds. For a weekend brunch or family get-together, make a batch of homemade biscuits to go with the marmalade. It's a wonderful treat that you won't soon forget.

You'll need to suprême oranges for this marmalade. It's an easy technique to master, and you'll find that you will use orange suprêmes in many more recipes than just this one. See the tip on the facing page to learn how.

MAKES SEVEN 8-OUNCE JARS (½ PINTS)

4 cups thinly sliced kumquats, seeds removed (about 1 pound)

3 cups julienned orange peel, most of white pith removed (about 3 to 4 oranges)

3 cups orange slices (suprêmes) (about 4 to 5 oranges)

½ cup freshly squeezed lemon juice

2 habaneros, trimmed, seeds and membranes removed, and cut into ⅛-inch dice (add seeds for more heat)

2 quarts water

About 10 cups granulated sugar

In a medium nonreactive stockpot with tall sides, combine all of the ingredients except the sugar, bring to a boil, and simmer for 5 minutes. Remove from the heat, cover, and refrigerate for 14 hours.

Measure out the fruit and liquid, then measure out 1 cup sugar for each cup of the kumquat mixture. Clip a candy thermometer to a clean medium stockpot, add the kumquat mixture and sugar, and bring to a rapid boil. Keep stirring until the mixture thickens, adjusting the heat to prevent boiling over but still keeping it at a boil, 30 to 45 minutes, skimming the foam as necessary. Once the mixture is thickened and reaches the gel point, or 220°F on the candy thermometer, remove the pot from the heat.

Ladle the marmalade into sterilized ½-pint jars (follow the instructions from the National Center for Home Food Preservation at http://nchfp.uga.edu/publications/publications_usda.html), leaving a ¼-inch headspace. Remove air from the jar by inserting a silicone spatula, wooden chopstick, plastic knife, or canning tool made especially for this task down the sides of the jar and around the fruit. Wipe the rims clean with a damp warm cloth. Seal the jars with sterilized lids and rims. Process in a water bath canner for 10 minutes (follow the manufacturer's instructions as well as

processing time if you are at a higher altitude). Remove the jars from the canner and allow them to sit untouched for 24 hours. Check to make sure the lids have "popped" and are sealed. Store in a cool, dark place. The preserves should last for 1 year un-opened.

CHEF'S TIP ❯ To suprême an orange, first cut off both ends so that the orange can stand upright on a cutting board. Using a Y-peeler and sharp paring knife, remove the peel and pith from the orange so that the flesh is exposed. The pith is bitter, so use the knife to remove it all before slicing the orange segments. With a sharp knife, carefully cut between the membrane that attaches the orange segments and release just the fruit into a bowl.

SPICY PICKLED OKRA

Southerners will take their okra almost any way they can get it, whether it's fried, in stews, grilled, roasted, or in dishes like Chorizo and Georgia Shrimp Dirty Rice (p. 149). Okra is another ingredient that I had never worked with until I moved to Kentucky. As an adopted Southerner, this Latino boy now loves his okra, too. Okra is abundant in the summer months, and at Seviche we find all sorts of ways to use what our farmers bring us. Pickling is one of the best methods of preserving one of summer's most prolific vegetables.

With a bit of heat and kick, these pickled okra are fun to serve in Bloody Marys or with a tray of charcuterie, local cheeses, and a dish of Pickled Jalapeño Pimento Cheese (recipe on p. 38). You can also add a little of the juice from this recipe to your next martini. If you use smaller okra for this recipe, you'll be able to fit more into the jars since they should be packed tightly.

MAKES 7 PINTS

3 to 3½ pounds okra, washed	2 teaspoons dill seeds
3 cups water	2 tablespoons crushed red pepper flakes
3 cups distilled white vinegar	1 tablespoon pickling spice
⅓ cup kosher salt	7 whole cloves garlic

Prepare 7 pint glass jars and lids for canning following the instructions for sterilizing from the National Center for Home Food Preservation (http://nchfp.uga.edu/publications/publications_usda.html). Trim the tops of the okra (without cutting into the pods) and pack into the sterilized jars.

Clip a thermometer to a medium nonreactive stockpot, then add the rest of the ingredients, except for the garlic. Stir to dissolve the salt and bring to a boil over high heat. Be sure the brine reaches at least 190°F.

Ladle the hot brine into the jars, leaving a ½-inch headspace; add 1 clove garlic to each jar. Remove air from the jar by inserting a silicone spatula, wooden chopstick, plastic knife, or canning tool made especially for this task down the sides of the jar and around the vegetables. Wipe the rims clean with a damp warm cloth. Seal the jars with sterilized lids and rims. Process in a water bath canner for 15 minutes (follow the manufacturer's instructions as well as processing time if you are at a higher altitude). Remove the jars from the canner and allow them to sit untouched for 24 hours. Check to make sure the lids have "popped" and are sealed. Store in a cool, dark place. Pickled okra should last for 1 year unopened.

MI CASA
ES SU CASA

MEALS WITH MY
FAMILY

MANY OF THE RECIPES in this chapter were inspired by what my mama used to cook for our family when I was a young boy, like Posole Verde (p. 217) and her chicken enchiladas (p. 226). My mama's food is what I crave.

Sunday suppers at home with the family started with my mama and sisters when I was younger. We'd save that day to catch up and spend time together after a busy week. I continue that tradition today with my family—we all have busy schedules that don't allow for a lot of time or meals together during the week, so we reserve every Sunday to gather together at the dinner table.

The recipes in this chapter are more casual than many of the others in the book and are some of the dishes I like to cook at home. These are simple comfort food dishes that any home cook can make for his or her family. Several of these dishes make large amounts (like the soup recipes), so →

One of my favorite sayings is, "Mi casa es su casa"—and I mean it. My boys' friends come over and ask if "Mr. Anthony" can come out and play, and the neighborhood kids want to eat at our house because they like my cooking.

there are leftovers to serve for another meal later in the week. One of the recipes, Billie's Steak with Red Sauce (p. 207), is a family favorite from my mother-in law.

There are many similarities between Southern and Latin cultures. In both, there's a real sense of hospitality that seems to center around food. Both Southerners and Latinos like to make more food than we need and invite people to share it with us. Next time you make a big pot of soup or stew, take some to your neighbor. It will make his day and you will help build a better community.

One of my favorite sayings is, "Mi casa es su casa"—and I mean it. My boys' friends come over and ask if "Mr. Anthony" can come out and play, and the neighborhood kids want to eat at our house because they like my cooking. Whether you come into my home or into my restaurant, I want you to feel at home and enjoy my food. I'll take it very personally if you don't.

ALBÓNDIGAS (MEATBALL) SOUP

Growing up, my mama would prepare this wonderful traditional Mexican soup because it's chock full of fresh vegetables and flavorful stock. It was also an economical way to extend a couple of pounds of ground meat. This recipe makes a large pot of soup, so it will feed your family for dinner and leave leftovers for another evening. Since my wife, Samantha, and I both have careers, I'm always thinking ahead when I cook at home and try to prepare meals that can be served twice during the week. I also like to enlist my boys, Ethan Diego and Ian Cruz, to help with rolling the meatballs and chopping the vegetables. This is a rustic soup, so the chopping doesn't have to be perfect; plus, cooking together is a great way to spend quality time with family, especially while my boys are young.

As with most soups, the flavor of this soup is even better the next day. Freeze any of the leftovers or share with friends and neighbors.

SERVES 10 TO 12

FOR THE MEATBALLS
2 pounds lean ground beef
1 cup cooked long-grain rice
1 tablespoon kosher salt
1 teaspoon freshly ground black pepper
1 tablespoon chopped fresh oregano

FOR THE SOUP
1 tablespoon canola oil
1 medium Spanish onion, cut into ¼-inch dice
1 chayote squash, peeled, pit removed, and cut into ¼-inch dice
2 medium carrots, sliced
3 large or 5 small stalks celery, sliced

2 small white potatoes, peeled and cut into ½-inch dice
¼ head cabbage, thinly sliced
3 cloves garlic, minced
1 tablespoon kosher salt
1½ tablespoons Homemade Sazón (p. 248)
3 quarts organic or homemade chicken stock
1 bunch cilantro, leaves only, and divided
2 tablespoons Posole Spice Mix (p. 242)
Juice of 2 limes
2 medium zucchini, cut in half lengthwise and then cut into half-moons
Chopped onion and lime wedges, for garnish

MAKE THE MEATBALLS

Line a baking sheet with parchment. Combine all of the ingredients for the meatballs in a large mixing bowl. Use your hands to mix well and shape into golf ball–size meatballs. Place on the prepared baking sheet and set aside. You can make the meatballs to this point, cover, and refrigerate for up to 8 hours.

MAKE THE SOUP

In a large stockpot over medium-high heat, heat the canola oil until hot but not smoking. Add the onion, chayote, and carrot. Sauté just until the onion becomes translucent, about 2 to 3 minutes. Add the celery, potatoes, cabbage, and garlic and sweat the vegetables for 4 to 5 minutes more. Season the mixture with the salt and Sazón and stir well to combine. Stir in the chicken stock and bring to a boil.

Once the mixture is boiling, add about a third of the cilantro. Reduce the heat and simmer for 20 minutes. Add the meatballs, return the soup to a boil, and then reduce the heat to a rolling simmer; cook for 20 minutes, skimming foam from the top, if necessary. Add the Posole Spice Mix, lime juice, and zucchini. Bring to a boil. Reduce the heat to a simmer and cook for another 5 minutes, or until the zucchini is tender.

Ladle the hot soup into serving bowls, garnish with some chopped onion and the remaining cilantro leaves, and serve with lime wedges for squeezing.

CHEF'S TIP > This dish is perfect paired with a Spanish Rioja or a Pinot Noir. Typically you would serve a red wine with a beef dish; because there's not a lot of fat in this dish and it's a soup, a light red is perfect. Rioja has the right amount of acid to complement the dish, but a Pinot Noir will work nicely, too, and it may be more accessible.

BILLIE'S STEAK WITH RED SAUCE

This is one of my family's favorite weeknight meals; my youngest boy, Ian Cruz, asks for this dish by this name. Bille is my mother-in-law, hence the name. Many of you probably know this recipe better as Swiss steak, and you may have grown up with your mother's own version. It reminds me a little of Carne Guisada (Puerto Rican beef stew), but without the olives and peppers. We never have any leftovers when I make it for my family.

I've made a few minor changes to Billie's original recipe, adding a little bit of heat and some fresh tomatoes to brighten up the flavor. You will need a pressure cooker to prepare the dish since cooking it with this method tenderizes an inexpensive and tougher cut of beef. Be sure to ask your butcher to tenderize the meat—a technique that breaks down the tissue so it will resemble a cube steak.

This simple and satisfying dish is great over steamed white rice. Serve with your favorite vegetable and a green salad for a comforting home-cooked supper that will take you back to your own childhood.

SERVES 4 TO 6

2 pounds top round steak, tenderized, cut against the grain in 1-inch strips
1½ teaspoons kosher salt
½ teaspoon freshly ground black pepper
1 tablespoon garlic salt
Canola oil
All-purpose flour
1 Vidalia onion, cut in half and sliced
2 cups crushed whole canned tomatoes

3 Roma tomatoes, peeled and quartered
¼ teaspoon crushed red pepper flakes
Steamed white rice, for serving

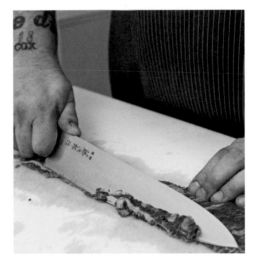

Pat the meat dry with paper towels. Season the meat with the salt and pepper and sprinkle with the garlic salt. Heat enough oil to just cover the bottom of a large skillet over medium-high heat. Lightly dredge the steak pieces in flour, shake off the excess, and then cook in batches in the hot oil, just until brown (this takes only seconds).

Place the meat, onion, canned and fresh tomatoes, and red pepper flakes in a pressure cooker and seal. Once it begins to hiss, cook for 18 minutes. Let the pressure cooker cool down until it's safe to open. Serve immediately over white rice.

CHEF'S TIP ❯ A big red meat dish needs a big wine to complement it. A French Bordeaux, which is a blend, makes a good pairing, but consider the blends of Spain or the United States, too. Try a California Meritage, which has a robust fruit aroma and layers of flavor. A more simple pairing is a Spanish Tempranillo.

BARRIO FRUIT SALAD

This recipe is my version of the fruit salads that I remember buying from street vendors and in Latin markets as a young boy in southern California and Mexico. A popular Mexican fruit salad topped with chile pepper, lime, and salt, this recipe is bursting with unexpected flavors and textures. There's sweetness from the fruit, tanginess from the fresh citrus, crunch from the jícama, and a salty component that brightens the salad, all topped with a bit of heat.

My boys love this salad, and they eat it the way most kids eat candy. They must have gotten this from me because I have always enjoyed all types of fresh fruit and will choose to nibble on fruit rather than some other snack foods.

While you will find many variations on this salad, it is always prepared with well-chilled ingredients and served soon after preparing. Some street vendors top it with a sweet, thickened tamarind fruit syrup; many use a prepared chile pepper powder mix. For my version, I season the mixture generously with lime, kosher salt, and some cayenne pepper. Fresh ripe mango, honeydew, or cantaloupe pieces are nice additions, as are some fresh shaved coconut pieces. Let the flavors spend just a few minutes together in the refrigerator before serving. As the juices are released from the fruits and veggies, the balance of flavors may change, so check again for seasonings and then serve immediately.

SERVES 4 TO 6

4 cups bite-size watermelon pieces, preferably seedless

½ small pineapple, peeled, cored, and cut into bite-size pieces (see the tip below)

1 medium cucumber, peeled, seeded, sliced in half and cut into bite-size pieces

1 small to medium jícama, peeled and cut into ¼-inch pieces

2 oranges, peeled and cut into suprêmes, juice from the pulp reserved (see p. 199)

1 medium mango, peeled, pit removed, and flesh cut into bite-size pieces (optional)

1 cup bite-size cantaloupe or honeydew melon pieces (optional)

½ cup fresh coconut pieces (optional)

Juice of 2 limes

1 tablespoon kosher salt

½ teaspoon ground cayenne

Chill all of the fruit. Combine the watermelon, pineapple, cucumber, jícama, and oranges in a large bowl, then sprinkle with the reserved orange juice. Add the mango, melon, and coconut, if using. Add the lime juice, salt, and cayenne and toss well. Cover and refrigerate for 10 to 15 minutes to let the flavors come together. Toss well and taste and adjust seasonings before serving. The fruit salad is best when well chilled.

CHEF'S TIP ❯ To core a fresh pineapple, first lay the pineapple on its side and slice off the crown, or top, and the bottom; discard. Hold the pineapple upright, resting its bottom on a cutting board, and slice off the skin (discard). Cut lengthwise pieces (¾ to 1 inch thick) down each side of the pineapple. Rotate the fruit as you slice, and repeat the process until you reach the core. (This works for mangos and cucumbers as well.) You can also make triangle-shaped pieces by cutting the pineapple in half lengthwise and then cutting each half into quarters. Remove the skin and slice out the core from each quarter, then slice the flesh into triangle-shaped pieces. Keep cut pineapple in a tightly sealed container in the refrigerator for several days.

CHICKEN RICE SOUP

A bowl of steaming hot chicken soup always brings back memories of growing up in California and of my mama cooking for long hours in the kitchen. She was a wonderful cook and even when we were better off financially, many of our meals were soups and stews that extended the ingredients. She was thrifty and never wasted anything. She passed that trait on to me, so I'm conscientious about utilizing every ingredient available and then using the leftovers as well.

This is one of my favorite go-to recipes for chicken soup when I'm cooking at home for my own family. It's simple to prepare, rustic, and flavorful. This version has Latin spice and more vibrant flavors than a traditional recipe, along with fresh citrus and cilantro. I also add chicken stock and more vegetables, making this an even heartier soup. It makes quite a large batch, so put some in the freezer or share some with neighbors. If you're going to make it a few hours or more before serving, wait to add the rice and cook it when you reheat the soup. Likewise, if you know that you will be freezing some of it, reserve the part to be frozen before adding rice and then add the rice when you reheat the soup. Be creative and use whatever vegetables you have on hand or the ones you prefer.

SERVES 10 TO 12

One 3½- to 4-pound whole chicken

3 quarts water

5 cloves garlic, smashed

1 tablespoon Posole Spice Mix (p. 242)

3½ tablespoons kosher salt

1 tablespoon freshly ground black pepper

3 bay leaves

1 tablespoon Homemade Sazón (p. 248)

½ bunch fresh cilantro, bottoms trimmed, but leave longer stems so they are easier to remove, plus chopped cilantro for garnish

1½ large onions, cut into ½-inch dice, divided

5 stalks celery, cut into ½-inch dice

6 small or 5 large carrots, cut into ½-inch dice

2 cups raw long-grain rice

3 small zucchini, cut in half lengthwise and then cut into ½-inch slices

½ medium head cabbage, sliced

1 quart organic or homemade chicken stock

3 limes, divided

Warm corn tortillas, for serving

In a large stockpot, combine the chicken, water, garlic, Posole Spice Mix, salt, black pepper, bay leaves, Sazón, and cilantro stems. Add more water to cover the chicken, if necessary. Bring to a boil and then add most of the onion, the celery, and carrot; reduce the heat, cover, and simmer for 45 minutes, skimming foam if necessary. Remove the chicken and let it cool. Once it's cool enough to handle, remove the skin and bones (and discard or save the bones for making stock), pull off the meat, and cut it into large chunks.

Skim the fat from the broth and remove and discard the cilantro. Add the chunks of chicken, the rice (if serving the soup right away), zucchini, cabbage, and chicken broth or stock and bring to a boil. Lower the heat, cover, and simmer for 15 to 20 minutes, until the rice is cooked and the vegetables are tender.

Right before serving, remove and discard the bay leaves, add the juice of 2 limes, and taste and adjust seasonings. You may need to add more salt to balance out the citrus.

Serve hot, garnished with the chopped cilantro and the remaining chopped white onion. Cut the remaining lime into wedges and serve alongside the soup with warm corn tortillas.

CHEF'S TIP ❯ While all recipes taste better when you use homemade chicken, beef, or vegetable stock, the reality is that most home cooks don't have time to make their own. For the recipes in this book, we suggest using homemade stock, organic store-bought stock, or an organic broth, like Swanson®. Organic stocks and broths have less sodium than other types and that's important, especially when trying to balance the flavors in your recipe.

CHORIZO HOME FRIES

These home fries are a Latino's answer to chili cheese fries. And who doesn't like french fries topped with spicy meat and lots of melted cheese? I make this dish at home and also prepare it for my staff at Seviche for an afternoon snack while everyone's in the kitchen prepping for dinner service.

You need to start with crispy, perfectly cooked french fries to make this dish exceptionally tasty. Start with freshly cut potatoes and leave the skins on. Cut them with a mandoline or by hand into ¼-inch sticks and then soak the potatoes in cold water for at least 4 to 6 hours or even overnight in the refrigerator. When you're ready to fry them up, use a deep fryer, large Dutch oven, or cast iron skillet, being certain to check the temperature of the oil with a good thermometer for accuracy.

They are twice-fried. This method of frying the potatoes twice is the best we've found at the restaurant and the one that Gwen found works best at home to ensure that the fries are crispy on the outside and light and delicious on the inside.

These fries make a great snack for entertaining or an afternoon of watching sports on television; be sure to serve them freshly made. Pop open a cold beer and enjoy!

SERVES 4 TO 6

2 russet potatoes (about 1½ pounds), scrubbed and cut into ¼-inch sticks	1 cup shredded grated Cheddar cheese
1 teaspoon kosher salt	Canola oil
½ pound Mexican chorizo	1 teaspoon Greek seasoning
1 cup shredded Manchego cheese	Sliced scallions (white and light green parts), sour cream, and Tapatio® Hot Sauce, for serving

Put the potatoes in a large bowl, cover with cold water, and add salt. Refrigerate for 4 to 6 hours or overnight.

When ready to cook the fries, heat a convection oven to 350°F. →

Heat a small skillet, add the chorizo, and cook over medium-high heat, breaking up the pieces with the back of a spoon, until it is brown and crumbly. Drain and set aside. In a medium bowl, combine the two cheeses and set aside.

Remove the potatoes from the refrigerator and drain on kitchen towels, patting dry with paper towels. Clip a thermometer to the side of a deep fryer or large Dutch oven, add a couple of inches of oil, and heat the oil to 300°F. Add the potatoes, working in batches so as not to crowd them, and fry for 3 to 4 minutes, just until they begin to cook. Remove with a slotted spoon or spider and drain on paper towels. Increase the temperature of the oil to 375°F. Working in batches, fry the potatoes until they're golden brown and crispy, about 2 minutes (this will depend on the oil temperature and how brown you like your potatoes). Be sure the temperature of the oil remains at a constant 375°F, adjusting the heat as needed. Remove immediately and drain on paper towels; continue to fry the rest of the potatoes.

If making single servings, portion the fries evenly among individual casserole or cast iron dishes, sprinkle with a little Greek seasoning, and top with the cooked chorizo. If serving at a party, place the fries in a 2-quart baking dish and top with the Greek seasoning and chorizo, and cook for 10 minutes. Top with the cheese mixture and cook for another 5 minutes, or until the cheese has melted. Serve with chopped scallions, sour cream, and Tapatio on the side.

CHEF'S TIP ❯ Russet, or Idaho, potatoes are high in starch and are denser than some other varieties of potatoes. Because they have less moisture, they are the best potato for frying and baking. Potatoes that are creamy in texture, like Yukon Gold, are better as mashed potatoes.

CUCUMBER SALAD

At home, we eat this salad like popcorn, and I prepare it as a snack for my family to share when we're watching television or cooking in the kitchen together. I love when my boys ask me to make healthy dishes like this one or the Barrio Fruit Salad (p. 208). My boys prefer to eat vegetables and fruit instead of sweet snacks; your children will too if you season the vegetables right and offer them often.

Be sure to make this in the summer or early fall, when you can use sweet and delicious heirloom cherry tomatoes from a local farmer. This is as simple and delicious as summertime gets.

SERVES 4 TO 6

4 medium cucumbers, chilled, peeled, seeded, and sliced thick

½ pint (8 ounces) heirloom cherry tomatoes or grape tomatoes, chilled and cut in half

½ cup red-wine vinegar

1 tablespoon kosher salt

Juice of 1 lemon

In a medium bowl, combine the cucumbers and tomatoes, cover, and refrigerate until very cold. In a small bowl, whisk together the vinegar, salt, and lemon juice. Pour over the vegetables and toss to combine well. Taste for seasoning and serve immediately.

CHORIZO AND EGG BURRITOS

I prepare this dish on a rare day off or on weekends. It's so simple but incredibly satisfying.

A note about a few of the ingredients. Tapatio Hot Sauce has great flavor and spices things up a bit. Mexican chorizo is a fresh, spiced sausage that is available either in links or in bulk at your local butcher shop, or it can be found in 1-pound packages at the grocery store. Chihuahua cheese, also a Mexican staple, is a mild melting cheese that is readily available in most markets, but if you can't find it, substitute Monterey Jack. It you like things spicier, use pepper Jack or habanero Jack. Be sure to include the avocado slices, as they add a fresh taste and creamy texture. Be creative and use your favorite cheeses or add other ingredients that you and your family will enjoy wrapping up in a flour tortilla.

If you have a little extra time, make a batch of Salsa Rojo (p. 242) to serve with the burritos. It adds a wonderful smokiness and richness to the flavor of the burrito.

SERVES 6 TO 8

1 pound Mexican chorizo, crumbled into smaller pieces (if you purchase chorizo with casings, remove the casings and dice or crumble the sausage before cooking)

12 large eggs, beaten

1 cup grated Chihuahua cheese

1 cup grated sharp Cheddar cheese

6 to 8 large (12-inch) flour tortillas

Tapatio Hot Sauce

2 to 3 ripe avocados, pitted, peeled, and sliced or cut into chunks

Heat a large nonstick skillet over medium-high heat until hot but not smoking. Add the chorizo, breaking it up into smaller crumbles. Reduce the heat to medium and cook until the chorizo is lightly browned, 4 to 6 minutes. If desired, remove the fat from the pan.

Add the eggs to the pan, stir to combine thoroughly, and scramble the eggs until they are soft set or cooked to your desired doneness. Add the cheeses and mix well until the cheeses are melted. Keep the egg and chorizo mixture warm over low heat.

Warm the tortilla slightly over an open flame or in a microwave (see p. 188). To assemble the burritos, place an even amount of egg and cheese mixture in the middle of each tortilla. Add a few dashes of Tapatio and layer several slices or chunks of avocado over the top. To roll the burrito, fold over the short bottom and top ends of the tortilla to the middle and then fold over the right side toward the middle and push the edge back up under the egg and chorizo mixture. Tightly roll up the burrito until it's a uniform shape and serve immediately.

MAMA'S POTATO SALAD

Potato salad is a casual get-together favorite, especially in the summertime at picnics and barbecues. My Mama's version includes sliced California olives, which add a unique twist and one that I loved as a boy. Growing up in Lindsay, California, olive groves were all around us, so Mama often used olives in her cooking. The lemon juice and fresh dill add brightness to the salad dressing, and dill pickle and celery add a bit of crunch. My family loves this recipe and so do guests who are always surprised at, but then converted by, the black olives in their potato salad. Bring it to your next potluck supper and I bet you'll get requests for the recipe.

If you prefer a drier potato salad, use a little less mayonnaise to start. As the salad chills, the potatoes will absorb some of the dressing.

SERVES 8

3 large russet potatoes (about 2¼ pounds total), peeled and cut into ½-inch dice

2 tablespoons kosher salt, divided

One 6.5-ounce can sliced California black olives, drained

3 stalks celery, cut into ¼-inch dice

2 whole dill pickles (or 8 spears), cut into ¼-inch dice

1 teaspoon Dijon mustard

1 teaspoon celery salt

½ teaspoon celery seed

1 tablespoon freshly ground black pepper

Juice and finely grated zest of 1 lemon

1 tablespoon snipped fresh dill

1½ to 2 cups mayonnaise (homemade, Duke's, or Hellmann's, not low-fat)

6 hard-cooked eggs, cut into ¼- to ½-inch dice

Fill a medium stockpot about three-quarters full with water and add 1 tablespoon salt; bring to a boil. Add the potatoes and cook until just tender, about 8 minutes. Drain and rinse in cold water. Cover and refrigerate until completely chilled, at least 2 hours.

In a large bowl, combine the olives, celery, pickles, mustard, celery salt, celery seed, black pepper, lemon juice and zest, dill, and the remaining 1 tablespoon salt. Stir in 1½ cups of the mayonnaise and mix to combine thoroughly. Gently fold in the cooked potatoes and diced eggs. If you like, add the additional ½ cup mayonnaise. Cover and refrigerate for at least 1 hour before serving.

POSOLE VERDE

To this day, Posole is one of my favorite dishes and one of my strongest food memories. My Mama would simmer the broth for hours, and the incredible aroma would permeate the house throughout the day. I can still smell that pot of Posole cooking. Having to be patient until the next day to enjoy the dish was nearly impossible, but always worth the wait. I couldn't sleep at nights with the smell of the herbs and spices simmering in the kitchen and thinking about the wonderful flavors of her Posole. She would tell me to go drink a glass of milk to ease the hunger pangs, just as I do today with my boys in the middle of the night, but nothing would do until I could eat Mama's Posole.

My version of Posole was dubbed "Latin hangover food" after I served it at Lambstock (an annual industry event for chefs and others in the culinary world) in Patrick Springs, Virginia. The dish was also mentioned in a *New York Times* article, and I talked about it on NPR's *All Things Considered* program. As with most soups and stews, it's even better after the flavors have spent the night together and had a chance to mingle. It also freezes well.

You might be more familiar with red Posole, or Posole Rojo, another version made with dried peppers. You can use the Salsa Rojo (p. 242) as a base for making red Posole. Serve Posole topped with thinly sliced cabbage, chopped fresh onion, chopped fresh cilantro, lime wedges, a little dried Mexican oregano, and warm corn tortillas. Be sure to get a little of each accompaniment in every bite—that's where the magic is. You'll get a little heat, crunch, and brightness from the citrus and tomatillos—it's truly an explosion of flavors in your mouth. Even if you don't have a hangover, it'll cure whatever else might be ailing you.

SERVES 8 TO 10

4 large poblanos (1 pound), trimmed, seeds and membranes removed, divided

1 pound tomatillos, peeled, divided

3 ounces garlic cloves (approximately 24 cloves)

2 quarts organic or homemade chicken stock, divided

2 pounds Boston butt or pork shoulder

2 to 3 tablespoons kosher salt, plus more for seasoning the meat

Freshly ground black pepper

2 tablespoons canola oil

1 large onion, cut into ½-inch dice

1 tablespoon plus 1 teaspoon Posole Spice Mix (p. 242)

1 large bunch fresh cilantro, ends trimmed and tied together as a bouquet garni

3 bay leaves

Juice of 4 limes

1 tablespoon House Seasoning Blend (p. 248)

One 25-ounce can hominy, drained (I prefer Juanita's Foods®)

One 14.5-ounce can peeled whole tomatoes, drained and pulsed in a blender or crushed with your hands

FOR SERVING

Thinly sliced red and white cabbage, chopped onion, chopped fresh cilantro, dried Mexican oregano, lime wedges, and corn tortillas (warmed and folded)

Roughly chop half of the poblanos and half of the tomatillos, then add to a high-speed blender (I use my Vitamix) with the garlic and 1 quart of the chicken stock. Pulse until the mixture is loose. Set aside. →

Chop the remaining poblanos and tomatillos into medium (½-inch) dice; set aside.

Let the pork come to room temperature, then pat dry with paper towels. Cut the pork into 2½- to 3-inch pieces. Season the meat with salt and black pepper.

Heat the oil in a large Dutch oven over medium-high heat until hot but not smoking. Add the pork pieces and sauté until brown, turning frequently, 5 to 7 minutes. Add the onion and sweat for 2 to 3 minutes, until it is almost translucent, scraping up any browned bits on the bottom of the pan. Add the reserved chopped poblanos and tomatillos and cook for another 2 minutes. Stir in the Posole Spice Mix and let cook for a few seconds until aromatic.

Pour in the remaining 1 quart chicken stock and the puréed poblano mixture. Bring to a boil and then add the cilantro, bay leaves, lime juice, 2 tablespoons salt, and the House Seasoning Blend. Stir well and add the hominy and tomatoes. Lower the heat and simmer for 1½ to 2 hours, until the pork is tender, skimming any foam from the top of the Posole as it cooks. Remove and discard the cilantro and bay leaves. Taste for seasonings and add the additional 1 tablespoon salt as needed.

If serving immediately, skim any fat from the surface of the Posole and ladle into individual bowls. Or refrigerate overnight, then remove the fat from the surface and warm just before serving. Place the garnishes in small bowls and serve at the table so guests can top their own Posole.

CHEF'S TIP ❯ The flavors of this dish are light and savory with a little spice, so serve a soft Pinot Gris from France or a wine from the Rueda region of Spain, which produces crisp white wines.

CHEF'S TIP ❯ Using enameled cookware is one of the healthiest ways to cook. While there are a number of manufacturers, Le Creuset® cookware has been some of the most prized and best loved cooking pieces by chefs and home cooks for decades. It is coveted for its ability to heat up quickly and maintain an even cooking temperature. The pieces are able to go from stovetop to oven, allowing cooks to achieve a beautiful sear on meats and poultry before being transferred to the oven and cooked on low heat for many hours. I recommend adding a few pieces to your home kitchen, in particular a Dutch oven and a braiser. They are versatile and can be used to prepare anything from soups, stews, and sauces to cooking a whole chicken in a pot.

MEET BOB HANCOCK & KIT GARRETT >
WILDWOOD FARM, GOSHEN, KENTUCKY

FROM ANTHONY

Bob Hancock and Kit Garrett are two of the hardest working people I know. Owners of Blue Dog Bakery and Café in Louisville since 1998, their very popular restaurant serves dishes made with many local ingredients, and their bakery provides artisan breads to their own restaurant and many other restaurants in Louisville. I met this duo when I first discovered their breads, but they also operate a farm where they raise pigs and grow produce to use at the restaurant. I buy my pigs from Bob and Kit and it's some of the best pork I have ever tasted and worked with.

FROM BOB

In 2008, Kit and I decided to lease some farmland and raise pigs after several trips to Spain to learn more about the curing process used to create one of the most sought-after types of ham, the famous Jamón Serrano. Our goal with this new project was to raise and harvest pigs that would replicate the prized ham. After studying the various breeds of pigs and trying to find the perfect breed that would recreate the right flavors, we started raising Red Wattel pigs. This is a heritage breed that at one time was endangered, but is known for having good genetics and large litters.

Red Wattel pigs can grow as large as 700 pounds for the females, or sows, and the males, or boars, can reach 800 to 900 pounds. The ideal weight for the pigs, butchered for fresh meat that we use in our restaurant and sell to a few local chefs, like Anthony, is between 300 and 350 pounds. This size pig has the perfect proportion of meat to fat.

For our charcuterie, the curing process draws moisture and weight out of the meat, so pigs raised for charcuterie will reach 400 pounds and will have more fat, allowing for the curing and aging process. Our pigs reach weight and muscle structure at about 18 months of age and this is when we harvest, which is the average age of the pigs harvested

in Spain. For comparison, commercially raised pigs in the United States are harvested at about 5 months. These pigs are fed a diet that packs on the weight and they are not permitted to roam free.

Our experiments to create a superior pig for charcuterie, one that would replicate the ham from the Black Iberian Pig from Spain, has involved working with the Red Wattel breed, the Duroc pig, another well-known heritage breed, and one of the rarest heritage breeds, the Mule Foot. With its likely ties to the prized Spanish hogs, the Black Iberian Pig, the Mule Foot's genetics are highly desirable.

During this time we also opened Red Hog, a tapas concept within Blue Dog Bakery, where we sold our aged hams and charcuterie. Anthony told me he will never forget the first time he tasted one of my hams. It was aged for 3 years and Anthony describes it as sweet, nutty, and buttery, not salty—like nothing he'd tasted before in the U.S. We're now opening Red Hog as a separate restaurant, which will feature our charcuterie.

In 2012, Kit and I left the city limits of Louisville to partner with Wildwood Farm in Goshen, Kentucky. This new space on 110 acres of beautiful farmland (we only utilize about 20 acres) has allowed us to spread out and rotate the pigs on pastures filled with foraged greens and

grass. We've created a specially formulated diet of non-soy, non-GMO wheat, barley, oats, and field peas along with a nutrient-rich blend of vitamins and minerals and even some restaurant scraps. Our animals are allowed to roam free and root around to their heart's content. Pigs will eat anything in their path 6 inches above and 6 inches or more below the ground, so once the earth is depleted, they are moved to another pasture and then a cover crop is sewn to stabilize and replenish the soil. With around 50 pigs at a time, we are focused on raising quality animals. While it's not cost effective, it's a passion and a labor of love.

Kit and I manage much of the upkeep of the farm in a bartering arrangement, which allows us to keep our pigs on the land and to grow produce for Blue Dog. We put in long and hard days, typically starting at 4 a.m. and ending around 9 p.m., but it's incredibly rewarding.

Pork is the best animal on the planet, and the pork we raise is different—it's sweeter. When you buy pork in Spain at a butcher shop and it's sitting next to the beef, you can't tell the difference based on color and texture. There are also different cuts of pork that we don't have here in the States. To most Americans, all they know about pigs is a pork chop, ham, and bacon. In a small way, we hope to change that.

POTATO TACOS WITH CORN TORTILLAS

These meatless tacos are rustic and satisfying. Most of the ingredients are probably in your pantry, so they're easy to throw together for a quick supper. They are especially delicious with freshly made tortillas smeared with a generous amount of Latino Butter or Salsa Verde. If you use Salsa Verde, top the potatoes with avocado slices mixed with fresh lime juice and salt and pepper. If you use the Latino Butter, you won't need the additional avocado.

If you're lucky, your city will have a local bakery that makes fresh tortillas where you can purchase them still warm. If you don't, it's really simple to make them at home using an inexpensive 8-inch tortilla press, which you can find at most housewares stores or at any Latin market. Make the tortillas ahead of time and store them in a plastic bag until ready to heat and fill. They will hold for a few days.

MAKES 8 TACOS · SERVES 4

FOR THE TORTILLAS
1 cup masa harina
1 teaspoon kosher salt
½ teaspoon vegetable shortening
⅔ cup water

FOR THE POTATOES
1 teaspoon kosher salt, plus more as needed
2 large russet potatoes (approximately 1½ pounds total), peeled and cut into ½-inch dice

2 to 4 tablespoons extra-virgin olive oil
½ Spanish onion, cut into ¼-inch dice (1 cup)
1 jalapeño, trimmed, seeds and membranes removed, and sliced into half-moons
¾ to 1 teaspoon freshly ground black pepper
Latino Butter (p. 236) or Salsa Verde (p. 243)

FOR SERVING
Chopped onion; chopped fresh cilantro; ripe avocado slices mixed with fresh lime juice, kosher salt, and freshly ground black pepper; and lime wedges (optional)

MAKE THE TORTILLAS

Put the masa harina, salt, and shortening in a medium bowl and mix with your hands, incorporating the shortening completely. Add the water, a bit at a time, and continue to mix with your hands until the dough forms a ball and is a soft consistency. It should hold together but not be too wet. You might not need the entire ⅔ cup water.

Cut the dough into 8 equal pieces (just eyeball them so they're close) and shape each into a ball by rolling it between your hands. Working with one ball at a time, place it between two pieces of wax paper on a tortilla press and flatten. Remove the dough and store between sheets of wax paper until ready to cook, covering them with a damp towel to prevent them from drying out.

MAKE THE POTATOES

In a medium saucepan, cook the potatoes in boiling salted water for about 8 minutes, or until the potatoes are just beginning to get tender (a knife inserted in a potato will meet with a bit of resistance). Drain, then return the potatoes to the pan, heating it over low and shaking the pan to dry the potatoes.

Heat 2 tablespoons of the oil in a large nonstick or well-seasoned cast iron skillet over medium high just until hot but not smoking. Add the onion and sauté for just a minute, then add the potatoes and jalapeño pieces; season with salt and black pepper and sauté until the potatoes are have a nice brown crust and are tender and the onion is nicely charred, 5 to 10 minutes. Reduce the heat and add a little more oil if the mixture becomes too dry, keeping a consistent temperature after each addition. Flip the potatoes over as they brown on one side. Once the potatoes are cooked, move the pan off the heat and keep them warm.

COOK THE TORTILLAS AND SERVE

Cook the tortillas, one at a time, in a dry, hot cast iron skillet or nonstick skillet, just until pliable and light brown spots appear, about 1 minute per side. Keep the cooked tortillas in a tortilla warmer or wrap in a clean kitchen towel while you finish cooking all of the dough. Smear the tortillas with Latino Butter or Salsa Verde, then fill each with equal amounts of the warm potato mixture. Top with chopped onion, chopped cilantro, and avocado slices (if using Salsa Verde). Serve immediately, with lime wedges on the side, if desired.

CHEF'S TIP ❯ You can also serve these potatoes as a tasty version of home fries with eggs for breakfast.

SAUTÉED SPINACH

Sautéed spinach is one of the quickest vegetable dishes to prepare. With so little cooking time involved, it is a perfect family and weeknight side dish, especially after a long day at work or afternoon running the kids around. While most kids may not like the idea of eating spinach, just as with any dish, if you season it right, they will come to love it.

I flavor the spinach with Greek seasoning, which I started cooking with while working with the Greek owner of Timothy's in Louisville. This seasoning is an easy way to add the right amount of spice to certain dishes, including this one. A little garlic, butter, olive oil, and white wine add richness to the spinach, and the fresh lemon juice brightens the flavors.

This spinach dish is a great accompaniment to family-friendly foods like Samantha's Meatloaf (p. 225), but you can also serve it as an accompaniment to more elegant dishes like seared scallops or Pan-Seared Halibut with Red-Chile Bluegrass Soy Butter (p. 164). The recipe can be doubled easily.

SERVES 2 TO 3

1 teaspoon olive oil	2 tablespoons dry white wine
1 pound fresh spinach, washed and trimmed of large stems	1 teaspoon Greek seasoning (I prefer Cavender's)
1 to 2 tablespoons unsalted butter, divided	½ teaspoon kosher salt
½ teaspoon minced garlic	½ lemon →

In a large skillet over medium heat, heat the oil until hot but not smoking. Add the spinach, packing it into the skillet, stirring as the first pieces begin to wilt, and cook for a minute. Add 1 tablespoon of the butter and the garlic, stir, and cook until the spinach is slightly wilted, just a few minutes. Don't overcook it. Add the white wine and sprinkle with the Greek seasoning and salt. Toss the spinach with tongs to coat with the liquid. Once the spinach has wilted, add the remaining 1 tablespoon butter, if desired. Remove the pan from the heat and squeeze the lemon over the spinach. Stir to combine well, taste and adjust seasonings, and serve immediately.

THE BEST MASHED POTATOES

Everybody thinks their recipe for mashed potatoes is the best, and of course, I'm no different. That's why this recipe is called The Best Mashed Potatoes!

Lots of butter, whole milk, and white pepper make this version stand out. There's not too much to say about making mashed potatoes other than to use firm russet potatoes that are free of blemishes, cook them just until tender, and then be sure that after you drain them you let them dry just a bit before mashing. You don't want any water in the pan.

Enjoy the mashed potatoes with Samantha's Meatloaf (on the facing page) or any other dishes that you like to serve with mashed potatoes, such as pot roast or roast chicken.

SERVES 4 TO 6

6 medium russet potatoes (about 3 pounds total), scrubbed, peeled, and cut into ½-inch dice

1 tablespoon plus 2 teaspoons kosher salt, divided

8 tablespoons unsalted butter, at room temperature

¼ cup milk, at room temperature

½ teaspoon ground white pepper, plus more to taste

Put the potatoes in a large stockpot or Dutch oven and cover by 2 inches with water. Add 1 tablespoon salt and bring to boil over high heat. Reduce the heat to a low boil, cover, and cook the potatoes until tender, 15 to 20 minutes. Drain the potatoes, then return them to the pot, heating over low and gently shaking the pot to dry them. Using a hand masher or a ricer, mash the potatoes. Add the butter, milk, the remaining 2 teaspoons salt, and ½ teaspoon white pepper; stir to combine well. Do not overwork the potatoes or they will become sticky. Taste and adjust seasonings. Serve immediately or keep warm until ready to serve.

SAMANTHA'S MEATLOAF

My wife Samantha makes a wonderful meatloaf, but when I make her recipe, I add in a little Latin love. I use a combination of ground beef and chorizo (I sneak this in, shhh…). I think the chorizo gives my version of her meatloaf more complexity and great flavor. I add a lot of seasonings, and the beef stock is another tasty addition that helps to keep the meat moist.

I top the meatloaf with ketchup or tomato sauce, which caramelizes during baking and becomes sweet. It's a nice contrast to the spiced meatloaf. A home-cooked meatloaf dinner wouldn't be complete without potatoes and a veggie, so try The Best Mashed Potatoes (facing page) and Sautéed Spinach (p. 223). Save the leftovers for one of my favorites, a meatloaf sandwich.

SERVES 8

Nonstick cooking spray, for the pan	½ teaspoon crushed red pepper flakes
1½ pounds lean ground beef	1 teaspoon kosher salt
½ pound ground Mexican chorizo	½ teaspoon freshly ground black pepper
1 teaspoon chopped fresh oregano	1 teaspoon Worcestershire sauce
1 teaspoon chopped fresh thyme	1 cup homemade dried breadcrumbs
1 teaspoon onion powder	2 large eggs, lightly beaten
½ teaspoon smoked Spanish paprika (pimentón)	½ cup organic or homemade beef stock
½ teaspoon smoked serrano chile powder	Tomato ketchup or tomato sauce

Heat a convection oven to 350°F. With the nonstick cooking spray, grease a rimmed baking sheet or loaf pan.

In a large bowl, combine all the ingredients except for the ketchup or tomato sauce. Mix everything together with your hands, just until incorporated—don't overwork the mixture. Turn out the mixture onto a plastic cutting board and shape into a loaf. Place on the prepared baking sheet or in the loaf pan. Top generously with ketchup or tomato sauce, then tent the meatloaf with foil.

Bake for ½ hour and then remove the foil. Bake for an additional 20 to 30 minutes, or until the meatloaf is done. The internal temperature should be 165° to 170°F on an instant-read thermometer. If you baked the meatloaf in a loaf pan, invert it onto a serving plate; slice and serve immediately.

CHEF'S TIP › Meatloaf is an everyday comfort meal, so pair it with a comfortable wine. In the warmer months, try an Italian Dolcetto or French Beaujolais; in the fall, an Argentinian or Chilean Malbec is a nice accompaniment. In the cold of winter, a spicy Zinfandel pairs well with the chorizo in the meatloaf.

MAMA'S CHICKEN AND MUSHROOM ENCHILADAS WITH MANCHEGO CREMA

. . . .

When I was a boy, this was one of my favorite dishes Mama made. She usually prepared enchiladas on special occasions, so they weren't regular weeknight suppers. Back in those days, cream of mushroom soup was quite popular and used by many home cooks. I have updated my Mama's recipe and I make my own sauce. This recipe is a variation of the one we serve at Seviche. At the restaurant, we make a cream sauce with mushrooms, fill the tortillas with sautéed mushrooms and chicken, and serve three enchiladas on a bed of yellow rice.

For the home version, this recipe is baked in a casserole dish, making preparation and cooking easier. The creamy cheese sauce is the perfect accompaniment to the filling of sautéed mushroom and chicken. You can certainly add mushrooms to the sauce, if you like. Leftover roasted chicken or store-bought rotisserie chicken is perfect in this recipe. Serve with Yellow Rice (see the facing page) and garnish with sour cream, chopped scallions, Salsa Verde (p. 243), and fresh tomatoes, if they're in season.

Use a combination of regular button mushrooms and portobello mushrooms or, if you prefer, add in some wild mushrooms that are in season at your local farmers' market.

SERVES 6

FOR THE FILLING AND ENCHILADAS

2 tablespoons extra-virgin olive oil

½ onion, diced (1 cup)

2½ cups sliced mushrooms (equal amounts of white button mushrooms and portobello mushrooms)

Kosher salt and freshly ground black pepper

2 cloves garlic, minced

2½ cups cooked, pulled chicken

½ cup organic or homemade chicken stock

⅓ cup sour cream

Canola oil, for frying

12 corn tortillas

Nonstick cooking spray, for the pan

FOR THE SAUCE

2 tablespoons unsalted butter

2 tablespoons all-purpose flour

1 teaspoon kosher salt

2 cups whole milk

¼ teaspoon ground white pepper

2 cups grated Manchego cheese, divided

FOR SERVING

Yellow Rice (see the facing page), sour cream, chopped scallions, Salsa Verde (p. 243), and chopped fresh tomatoes

MAKE THE FILLING AND STUFF THE ENCHILADAS

In a large skillet, over medium-high heat, heat the olive oil until hot but not smoking. Add the onion and sweat for 2 to 3 minutes, then add the mushrooms. Sprinkle with a little salt and black pepper and sweat the mushrooms for another 2 minutes, until they begin to brown and release their juices; reduce the heat if necessary. Add the garlic and cook for another 30 seconds, then add the chicken, stock, and sour cream; stir well to combine. Heat the mixture through and set aside off the heat.

In a medium skillet over medium-high heat, add a thin layer of canola oil to cover the bottom of the pan and deep enough to cover the tortillas. When the oil is very hot, add the tortillas, one at a time, and fry for 10 to 15 seconds, just enough to warm and soften the tortillas. Drain on paper towels. Alternatively, hold a tortilla with tongs over an open flame on the stove. The tortilla will soften in mere seconds.

When ready to fill the tortillas, place approximately ¼ cup of the chicken and mushroom mixture in the middle of each tortilla and roll up.

MAKE THE SAUCE

In a medium saucepan over medium-high heat, heat the butter until melted and the foaming subsides. Quickly add the flour and salt and whisk constantly for about a minute to make a roux. Slowly pour in the milk, whisking constantly to create a smooth sauce. Stir in the white pepper. Cook for about 5 minutes, whisking frequently until the mixture is smooth and thickened and almost to boiling. Lower the heat and add in 1½ cups of the grated Manchego; whisk until the cheese is melted and the sauce is smooth. Do not let it boil. (If the sauce sits, it will thicken. If desired, thin with a little milk.)

ASSEMBLE AND COOK

Heat a convection oven to 350°F. Grease a 9 x 13 x 2-inch pan.

Spread about ½ cup of the sauce evenly over the bottom of the pan. Arrange the rolled tortillas, seam side down, in the pan so that they cover almost the entire bottom. Pour the cheese sauce evenly over the top of the enchiladas, then sprinkle with the remaining ½ cup of grated Manchego.

Bake for 30 to 35 minutes, or until the casserole is bubbly and the enchiladas are heated through. If you like the top well browned, place the casserole under the broiler for a few seconds.

Serve family style, with the garnishes on the side.

YELLOW RICE

SERVES 6

1 tablespoon canola oil	2 cups homemade or organic chicken stock
1 cup raw long-grain rice	1 teaspoon tumeric
¼ onion, cut into ¼-inch dice	¼ teaspoon white pepper
1 clove garlic, minced	1 teaspoon kosher salt

In a medium saucepan over medium-high heat, heat the oil until hot but not smoking. Add the rice and cook, stirring, for 2 minutes. Do not brown the rice. Add the onion and stir; cook for another 2 to 3 minutes to sweat the onion. Add the garlic, stir, and cook for another 30 seconds, just until aromatic. Add the chicken stock, turmeric, white pepper, and salt (depending on how salty the chicken stock is). Bring to a boil, stir, and cover. Simmer for 15 minutes, or until stock is absorbed. Fluff with a fork and serve.

THE SECRET INGREDIENTS

SAUCES, SEASONINGS & RUBS

W E CALL THESE RECIPES
"secret" for a reason. Most of
these sauces, butters, and rubs are
the key ingredients to many of the
dishes and recipes in the book. As I
have mentioned in other chapters, my
food is all about the layering of flavors
and textures. While a marinated and
grilled piece of salmon or beautifully
brined and seared chicken breast
might be delicious on its own, it can be
elevated to spectacular with just a little
bit more love. Add in some vegetables
for texture or a luscious buttery sauce
for silkiness and you've created something really special.

When I first became really interested
in food in my teens, I instinctively knew
the importance of rubbing steaks or
other cuts of beef first with a seasoning
blend like Adobo Rub (p. 245) to layer in
the flavors and then serving them with
a bright and fresh sauce like Chimichurri (p. 249). I've carried that sense of
elevated flavors throughout my career.

While most of the recipes in this
chapter are part of composed dishes →

in recipes throughout the book, there are some other suggested uses. Some are more time-consuming to prepare, like the demi-glace (p. 238), but it will hold in your freezer for months and will completely change the complexity of flavors in dishes that it's added to, such as beef stew, beef stroganoff, or chili.

The dried spice mixtures can be made ahead and kept in an airtight container in your pantry. You never know when you'll want to make a batch of Posole (p. 217), so be sure to have some Posole Seasoning Mix (p. 242) on hand, especially when it's time for fall comfort food.

Make up one or two of the compound butters and store in your refrigerator (or freezer for longer storage) to perk up foods like steaks on the grill or steamed vegetables.

As with all cooking, these recipes and headnotes are guidelines. Get creative and have fun in the kitchen, and try your hand at pairing these exciting flavors and textures with some of your favorite family dishes.

> Get creative and have fun in the kitchen, and try your hand at pairing these exciting flavors and textures with some of your favorite family dishes.

AJI PANCA SAUCE

A popular pepper grown in Peru, aji pancas (see p.10) are primarily grown to be dried, so the fresh peppers never leave the farms where they're harvested. A deep red or burgundy color at full maturity, these peppers are used in aji panca paste, which is the primary ingredient in this recipe. It can be found at Latin or international markets or ordered online (see Resources on p. 277). These peppers have almost no heat, but they are a bit smoky and sweet, making them a perfect pairing for the Chicken Liver Anticuchos (p. 26).

Like my other sauces, this one gets its smooth texture from using a high-speed blender, so if you own one, use it to blend the ingredients. If you don't own one, then purée the mixture in a regular blender until the sauce is very smooth.

MAKES ABOUT 2 CUPS

8 ounces aji panca paste	¼ Spanish onion, roughly chopped
1 cup organic or homemade chicken stock	2 teaspoons kosher salt
2 cloves garlic, roughly chopped	Juice of 1 lime

Purée all the ingredients in a high-speed blender until smooth. Taste and adjust seasonings. Transfer to an airtight container and store in the refrigerator. The sauce will hold for several days.

LEMON—TOMATO BUTTER

I love this lemony tomato and butter sauce paired with the Country Ham and Spinach–Stuffed Chicken Breasts (p. 116). The saltiness of the ham and Manchego cheese are absolutely delicious with the brightness of this sauce; it's really a nice balance of flavors. Taste the country ham first to see how salty it is, and then you can adjust the amount of salt needed for this sauce. You'll want to adjust the amount of salt in the sauce based on what it will be served with.

MAKES 1½ CUPS

½ cup dry white wine
Juice and peeled zest of 1 lemon
1 small shallot, sliced
½ cup heavy cream
¼ cup tomato paste

¾ teaspoon kosher salt, plus more as needed
2 teaspoons cornstarch slurry (p. 118), as needed
8 tablespoons unsalted butter, sliced

In a small saucepan, combine the wine, lemon juice, lemon zest, and the shallot. Bring to a boil, then lower the heat to medium and cook until the mixture is reduced by half, 3 to 4 minutes. Add the cream, tomato paste, and salt; whisk together and bring to a boil. Reduce the heat to low and slowly add the cornstarch slurry, a little at a time, whisking constantly, until the sauce is smooth and semi-thick. Off the heat, or over low heat, whisk in one slice of butter at a time, until all the butter has been incorporated and the sauce is smooth. Strain through a fine-mesh sieve or chinois. Keep warm until ready to serve.

BEURRE BLANC

BEURRE BLANC, meaning "white butter" in French, is a classic butter sauce that is made by reducing a liquid, traditionally white wine or vinegar, and then adding butter, a pat at a time, until a silky-smooth consistency is achieved. Additional seasonings, such as shallots or herbs, are added to create a beautiful and luscious sauce that makes a perfect accompaniment to seafood and shellfish or to meats and vegetables. We use several beurre blanc sauces at Seviche.

While a French butter sauce sounds difficult to make, it is actually quite simple to prepare. The key to these sauces is to not leave them on the stove once all of the butter has been incorporated. They will break down quickly and while they can be recovered, you don't want to get to that point. My suggestion is to prepare them at the last minute and then serve them immediately for the best results. If they have to be held even for a few moments, the best way to do that is over a double boiler; whisk before serving.

CUMIN—LIME AÏOLI

This simple aïoli is the secret to the exceptionally tasty Baja-Style Fish Tacos (p. 147). You can also serve this delicious sauce with Crab Cakes (p. 153) and any other seafood, such as grilled shrimp. We also serve it with our Duck Nachos at Seviche. If you're a purist, then make your own homemade mayonnaise, but a good store-bought version will work as well in a pinch. I prefer Duke's or Hellmann's.

MAKES 1 CUP

1 cup mayonnaise, homemade or store-bought (not low-fat)	1½ teaspoons Adobo Rub (p. 245)
1 clove garlic, minced	Juice of 1 lime

In a small bowl, whisk together all the ingredients until well blended. Cover and refrigerate for up to a day.

MOJO DE AJO

At Seviche, we serve this pungent sauce with the Puerto Rican Mofongo (p. 126). Spanish for "garlic sauce," Mojo de Ajo really brightens up the flavor of the roasted pork and adds an acidic balance to the richness of the buttery, sweet plantains in the Mofongo.

Many recipes for Mojo de Ajo use quite a bit more garlic than this one does, but I prefer this version, which is my interpretation of a classic Latin sauce. Homemade Sazón (p. 248) gives the sauce its vibrant color. Mojo de Ajo is a great marinade for pork roast or chops, chicken, or grilled shrimp. It will hold for several days in the refrigerator, but will separate, so stir it well before using if it's been sitting for a few days. You can also add about ¼ teaspoon xantham gum to the sauce to stabilize it, adding a little at a time to reach the desired consistency. It won't take very much to thicken the sauce.

MAKES ABOUT 2 CUPS

Juice of 5 limes	1 teaspoon kosher salt
Juice of 2 oranges	½ teaspoon (or less) orange oil (see Resources on p. 277), or finely grated zest of 1 orange
5 cloves garlic	
½ cup red-wine vinegar	½ cup extra-virgin olive oil
4½ teaspoons Homemade Sazón (p. 248)	¼ teaspoon xantham gum, as needed to stabilize the sauce (optional)

Put all the ingredients except the oil and xantham gum in a high-speed blender (like a Vitamix) and blend well. With the machine running, add the oil slowly until the sauce comes together and emulsifies. Add the xantham gum, if desired, to keep the sauce from separating as it sits. Cover and refrigerate for several days.

—

JALAPEÑO—MINT PESTO

At Seviche, we serve this version of a spicy mint pesto with Albóndigas, our lamb meatball appetizer (p. 19). The spices in the ground lamb mixture and fresh lemon juice and zest pair beautifully with this pesto. Lamb can hold up to bold flavors, so this is the perfect combination of seasonings.

You can also serve this pesto with grilled lamb chops or leg of lamb. Try it in place of the Jalapeño—Basil Pesto on *cocas* (p. 191). It would be great with fresh ricotta cheese, halved heirloom cherry tomatoes, and lemon zest. If not using all the pesto right away, follow the directions for longer storage in the headnote for Jalapeño—Basil Pesto (p. 178).

MAKES ABOUT 2 CUPS

2 cups fresh mint, tightly packed
¼ cup grated Parmigiano-Reggiano or Manchego cheese
3 cloves garlic, chopped
2 jalapeños, trimmed and sliced, with seeds
¼ cup pine nuts, toasted

2 teaspoons kosher salt, plus more as needed
1 cup extra-virgin olive oil

Combine all of the ingredients, except for the olive oil, in a high-speed blender. Pulse several times to combine. With the machine running, slowly add the olive oil in a steady stream through the feeder tube until the pesto is smooth and emulsified. You may need to stop the blender a few times to push down the dry ingredients. Transfer the pesto to a small container. If not using immediately, refrigerate the pesto covered with a thin layer of olive oil for up to 1 day. Freeze for longer storage.

CHARRED CORN SALSA

We love our fresh corn in Kentucky in the summertime, and since the season is so short, I use it in as many dishes as possible. Corn from our neighboring state of Indiana is some of the best I've ever had. I use both the yellow corn and Silver Queen corn, depending on the recipe. For this corn salsa, yellow corn is best, as it will hold up to grilling because the corn is starchier. The combined colors with the fresh tomatoes and spicy jalapeños are very bright and attractive, especially when entertaining.

Make a batch of this fresh salsa and serve it with the Pork Loin with Chipotle–Orange Bourbon Glaze (p. 133) and Roasted Poblano and Manchego Weisenberger Grits (p. 160). The salsa also pairs well with grilled meats like chicken or pork chops or with homemade tortilla chips and guacamole as an appetizer. Add the fresh cilantro right before serving, as it will lose its flavor if it sits in the salsa too long.

MAKES ABOUT 2 CUPS

3 medium ears fresh sweet corn, shucked	Juice of 2 limes
½ red onion, cut into ¼-inch dice	1 teaspoon kosher salt
1 large tomato, cut into ¼-inch dice	½ teaspoon freshly ground black pepper
1 jalapeño, trimmed and cut into ⅛-inch dice (with seeds, if you like more heat)	1 tablespoon extra-virgin olive oil
	¼ bunch fresh cilantro, trimmed and chopped

Heat a gas or charcoal grill over high heat. Lay the ears of corn on the grates, leave the lid open, and grill the corn, turning occasionally, until some but not all of the kernels are charred. This can take up to 10 minutes, depending on your grill. When cool enough to handle, remove the corn kernels from the ears (see p. 75).

Combine the corn kernels and the rest of the ingredients, except for the cilantro, in a medium bowl. Mix well; taste and adjust seasonings. Cover and chill until ready to use.

When ready to serve, stir and again check for seasonings. When the salsa sits and the vegetables release their juices, it will need additional salt and sometimes black pepper. Add the chopped cilantro and mix well.

LATINO BUTTER

I grew up eating avocados and using them as you would butter. We had an avocado tree in our yard in central California, and avocados were one of the main agricultural products grown in the region. When I was a kid, my mama made this "butter"—really avocado–jalapeño purée—and I would eat it out of the bowl like most kids eat cake batter. Today, I make this and smear it on a tortilla or baguette. My younger son, Ian Cruz, loves it too.

At Seviche, we serve Latino Butter with a number of dishes, including Kentucky Bison Empanadas (p. 35) and Beef Tostados. It's great with tacos and a number of other recipes in this book, but it's also deliciously good on its own.

MAKES 1 PINT

2 ripe avocados, peeled and pitted, cut into slices	1 jalapeño, trimmed, with seeds
	2 cloves garlic
1 bunch fresh cilantro, trimmed of stems	4 ounces ice water, plus more if needed
Juice of 1 lime	2 teaspoons kosher salt

Put all the ingredients in a high-speed blender like a Vitamix and purée until smooth. If the ingredients get stuck and won't blend, push them down the sides using the

COMPOUND BUTTERS

WE MAKE A NUMBER OF COMPOUND butters at Seviche. It's amazing how something as simple as a pat of melting butter that's been enhanced with bright and bold seasonings can elevate the flavors of basic dishes like grilled meats, roasted vegetables, and rice.

I've included three of our favorite compound butters (see the two butters in this chapter and another on p. 171) and suggested uses, but let these be guidelines. Get creative in your own kitchen with leftovers and see where you can add some unique flavors.

We prepare the butters in 1-pound logs at Seviche, and we also store them in containers since we use them so much. When you're mixing the ingredients together to form a

log, some of the citrus juices will not completely incorporate (think of oil and water), but do your best. Mixing the butters by hand with disposable kitchen gloves is the preferred method.

These butters will hold for several weeks in the refrigerator. For longer storage (up to 2 months), wrap them tightly in plastic and freeze. You never know when you just might want that extra-special something to finish your dish, like a simple grilled chicken breast topped with Pernod Citrus Butter (p. 237) or a grilled pork chop topped with a smoky Chipotle–Pecan Butter (p. 240). They also make great gifts to share with friends. Make the larger recipe into two smaller logs; keep one for yourself and give the other as a gift.

push tool. Add more water, a drop at a time, as necessary to achieve a proper consistency. Transfer to an airtight container and then lay a piece of plastic wrap against the surface to prevent browning. Cover and refrigerate. This is best served the same day.

CHEF'S TIP ❯ If you've ever wondered why soups, sauces, and dressings in restaurants are incredibly smooth, frothy, and luscious, it's probably because a high-speed blender was used to achieve that texture. Regular blenders don't have the power that these machines do; we use a Vitamix high-speed blender at Seviche to make all of the sauces and soups.

PERNOD CITRUS BUTTER

We pair this wonderful bright and citrusy butter with Classic Carolina Gold Rice and Sea Island Red Peas (pp. 131–132), but it can be paired with so many other foods. It's our house butter at Seviche, so we always have it on hand.

It's perfect with fresh steamed or grilled veggies, grilled fish or chicken, and white rice or other grains. I especially like it with steamed artichoke hearts.

You can make a half recipe or make the whole thing and freeze half. If you're going to freeze the butter, don't add the parsley. You can add it later when you add the butter to whatever you prepare with it. The parsley will turn dark green and break down in the freezer.

MAKES A 1-POUND LOG

1 pound unsalted butter, softened	½ teaspoon Pernod
Finely grated zest of 1 orange	1 teaspoon minced garlic
Finely grated zest of 1 lime	2 teaspoons kosher salt
Finely grated zest and juice of 1 lemon	¼ teaspoon ground white pepper
Juice of ½ orange	2 tablespoons chopped fresh curly
Juice of ½ lime	parsley (if the butter will not be frozen)

In a medium bowl, use your hands or an electric handheld mixer fitted with wire beaters to gently combine all the ingredients until well blended. Lay a large piece of parchment on the counter and, with a spatula, scrape the butter mixture in the center. Shape the butter into a log and wrap in the paper, twisting the ends to tighten. Wrap in a piece of plastic wrap to keep it airtight. Refrigerate for at least 2 hours to firm before using. The butter will hold in the refrigerator for a few weeks or put it in a zip-top plastic bag and freeze for up to 2 months. Alternatively, you can store the butter in an airtight container.

COUNTRY HAM CHIPOTLE DEMI-GLACE

Homemade demi-glace may sound a little daunting, but this is a project that's worth the time and effort. There are two recipes that use demi-glace in the book, Pan-Seared Duck Breast with Bourbon–Country Ham Chipotle Demi-Glace (p. 129) and Roasted Leg of Lamb with Lemon–Rosemary Demi-Glace (p. 121). If you've never made demi-glace from scratch, now's the time to start.

Prepared from roasted veal bones that are then simmered in their stock for 24 hours, demi-glace is an incredibly rich, concentrated, and gelatinous sauce that adds a beautiful texture and complexity to dishes. This version has just a hint of heat and smokiness from the chipotle purée and a bit of Southern flair from the country ham, which gives it another layer of flavor.

In addition to creating the beautiful pan sauces that are paired with the Pan-Seared Duck and Leg of Lamb dishes mentioned above, you can add demi-glace to many other dishes to enhance their depth of flavor. Freeze it in smaller amounts so that you can add a little at a time to beef soups, stews, and pot roasts. You can also add a little demi-glace to beef stroganoff, chili, or Boeuf Bourguignon. Add a little horseradish and serve it with prime rib. Once again, get creative and think of the different uses for this liquid gold.

MAKES ABOUT 3½ QUARTS

9 pounds veal bones	2 cups dry red wine
2 carrots, roughly chopped	3 tablespoons Chipotle in Adobo Purée (p. 114)
4 stalks celery, roughly chopped	One 12-ounce slice Kentucky country ham, with bone
1 large Spanish onion, roughly chopped	1 tablespoon whole black peppercorns
1 cup tomato paste	4 bay leaves

Position a rack in the center of a convection oven and heat the oven to 500°F. In a large roasting pan, spread the veal bones and roast for 1½ hours. Remove the pan from the oven and add the vegetables and tomato paste. Stir to combine with the accumulated fat and pan juices. Return the pan to the oven and roast for another 30 minutes. Add the red wine to deglaze the pan.

Combine the veal bones and all of the vegetables, pan juices, and browned bits in a large 20-quart pot. Cover with cold water by 1 to 2 inches above the veal bones. Add the remaining ingredients and bring to a low simmer over medium-high heat. Simmer for 24 hours. (Yes, that means overnight.)

After 24 hours, strain the demi-glace through a fine-mesh sieve into an 8-quart stockpot. Bring to a low boil, reduce the heat, and simmer for 4 hours, or until the mixture has a thin gravy-like consistency. Let cool slightly and then transfer to airtight containers for longer storage, stirring the mixture from the bottom of the pan to distribute the flavors evenly as you transfer it. You can reduce the demi-glace or add it to sauces as is. Store in the refrigerator for up to 2 weeks or in the freezer for 6 months.

CHEF'S TIP > Veal bones can be sourced through a local butcher or restaurant. If you know a chef at an upscale restaurant close to home, then contact him and see if he can order in some extra veal bones for you. Beef bones don't create the same consistency or flavor in demi-glace, so make an effort to find veal bones.

CHIPOTLE—PECAN BUTTER

A slightly spicy compound butter, I use this to flavor the Roasted Sweet Potatoes with Sorghum (p. 99). It's also great added to roasted Brussels sprouts, grilled pork chops, or to season toasted French bread slices. The smoky, nutty combination can turn all kinds of dishes into something unique and flavorful.

We make a small amount of this butter because it has toasted pecans, which will become mushy over time. The quicker you use the butter, the better it will be. The butter will keep in the refrigerator for a few weeks, but when wrapped well, it will keep in the freezer for up to 2 months.

MAKES ONE ½-POUND LOG

½ pound unsalted butter, softened	½ cup chopped pecans, toasted
Juice of 1 lemon	¼ cup Chipotle in Adobo Purée (p. 114)
1 teaspoon kosher salt	

In a medium bowl, using your hands or an electric handheld mixer fitted with wire beaters, gently combine all the ingredients until well blended. Lay a large piece of parchment on the counter and, with a spatula, scrape the mixture onto the center of the paper and shape it into a log. Wrap and tighten the ends, twisting to seal tightly. Wrap the parchment in a piece of plastic wrap to keep it airtight. Refrigerate for at least 2 hours to firm before using. The butter will hold in the refrigerator for a few weeks, or put it in a zip-top plastic bag and freeze for longer storage. Alternatively, you can store the butter in an airtight container.

PICO DE GALLO

As the Pico de Gallo sits, the tomatoes will release juices and the seasonings may need to be adjusted before serving. Also, add the cilantro just before serving, as its bright flavor will be lost if it's added to the rest of the ingredients and allowed to sit in the juices. When tasting for seasonings, the amount of salt needed will depend on what you're serving the Pico de Gallo with. If you're serving it as an appetizer with guacamole and salty chips, it might not need as much salt as when you're using it to top Baja-Style Fish Tacos (p. 147) or another dish.

3 medium or 2 large ripe, but still firm tomatoes (about 1 pound), cut into ¼-inch dice

¼ red onion, cut into ¼-inch dice

1 jalapeño, trimmed, seeds and membranes removed, and cut into ¼-inch dice

Juice 2 lemons

Juice of 2 limes

5 shakes Tabasco, optional (add for a spicier Pico de Gallo)

1 tablespoon extra-virgin olive oil

2½ teaspoons kosher salt, plus more as needed

1 teaspoon freshly ground black pepper

1 small bunch cilantro, trimmed and chopped

In a medium bowl, combine all of the ingredients, except the cilantro. Mix well, cover, and let sit for several hours in the refrigerator. Right before serving, add the cilantro and taste again for salt, then adjust seasonings. Serve immediately.

WILD RAMP CHIMICHURRI

For a unique take on chimichurri sauce, I look to my Southern backyard. We are very fortunate to get wild ramps in Kentucky. This wild green onion arrives in early spring and has a great subtle flavor that can be used in many ways. We pickle and preserve them to serve at other times throughout the year. You can use spring onions or scallions to achieve a very similar, but slightly more oniony flavor. If you are lucky enough to find wild ramps at your local farmers' market or grocery store in the springtime, don't miss the opportunity to try them. Their season is short.

This chimichurri is served with the marinated and grilled tri tip (p. 123), but it can be used to enhance any grilled steak or other cut of beef, such as London broil or hanger steak.

MAKES 2½ TO 3 CUPS

1 cup chopped wild ramps, spring onions, or scallions (including the tender green tops)

1 bunch fresh cilantro, trimmed

1 bunch fresh curly parsley, trimmed

1 tomato, roughly chopped

1 teaspoon crushed red pepper flakes

4 cloves garlic, minced

2 teaspoons kosher salt

½ to ¾ cup red-wine vinegar

½ to ¾ cup extra-virgin olive oil

Add all of the ingredients to a high-speed blender, starting with ½ cup of vinegar and ½ cup of olive oil. Purée until the mixture is loose. Add more vinegar and oil if necessary. Taste for seasonings. Transfer to a container and refrigerate for 30 minutes prior to serving. The chimichurri is best used the same day it's made.

SALSA ROJO

Smoky and earthy, the flavors in this gorgeous and mildly spicy red salsa, which is made with two varieties of dried chiles, just explode. To read more about pasilla and guajillo chiles, see pp. 11–12.

This salsa is best made a day ahead and served with roasted pork, in tacos, or with Chorizo and Egg Burritos (p. 215) for a special weekend breakfast with family. This sauce will hold for several days in the refrigerator.

MAKES ABOUT 3 CUPS

8 dried pasilla chiles	Juice of 2 limes
8 dried guajillo chiles	2 tablespoons kosher salt
1 teaspoon House Seasoning Blend (p. 248)	½ cup reserved soaking water from chiles, plus more as needed
3 cloves garlic	
¼ medium onion	½ cup extra-virgin olive oil

Soak the dried chiles in just enough hot water to cover them until they are softened; this should take 5 to 10 minutes. Remove the chiles and reserve the water. Trim the chiles and remove the seeds and membranes.

Put the chiles and the rest of the ingredients except the olive oil in a high-speed blender and pulse until the mixture becomes smooth. Slowly add the oil through the feeder tube until the sauce is emulsified. If desired, add a bit more of the chile soaking water to get the consistency you like.

POSOLE SPICE MIX

Most Mexican home cooks have a jar of Posole spice mix sitting on their counters. Unique to each cook, you will find that many dishes, such as traditional Posole, will have a very different flavor from one home to another based on the blend of spices the cook chooses to use. The basis for my Posole Spice Mix (or Menudo) is a homemade Adobo Rub (p. 245), which is another seasoning I use often in my recipes. If you don't want to make your own homemade version of these two seasoning mixes, you can purchase them at most Latin or international markets.

Just as Mexican cooks have their own particular blends, you will find that different store-bought brands will vary greatly. Try a few or create your own to add complex flavors to your own dishes.

These spice blends will hold as long as your regular spices (about 6 months) as long as they're sealed tightly in an airtight container. Be sure to use fresh and aromatic spices to make these blends, as they will only be as good as the ingredients they're made with.

3 ounces homemade Adobo Rub (p. 245)

3 tablespoons dried Mexican oregano

10 dried bay leaves, crushed in a spice grinder

1 tablespoon crushed red pepper flakes

1 tablespoon whole black peppercorns, crushed in a spice grinder

1 tablespoon dried onion flakes

1 tablespoon dried garlic flakes

1 tablespoon epazote, crushed with your fingers

1 teaspoon onion powder

¼ teaspoon granulated sugar

½ teaspoon dried basil

¼ teaspoon dried thyme

¼ teaspoon allspice

In a small bowl, blend together all ingredients. Transfer to an airtight container to store.

SALSA VERDE

Tomatillos, the primary ingredient in this salsa, are a member of the gooseberry family. This traditional green sauce is great with chips, served over grilled steak, with fresh tacos (use the leftover roasted pork from the roasted pork loin; p. 133), paired with Mama's Chicken and Mushroom Enchiladas (p. 226), and also as a sauce for the Black Bean Tortilla Lasagna (p. 184). Salsa Verde adds a unique layer of acid and spice to other dishes. It's best when fresh and used immediately, but can be stored for up to a day in the refrigerator. To give it a creamy and rich texture, add diced avocado.

MAKES ABOUT 2 CUPS

½ bunch fresh cilantro, trimmed

½ pound tomatillos, peeled and quartered

1 large jalapeño, trimmed and sliced, with seeds (or 2 small, without seeds)

¼ cup chopped onion

1½ cloves garlic

Juice of 1½ limes

1 teaspoon kosher salt

2 tablespoons water, plus more as needed

¼ cup extra-virgin olive oil

Combine the cilantro, tomatillos, jalapeño, onion, garlic, lime juice, salt, and water in a high-speed blender and pulse until combined. You may need to stop the machine and push the vegetables down once or twice. With the machine running, slowly pour in the oil in a steady stream until the sauce is emulsified. Add more water, 2 tablespoons at a time, up to ¼ cup, if needed. The salsa will be loose and not completely smooth. Taste and adjust the seasonings. Store for up to 1 day in the refrigerator.

SOFRITO

Sofrito is the basis of many Latin and Caribbean dishes. Just as a complex French dish or soup or stew would start with mirepoix (a mixture of chopped celery, carrot, and onion) or earthy dishes in Creole or Cajun cuisine begin with the "Holy Trinity" (chopped onion, bell pepper, and celery), this mixture of various chopped and gently cooked vegetables, peppers, citrus, and spices is the secret of many Latin dishes.

There are countless versions of Sofrito that include various ingredients, depending on the country where they originated. They are often the first step in cooking and the foundation for building a particular dish. Usually, the mixture is cooked in hot oil or fat until aromatic and then other ingredients are added, just as you would begin with mirepoix. You can add Sofrito to dishes as they are cooking, such as Chorizo and Georgia Shrimp Dirty Rice (p. 149). Use this as a dipping sauce for Crispy Chicken Liver Anticuchos (p. 26), as an alternative to the Aji Panca sauce.

Sofrito will last for several days in the refrigerator, or you can freeze it for longer storage.

MAKES ABOUT 2½ CUPS

1 tablespoon extra-virgin olive oil

1 Spanish onion, cut into ¼-inch dice

2 ounces chopped garlic (about 16 cloves garlic)

2 red bell peppers, trimmed, seeds and membranes removed, and cut into ¼-inch dice

2 tomatoes, cut into ¼-inch dice

3 tablespoons Homemade Sazón (p. 248)

4 teaspoons kosher salt

¼ teaspoon achiote powder

Juice of 2 limes

½ cup extra-virgin olive oil

Heat the tablespoon of olive oil in a medium skillet over medium heat until hot but not smoking. Add the onion and sweat for 2 to 3 minutes. When the onion is translucent, add the rest of the vegetables and cook for another 2 minutes. Remove from the heat, let cool, and then transfer the mixture to a high-speed blender, adding the Sazón, salt, achiote, and lime juice. Pulse to combine and then slowly add the ½ cup olive oil, puréeing until smooth. Transfer to an airtight container and refrigerate until ready to use.

ADOBO RUB

This basic Adobo Rub is the primary ingredient in the Posole Spice Mix on p. 242. Another classic Latin seasoning, prepared versions of these are sold at Latin markets or in grocery stores, but I say, make your own. It's so easy and will be fresher than store-bought.

This rub can be used dry or you can mix it with a little olive oil and fresh citrus juice as a wet rub. It's delicious with pork or chicken. You can also add a little more salt if you're marinating the meat overnight. The salt will help break down the tissues of less tender cuts of meat and will enhance the juiciness of the meat; however, I never apply salt to the meat just before cooking. If you're going to salt, salt early.

MAKES ABOUT ¾ CUP

¼ cup chile de arbol or ground cayenne

¼ cup cumin seeds, toasted and ground

¼ cup coriander seeds, toasted and ground

1 tablespoon kosher salt

In a small bowl, blend together the ingredients. Transfer to an airtight container and store for several months, as you would any spice blend.

FROM ANTHONY

Matt Jamie is one of Louisville's best-known specialty and artisan food producers and entrepreneurs. A good friend, Matt is the owner of Bourbon Barrel Foods and the creator of the first ever small-batch soy sauce produced in the United States. His Bluegrasss Soy Sauce, a chef favorite, is made with Kentucky-grown non-GMO soybeans and is fermented in repurposed Kentucky bourbon barrels from Woodford Reserve. The flavor is outstanding. Matt's ever-expanding line of artisan food products is truly unique.

FROM MATT

I've always said that Louisville is a small town and that people are often connected by where they went to high school. I'm pretty closely connected to Anthony because I went to school with his brother-in-law. One evening while I was dining at Seviche, a favorite restaurant in Louisville, I introduced myself to Anthony, and we've been friends ever since.

It's a rather interesting story how I first created Bluegrass Soy Sauce. It began over oysters and beer while out with some friends at a dive spot in Gainesville, Florida, called Calico Jack's. Maybe we had a few too many beers, but I came up with the idea that evening to make a local soy sauce in the fashion of small soy breweries in Japan, and what better place to age the soy than in the ultimate Kentucky aging vessel, bourbon barrels?

That was in 2003. I was a chef in Gainesville at the time and married with a child. When my young son would fall asleep at night, I'd go online and look up everything I could find about how to make soy sauce just as they do in Japan. After I moved back to Louisville, I began

brewing the stuff in my basement and then in 2006, after perfecting the technique, I started Bourbon Barrel Foods. The first bottle of Bluegrass Soy Sauce was sold in 2008.

When I first met Anthony, he was already using quite a bit of my soy sauce in his dishes, so I asked him to try my sorghum. We source Denny Ray Townsend's sorghum from Jeffersonville, Kentucky. The sorghum cane is grown, milled, and cooked down to a syrupy consistency and color that's a cross between maple syrup and molasses, but far more complex in taste. With the continued popularity of Southern cooking and ingredients and the unique taste of sorghum, more people across the country are now discovering this Southern sweetener. Along with Bluegrass Soy Sauce, I'm proud that I've been able to introduce sorghum to many chefs who might not have known about it.

While I love what many chefs are doing with our products, two of my favorites are what Anthony creates. He makes an amazing soy powder from our Bluegrass Soy Sauce thanks to a little molecular magic, and he uses liquid nitrogen to create frozen caramel popcorn with the Kentucky sorghum.

It's exciting to see our business continue to evolve and grow. We now partner with Woodford Reserve on a number of products, like several flavors of bitters and

bourbon cherries. We also have our own smokers in-house and developed a line of bourbon-smoked spices, including pepper, sea salt, and paprika.

One of the most exciting things we've done in the past several years is to open The Kitchen Studio at our warehouse location in the historic Butchertown Market. It's here in the professional kitchen and open space that we hold cooking classes, special events, tastings, and dinners; we're able to introduce people to the history of bourbon in Kentucky and the many uses for bourbon-inspired ingredients in our Eat Your Bourbon Chef Series, featuring demonstrations by local chefs. Bourbon is tasty in all sorts of recipes from cocktails to breakfast items and from main dishes to desserts, and these events allow us to showcase bourbon as a culinary ingredient.

It's exciting to have chefs use my products. We all share the same passion around great ingredients and great food, and we respect and support each other in this industry. Chefs are picky with the ingredients they source, and the fact that they use my products is a reflection of the pride and care that I put into making them. We are a group of high-caliber people who work really hard at what we do. It's a nice family to be a part of.

HOMEMADE SAZÓN

Sazón is a popular seasoning in Latin cooking and is available commercially at Latin markets or in the International section of your grocery store. Many Latin cooks use the version with achiote powder (from ground annatto seeds) to achieve the vibrant orange color in foods. I like to use Sazón to season and give color to meats like the roasted pork in the Pork Loin with Chipotle–Orange Bourbon Glaze (p. 133). I also use achiote powder by itself to give the beautiful reddish color to the sautéed shrimp in Nuevo Latino Shrimp and Grits (p. 157).

This homemade Sazón brightens up foods and gives them more depth of flavor. For reference, 1½ teaspoons of Homemade Sazón equals 1 package or envelope of store-bought Sazón with cilantro and achiote.

MAKES ABOUT ⅓ CUP

1 tablespoon ground coriander
1 tablespoon ground cumin
1 tablespoon garlic powder

1 tablespoon achiote or ground annatto seeds
1 tablespoon kosher salt

In a small bowl, combine all of the ingredients and mix well. Store in a small, airtight container as you would any other spice or spice blend for up to 6 months.

HOUSE SEASONING BLEND

Many chefs have a go-to house seasoning mix. This is a version of ours, and it's used in a number of recipes throughout the book. When you taste a dish or sauce and it's missing that certain something, try adding a pinch of this to wake up the flavors. You might find that it's just what the chef ordered to enhance many of your dishes.

MAKES ABOUT ¾ CUP

10 tablespoons onion powder
1 tablespoon garlic powder
1 tablespoon ground white pepper

1 tablespoon kosher salt
1 teaspoon granulated sugar
1 teaspoon freshly ground black pepper

In a small bowl, combine all of the ingredients and mix well. Store in an airtight container or spice jar. The seasoning will keep for up to 6 months, just like any other spice blend.

CHIMICHURRI

People come to Seviche just for our steak with chimichurri. With its origins in Argentina, this popular sauce is usually served with grilled meats and can be made with varying combinations of parsley, cilantro, and oregano. Argentineans will eat it just as Americans eat ketchup, even with french fries. It is garlicky, bright, and tangy with the acidity created by the addition of red-wine vinegar. Any number of other spices and seasonings can be added to the basic recipe, depending on what you're serving it with. For a Southern twist, I make a Wild Ramp Chimichurri (p. 241) when ramps arrive in early spring.

I like the consistency of my chimichurri to be "loose"—the cilantro and parsley are finely minced, yet there is still texture to the sauce and it's not completely puréed.

MAKES 2 CUPS

1 bunch fresh cilantro, trimmed
1 bunch fresh curly parsley, trimmed
2 large cloves garlic, chopped
2 teaspoons kosher salt

½ teaspoon crushed red pepper flakes
¾ cup red-wine vinegar
¾ cup extra-virgin olive oil

Purée all of the ingredients in a high-speed blender until the mixture is loose. Taste for seasonings. Transfer to a container, cover tightly, and refrigerate for 30 minutes prior to serving. Chimichurri is best made when served immediately and will not hold beyond the same day.

CHEF'S TIP > Be sure to trim the bunches of parsley and cilantro so that you are left with mostly leaves and not a lot of the stems. An average bunch of curly parsley, before trimming, should weigh just over 5 ounces; cilantro should weigh about 4 ounces.

SWEET ENDINGS

DESSERTS & TREATS
TO WRAP THINGS UP

I WASN'T MUCH of a dessert eater as a kid, but all that changed as an adult. Please pass me the cobbler, cake, and flan! My mama didn't usually serve desserts after dinner, except on special occasions, so I didn't grow up around them, nor did I have lots of sweets as a kid. I do think that a little something sweet at the end of the meal finishes things off right; even something as simple as a really nice piece of dark chocolate. Some people might even argue that you should skip the dinner and go right for the dessert. With some of the recipes in this chapter, I just might have to agree with that notion.

My pastry chef at Seviche, Steve Rappa, was the first friend I made in Louisville when I moved to town many years ago. He even gave me the first piece of furniture that I had in my apartment. We worked together at Lily's Restaurant and then crossed paths many times at various restaurants in Louisville over the years. No matter where we were in our careers, we always kept in touch. He came →

251

Some people might even argue that you should skip the dinner and go right for the dessert. With some of the recipes in this chapter, I just might have to agree with that notion.

to work with me at Seviche in 2011 and eventually became our pastry chef.

Many of the dessert recipes in this chapter are a collaborative effort between us, and some are updated family recipes, like Steve's grandmother's Peach Cobbler (p. 267) and my aunt's Coconut Flan (p. 258). I like to come up with concepts and ideas for desserts and then together Steve and I create the desserts at Seviche. Steve's latest specialty is his extensive ice cream and sorbet selection, which is

ever-changing with the seasons. We have included two of our favorites in this chapter, Brown Butter–Macadamia Nut Ice Cream (p. 257), an incredibly decadent, smooth, and rich ice cream that's perfect for fall, and our award-winning Avocado Ice Cream (see the facing page). These little chocolate shells resembling an avocado half, filled with ice cream and complete with a Bourbon Dulce de Leche "pit," traveled in dry ice all the way from Louisville to New York City in July of 2014

to our Sustainable Seafood Dinner at the James Beard House.

For chocolate lovers, try Double Chocolate Espresso Brownies with Toasted Georgia Pecans (p. 260), probably some of the best brownies you'll ever eat. Moist and chocolaty, they are incredibly rich. The Flourless Chocolate Cake with Kahlúa® Ganache (p. 263) is always popular. Serve it warm with freshly whipped cream, fresh seasonal berries, and a sprig of mint for an elegant ending to a dinner party.

There is truly something for everyone in Sweet Endings. No matter which recipes you prepare, we hope they'll become favorites with your family and friends.

AVOCADO ICE CREAM

I grew up surrounded by avocado groves in central California. In fact, when I was a kid, I had an avocado stand and sold avocados, just as most kids had lemonade stands. Leave it to a Latino to sell free avocados falling from the trees! They were always one of my favorite foods, and, when time was short to prepare something to eat, my mama would serve us avocado sandwiches sprinkled with just a bit of salt and fresh squeezed lime juice. To this day, I still enjoy the same snack and so do my boys.

We serve this ice cream at Seviche in a chocolate shell shaped like an avocado and then place a Dulce de Leche "pit" that is encased in chocolate on the top of the ice cream. It was featured on "America's Best Bites" on The Cooking Channel and was named the "Best Ice Cream Treat in Kentucky" by *Food Network Magazine*. This ice cream's unique flavor is similar to banana ice cream and it will surprise your guests when they find out it's made from fresh avocados.

You can re-create this treat at home with a simpler version, adding dark chocolate shavings to the ice cream while it's churning in the ice cream freezer insert and then drizzling with Dulce de Leche when serving (see the Variation below). Either way, the flavors are addictive.

MAKES 1½ QUARTS

2 cups heavy cream

2 cups half-and-half

2 ripe avocados, skinned, pitted, and cut into thin slices (see the tip on p. 57)

1 cup granulated sugar

Chocolate sauce or Bourbon Dulce de Leche (p. 275), for serving

Combine the cream, half-and-half, avocados, and sugar in a high-speed blender and purée until smooth. Transfer to the freezer insert of an ice cream maker and freeze according to the manufacturer's directions. Transfer to a freezer-safe container and freeze for several hours before serving with a drizzle of chocolate sauce or Bourbon Dulce de Leche.

VARIATION ❯ Add ½ cup or more dark chocolate shavings during the last few minutes of the churning cycle, or according to the manufacturer's directions for adding mix-ins.

BANANA—RUM PUDDING WITH TOASTED COCONUT

Our riff on a Southern favorite, this elevated version of old-fashioned banana pudding adds in some bright tropical flavors and spiced dark rum, shaved, toasted coconut, and homemade vanilla cake for a long overdue update on the original.

While this recipe is made in a large pan, you can get fancy and prepare the dessert as we did for the photo. If you decide to do that, use an 8-inch square pan to bake the vanilla wafer crust. It will take a few extra minutes to bake since it is thicker. You will also have some pudding and whipped cream left over, but no one in your family will complain about that.

When you make this as the recipe suggests, in a 9 x 13 x 2-inch pan, you can prepare it a day ahead. In fact, the flavors get better after they've spent some time together. If you're not going to serve the whole dessert at the same time, add the fresh banana slices and toasted coconut on the portions that will be cut and served.

MAKES ONE 9 X 13 X 2-INCH PAN · SERVES 12

Nonstick cooking spray or softened unsalted butter, for the pan

FOR THE VANILLA WAFER CRUST
1½ cups all-purpose flour
½ teaspoon baking powder
¼ teaspoon kosher salt
8 tablespoons unsalted butter, softened
½ cup granulated sugar
4 yolks from large eggs
2 tablespoons honey
1½ tablespoons pure vanilla extract
1½ ounces (about 3½ tablespoons) heavy cream, plus more for brushing the crust

FOR THE RUM PUDDING
3 cups whole milk, divided
¾ cup granulated sugar
¼ cup cornstarch
4 yolks from large eggs
½ teaspoon kosher salt
1½ teaspoons pure vanilla extract
¼ cup Gosling's Black Seal® rum

FOR THE WHIPPED CREAM
2½ cups heavy cream
4 tablespoons confectioners' sugar
1 teaspoon pure vanilla extract

5 to 6 medium-ripe bananas
½ cup (or more) shaved coconut, toasted

MAKE THE VANILLA WAFER CRUST

Position a rack in the center of a convection oven and heat the oven to 325°F. Spray or lightly grease a 9 x 13 x 2-inch pan and set aside.

In a small bowl, combine the flour, baking powder, and salt. Mix well and set aside. In the bowl of a stand mixer fitted with the paddle attachment, combine the butter and sugar. Cream together until combined and pale yellow. Add the egg yolks, one at a time, beating on low speed after each addition and scraping down the sides of the bowl, if necessary. Add the honey and vanilla and mix on low speed until incorporated. With the mixer running on low speed, add a third of the flour mixture alternately with a third of the heavy cream, blending well after each addition. Do this two more times until all of the flour and cream are added and the batter is smooth.

Using a silicone spatula, transfer the batter to the prepared pan, spreading it evenly. The batter is sticky and firm, so you can also lay a piece of lightly sprayed parchment on top of the batter and rub all over with your hand to smooth the batter; remove the parchment before baking. Brush the top lightly with heavy cream and bake for 15 minutes, or until just set and golden brown.

MAKE THE RUM PUDDING

In a medium saucepan over medium heat, bring 2 cups of the milk just to the point where bubbles form around the edges and it's steaming. Meanwhile, in a medium bowl, combine the remaining 1 cup milk with the sugar, cornstarch, egg yolks, salt, and vanilla. Whisk well or use an electric handheld mixer fitted with wire beaters to combine. Slowly add the hot milk, tempering the mixture, while whisking constantly.

Once the mixture is thoroughly combined, transfer to a clean medium saucepan and cook over medium heat, whisking constantly, until the pudding boils. Continue cooking and stirring constantly for 1 minute, until thickened. Immediately remove from the heat, add the rum, and stir well. Transfer to a medium bowl and place a piece of plastic wrap directly on the surface of the pudding so a skin doesn't form. Refrigerate for several hours or overnight until cool.

ASSEMBLE THE PUDDING

The day before serving, stir the pudding well and then layer the pudding over the top of the vanilla wafer crust. Cover with plastic wrap and refrigerate overnight.

Several hours before serving, make the whipped cream. In a chilled bowl of a stand mixer fitted with the whisk attachment, combine the heavy cream, confectioners' sugar, and vanilla. Beat on high just until stiff peaks form.

Remove the pudding from the refrigerator and spread the whipped cream evenly over the top with a silicone spatula. Cover and return the pudding to the refrigerator until ready to serve.

When ready to serve, arrange the sliced bananas (tossed in a little lemon juice, if desired, to prevent browning) evenly on top of the whipped cream. Sprinkle with the toasted coconut. Slice into 12 equal squares and serve immediately.

CHEF'S TIP ❯ To toast coconut, spread on a baking sheet and bake in a 300°F convection oven for 5 to 10 minutes, or until it smells nutty and is lightly golden brown (stir and check after 5 minutes). To toast on the stovetop, spread the coconut in a dry skillet and heat over medium low for 5 to 10 minutes, stirring frequently, just until toasted.

BROWN BUTTER—MACADAMIA NUT ICE CREAM

The extraordinary texture of this nutty, rich, and incredibly smooth ice cream is achieved by using a Vitamix or other high-speed blender to combine the ingredients. This decadent ice cream is one that you will not soon forget and will want to make time and again. And if it's not decadent enough as is, you can top it with a drizzle of Bourbon Dulce de Leche (p. 275). The flavors of the bourbon and caramel pair beautifully with the brown butter and nuts, making it a Latin version of pecan praline ice cream.

As with most homemade ice creams, this is best served within a few days of making it. Keep it tightly covered with plastic wrap on the surface of the ice cream and then sealed in an airtight container in your freezer until you devour the rest of it.

MAKES 1 QUART

½ pound unsalted butter	1 cup heavy cream
6 yolks from large eggs, at room temperature	2 cups half-and-half
	Pinch of kosher salt
1 cup granulated sugar	½ cup chopped macadamia nuts, toasted

Put all of the butter in a medium light-colored skillet (so you can see the color of the butter and brown bits forming) and cook over medium-low heat and cook, stirring or swirling frequently, until the butter has an amber color and smells nutty. Keep a watchful eye toward the end of the cooking, as it's easy to go from brown to burnt. Reduce the heat if the butter begins to burn. Once the butter is browned, skim the solids and then strain through a fine-mesh sieve into a small clean bowl, leaving the brown bits behind to create a smooth finish. Alternatively, you can leave the brown bits in the ice cream.

Put the egg yolks in a blender with the sugar and blend until smooth. Temper the egg yolks with the hot butter, adding in just a bit and blending constantly; slowly and gradually add the remaining butter through the feeder at the top of the blender. Meanwhile, combine the heavy cream and half-and-half in a medium saucepan and bring to a simmer over medium heat. Remove the pan from the heat and then gradually add the cream mixture to the blender, along with a pinch of salt. Process until the mixture is completely smooth and blended and then transfer to a clean medium saucepan.

Cook the mixture over medium-low heat, stirring constantly, until the custard is slightly thickened and coats the back of a spoon, 2 to 4 minutes. (The temperature should be no more than 170°F on an instant-read thermometer; otherwise the eggs will curdle.) Remove the pan from the heat and quickly strain the custard through a fine-mesh sieve into a clean large bowl, if not using brown bits. →

Refrigerate the mixture overnight or until very cold, at least 6 hours. Process in an ice cream maker following the manufacturer's directions. Add the chopped macadamia nuts at the end of the churning cycle or according to the manufacturer's directions for adding mix-ins. Transfer the ice cream to a freezer-safe container and cover tightly with plastic wrap pressed against the ice cream. Serve within a couple of days.

COCONUT FLAN

This is my tia's (or aunt's) recipe for flan that I grew up with—our Latin version of custard. I always thought my tia's recipe was the best one I'd ever tasted, even after trying flan in my travels all over the world. This is truly one of the smoothest and most delicious flans I've ever eaten.

The only change we made from my tia's recipe is the addition of rum. Gwen decided we needed to add just a little, since coconut pairs perfectly with rum. It gives the flan a tropical flair.

This elegant dessert is simple to prepare and can be made earlier in the day you want to serve it or the day before. When serving, unmold it onto a plate large enough for the decadent caramel to spill onto. Be sure to scoop up some of the caramel sauce with each slice of flan.

For those of you who are fortunate to source pawpaws where you live, I have included a version of the flan with fresh pawpaw purée. I discovered pawpaws when I moved to Kentucky, a tropical-like fruit that is available for just a few weeks during late summer. With a flavor that's a cross between mango, banana, and pineapple, pawpaws make a unique and delicious flan. At Seviche, we serve it garnished with candied pecans.

MAKES ONE 9-INCH FLAN

½ cup water	One 14-ounce can sweetened condensed milk
1 cup granulated sugar	1 tablespoon rum (I like Myer's®)
12 yolks from large eggs	½ teaspoon pure vanilla extract
One 13.5-ounce can coconut milk (I use Goya)	Pinch of kosher salt

Position a rack in the center of a convection oven and heat the oven to 325°F.

In a small heavy saucepan over medium-high heat, heat the water and the sugar, stirring until the sugar is dissolved. Cook without stirring, brushing down any sugar crystals from the side of the pan with a pastry brush dipped in cold water and swirling the pan occasionally so the caramel browns evenly, until the caramel is dark amber in color. Immediately pour the caramel into a 9-inch cake pan, swirling the pan so the caramel coats the bottom and about ⅛ inch up the side of the pan.

In a large bowl, combine the remaining ingredients and blend well using a handheld electric mixer fitted with wire beaters or with a wire whisk, until the mixture is very smooth and the yolks are completely incorporated. Pour the mixture through a fine-mesh sieve or chinois and into a clean large bowl, then scrape the custard into the caramel-lined cake pan.

Place the pan in a large roasting pan (be sure the cake pan sits flat on the bottom of the larger pan) and pour hot water into the roasting pan so it comes halfway up the sides of the cake pan. Cover the roasting pan with aluminum foil and then cut several small air vents into the top of the foil.

Bake for 65 to 70 minutes, or until the center of the custard is just set and barely jiggles in the middle when nudged. Remove the roasting pan from the oven, uncover, and leave the flan in the water bath for 10 minutes. Remove the cake pan and let cool on a wire rack.

Once completely cooled, cover the flan and refrigerate for several hours until chilled or overnight. When ready to serve, unmold by dipping the bottom of the pan in warm water and gently running a small knife around the inside to break the seal. Holding a large plate over the top of the cake pan, invert the flan, quickly flipping the plate and pan together. Leave the flan pan on top of the serving plate for a few minutes to let the caramel run over the flan. Remove the cake pan, cut the flan into wedges, and serve immediately.

VARIATION > Pawpaw Flan Prepare the caramel as directed for the Coconut Flan. Position a rack in the center of a convection oven and heat the oven to 325°F. In a large mixing bowl, whisk together 2 cups pawpaw purée (excess water removed) and 10 large egg yolks until combined. Add in one 14-ounce can sweetened condensed milk, one 12-ounce can evaporated milk, and 1 teaspoon pure vanilla extract. Whisk again until everything is blended together and then strain the mixture through a fine-mesh sieve and into the caramel-lined pan. Bake as directed for the Coconut Flan in a hot water bath, checking after 55 to 60 minutes. The flan should be set but still jiggle a little in the middle. If a little moisture has accumulated on the top (due to the juice from the pawpaws) and the flan needs more time to set properly, uncover the flan and bake uncovered for another 5 to 10 minutes. Remove immediately from the hot water bath and transfer to a wire rack. Cool and chill as directed above. Serve garnished with candied pecans.

You can order frozen pawpaw purée from Earthy Delights (see Resources on p. 277) or use fresh pawpaws in season. To make your own pawpaw purée, peel and seed a ripe pawpaw, then mash the fruit. The seeds are difficult to remove, so rub the flesh over the grates of a fryer basket (or something similar) to separate the flesh from the seeds. Work quickly since the beautiful bright yellow-orange flesh will turn brown quickly.

DOUBLE CHOCOLATE ESPRESSO BROWNIES WITH TOASTED GEORGIA PECANS

This recipe makes a very moist and chocolaty brownie. The goal was to have an intense chocolate flavor enhanced with espresso. I think you will agree we've achieved that with melted chopped semisweet chocolate and another hit of chocolate from cocoa powder. The texture is perfect—a soft center, crunch from Georgia pecans, and extra chocolaty goodness from the chocolate chips added to the batter.

We make our brownies thinner since we serve them warm and topped with homemade vanilla ice cream or Brown Butter–Macadamia Nut Ice Cream (p.257) for a completely decadent dessert. Don't forget the Bourbon Dulche de Leche (p.275) if you want to serve something that's downright outrageous.

This recipe makes enough brownies so that you can enjoy a batch and then share some with friends and neighbors.

MAKES TWO 9 X 13 X 2-INCH PANS (OR 1 HALF-SHEET PAN)

1½ cups all-purpose flour	2 teaspoons pure vanilla extract
2 tablespoons cocoa powder	6 large eggs
½ teaspoon kosher salt	1½ cups granulated sugar
16 tablespoons unsalted butter, plus more for the pans	½ cup lightly packed light brown sugar
10 ounces semisweet chocolate baking bars, chopped	1½ cups semisweet chocolate chips, divided
1½ teaspoons espresso powder	1½ cups toasted chopped pecans

Position a rack in the center of a convection oven and heat the oven to 350°F. Grease two 9 x 13 x 2-inch baking dishes or a half-sheet pan.

In a small bowl, combine the flour, cocoa powder, and salt. Set aside.

In a double boiler, melt the butter and chopped chocolate over a pan of simmering water. Stir occasionally while the mixture is melting and then whisk until smooth once the butter and chocolate have completely melted. Remove from the heat. Add the espresso powder and vanilla and whisk again to combine. Set aside.

In a large mixing bowl and using a handheld electric mixer fitted with wire beaters, beat the eggs and sugars until the mixture is pale yellow and the sugar is dissolved.

With the mixer on low speed, or using a whisk, gradually add the chocolate mixture to the egg mixture, tempering the eggs and blending well after each addition to combine. Add the flour mixture in three equal parts, blending well after each addition. Once the mixture is thoroughly blended, fold in by hand the chocolate chips and chopped nuts. Pour the batter into the prepared pans and smooth the top with a knife, if necessary.

Bake for 25 to 30 minutes, testing for doneness with a toothpick inserted near the center at 25 minutes. Once the toothpick comes out with just a few crumbs attached, the brownies are done. Do not overbake them.

Move the pan to a wire rack to cool. If you can wait, let the brownies come to room temperature before cutting them. If you can't wait, enjoy them while they're warm! Store, covered tightly, for several days at room temperature.

CHEF'S TIP > There is a difference in saltiness between types of salts (kosher, table, and sea salt), but even different brands of the same type of salt create a different saltiness because of the size and texture of the crystals. I prefer Diamond Crystal® kosher salt for cooking. Morton® kosher salt is almost twice as salty as Diamond Crystal, so you will have to adjust recipes depending on the salt you use.

SMOKED SERRANO GEORGIA PECAN BRITTLE

If you've never made homemade brittle, you'll be surprised how easy it is. We serve this brittle with several desserts at Seviche, but it's also delicious all by itself. Make several batches during the holidays to give as gifts to neighbors and friends. They will wonder what ingredient elevates the buttery and nutty caramel flavor and gives the brittle a kick. Smoked serrano powder is the not-so-secret secret ingredient that gives this brittle its uniquely wonderful back heat. If you're afraid of spice, use a little less than what's called for, but we think the amount is perfect as is.

You will need a candy thermometer to measure the temperature of the brittle, and you'll need to work quickly to incorporate all of the ingredients and then spread the mixture onto a sheet pan. I like to add the second half of the nuts to the mixture in the pan while it's still hot and pliable, pressing them in to give the brittle more texture and crunch.

MAKES APPROXIMATELY ONE 15 X 10-INCH SHEET PAN

Softened butter, for the pan	2 cups Georgia pecans, toasted and roughly chopped, divided
2 cups granulated sugar	
1 cup corn syrup	4 tablespoons unsalted butter
½ cup water	2 teaspoons baking soda
½ teaspoon kosher salt	1 teaspoon smoked serrano powder

Grease a 10 x 15-inch baking pan with butter.

In a large saucepan over medium heat, cook the sugar, corn syrup, and water until the mixture boils and the temperature reaches the hard crack stage (325°F) on a candy thermometer, stirring as needed to prevent the mixture from boiling over.   →

SMOKED SERRANO GEORGIA PECAN BRITTLE, continued

Quickly stir in the rest of the ingredients, except for 1 cup of pecans. Mix thoroughly and then pour on the prepared pan and spread thin. Working quickly, add the remaining nuts, pressing them into the brittle. Let the brittle cool completely (about ½ hour), then break it into pieces. Store pieces, covered, separated by parchment or wax paper, in an airtight container for up to 1 week.

FLOURLESS CHOCOLATE CAKE WITH KAHLÚA GANACHE

A classic flourless chocolate cake, this recipe is really simple to make and quite impressive to serve. The soft-centered and rich chocolate cakes are baked in individual springform pans so that they can be removed easily from the pans once cooled. The cakes are large enough to share, if you are willing to do so, but you may want to have one all to yourself.

You will need an instant-read thermometer to accurately check the temperature of the middle of the cake (see p. 135 for more information about this tool). You'll remove the cakes from the oven when the temperature reaches 140°F, which is slightly underdone. They will continue to cook as they cool and you'll end up with wonderful texture.

The ganache is thin, so use a little less liquid if you want it a bit thicker. You won't use it all, so wrap the rest tightly and refrigerate; serve over vanilla ice cream another evening. Serve these cakes slightly warm for an intense chocolate flavor.

Most dessert wines will pair well with any of the recipes in this chapter; however, for this dessert, Rosa Regale, a sweet aromatic sparkling Italian wine, makes this dessert extraordinary.

MAKES 4 CAKES

Nonstick cooking spray or softened butter, for the pans

FOR THE CAKE

¾ pound semisweet chocolate, chopped

12 tablespoons unsalted butter

6 large eggs

FOR THE KAHLÚA GANACHE

1 cup semisweet chocolate chips

⅓ cup heavy cream

⅓ cup Kahlúa

Fresh raspberries or other in-season berries, sweetened whipped cream, and fresh mint, for garnish

MAKE THE CAKE

Position a rack in the center of a convection oven and heat the oven to 325°F. Lightly grease 4 individual springform pans (4½ inches by 1½ inches). Cut a piece of parchment to fit the bottom of each mold. (Place a pan on the parchment, use a pencil to trace around it, then cut it out.) Grease the paper, put it in the pans, then put the pans on a baking sheet and set aside.

Combine the chocolate and butter in a small saucepan or heatproof bowl and place over a pan of simmering water. Stir occasionally while the mixture is melting and then whisk until smooth once the butter and chocolate have completely melted. Remove the chocolate mixture from the heat, and let cool. Transfer the chocolate mixture to a large bowl.

In the bowl of a stand mixer fitted with the whisk attachment, whip the eggs for 5 to 8 minutes at high speed until doubled in volume. They will be pale yellow and frothy. Gently fold the whipped eggs into the chocolate mixture, a third at a time, until all the eggs are incorporated. Ladle the mixture evenly into the springform pans and bake for

15 minutes, or until a thermometer reads 140°F inserted in the center of a cake. Transfer the cakes to a wire rack to cool.

MAKE THE KAHLÚA GANACHE

Combine all of the ingredients in a small saucepan or heatproof bowl and place over a pan of simmering water, whisking until smooth. Remove from the heat and set aside.

FINISH THE CAKES

When the cakes are almost cool, run a knife around the inside to release the cake from the pan, then open the clasp gently and remove the cakes from the pans. Place on serving plates. Carefully remove the cakes from the parchment, using a thin knife, if necessary, to release the cake from the paper. Whisk the ganache, then pour it evenly over the top of each cake, smoothing with an offset spatula or icing knife. Serve warm, garnished with fresh berries, sweetened whipped cream, and fresh mint.

RHUBARB AND BLUEBERRY SOUR CREAM PIE

Fresh rhubarb first arrives in late spring and is available in markets through the beginning of fall. If you're not familiar with rhubarb, it is quite tart by itself, but really wonderful when combined with other fruits and, of course, a good bit of sugar. Similar in appearance and texture to celery and mostly bright red (with some green) in color, rhubarb is especially delicious in the summer when baked with local blueberries in a fresh fruit pie.

This pie combines a custard filling with fresh fruit for a unique twist on a more traditional baked fruit pie. The brown sugar crumble adds another flavor component and a crumbly texture to the creamy, fruity filling. There's just the right amount of sweetness and a nice balance of flavors in this pie. The recipe makes a true deep-dish pie, so be sure to use a deep-dish pan and your favorite recipe for piecrust that will be large enough to fit the pan.

This is a great dessert to prepare early in the day to serve at a summer barbecue or get-together that evening. Use summer's sweetest blueberries to make this pie really shine.

→

MAKES ONE 9-INCH DEEP DISH PIE

FOR THE PIE
One 9-inch deep-dish unbaked piecrust (homemade or store-bought)
1½ cups granulated sugar
⅓ cup all-purpose flour
Pinch of kosher salt
Juice and finely grated zest of 1 lemon
1 large egg, lightly beaten
1 cup sour cream

3 cups ¾-inch pieces fresh rhubarb (about 1 pound)
1 cup fresh blueberries

FOR THE BROWN SUGAR CRUMBLE
4 tablespoons unsalted butter, softened
½ cup light brown sugar
½ cup all-purpose flour
¼ teaspoon ground cinnamon

MAKE THE PIE

Position a rack in the center of a convection oven and heat the oven to 425°F. Put the piecrust in a 9-inch deep-dish pan and crimp the edges. Prick the bottom and sides all over with a fork.

In a large bowl, combine the sugar, flour, salt, and lemon zest. Add the lemon juice, egg, and sour cream. Combine until blended with an electric handheld mixer fitted with wire beaters or by hand with a whisk. Fold in the rhubarb and blueberries and scrape the mixture into the prepared piecrust, being careful not to overfill.

MAKE THE BROWN SUGAR CRUMBLE AND FINISH THE PIE

In a small bowl, mix the butter and brown sugar with a fork until combined. Add the flour, a little at a time, until it's fully incorporated and the mixture is crumbly. Add the cinnamon and mix well. Sprinkle the crumb mixture evenly over the top of the pie.

Bake for 15 minutes at 425°F, then reduce the heat to 325°F and bake for another 35 to 45 minutes, or until the filling is set. If the crust browns too quickly, cover the edges with aluminum foil. Transfer the pie to a wire rack and let cool completely. Serve at room temperature or chilled. Store any leftover pie in the refrigerator.

CHEF'S TIP ❯ When buying rhubarb from a farmers' market, it typically comes with some of the leaves still attached. Be sure to cut all parts of the leaves off the stalk and discard before using because rhubarb leaves are poisonous.

MAMAW'S PEACH COBBLER

Steve Rappa is Seviche's pastry chef, and Mamaw is Steve's grandmother. This is her original cobbler recipe that Steve put his own delicious spin on, adding Grand Marnier®. After all, Grandma wouldn't have been caught adding a nip of booze to her cobbler, now would she? The Grand Marnier elevates this traditional peach cobbler, giving it an elegant finish. The generous yet light topping soaks up some of the wonderful juice from the fruit, so don't miss getting a biscuit (or two) all to yourself.

Peaches are grown in 23 states, but you'll find some of the best and sweetest peaches in South Carolina and Georgia. Our neighboring state of Indiana also has some great peaches. Buying fruit grown thousands of miles away means that they were picked before they're vine-ripened and are forced to ripen during transporting. Those peaches don't have the same sweetness and flavor as locally grown peaches and often are mealy in texture. Regardless of where you live, look for locally grown fruit. $\longrightarrow$

SERVES 6

Softened butter, for the pan

FOR THE PEACHES

6 cups peaches (approximately 6 peaches), blanched, peeled, pitted, and sliced (use peaches that are ripe, but still firm)

Juice of ½ lemon

1 tablespoon cornstarch

1¼ cups granulated sugar

¼ cup Grand Marnier

FOR THE COBBLER TOPPING

1 cup all-purpose flour

2 teaspoons baking powder

¼ teaspoon kosher salt

3½ tablespoons unsalted butter, chilled

3½ tablespoons shortening, chilled

1 large egg, lightly beaten

⅓ cup buttermilk

Granulated sugar, for dusting

Vanilla ice cream, for serving

Position a rack in the center of a convection oven and heat the oven to 400°F. Butter an 8-inch square baking dish and set aside.

PREPARE THE PEACHES

In a large mixing bowl, combine the peaches and lemon juice. Toss carefully to combine. Sprinkle the cornstarch over the peaches, then add the sugar and Grand Marnier. Combine gently with a spatula, mixing everything together. The mixture will be syrupy. Scrape the peaches and sauce into the prepared baking dish and bake for 20 minutes.

MAKE THE COBBLER TOPPING

While the peaches are baking, combine the flour, baking powder, and salt in a medium bowl and stir well. Cut in the butter and shortening using a pastry blender or two knives until the mixture is crumbly. In a separate small bowl, whisk the egg and buttermilk until blended. Slowly add the wet ingredients to the dry, mixing just until combined. The dough will be wet. (Note: Do not prepare this in advance.)

Remove the peaches from the oven and evenly distribute the dough in dollops over the top. It will cover most of the pan. Sprinkle lightly with sugar, return the cobbler to the oven, and bake for another 15 to 20 minutes, until the cobbler topping is lightly browned. Remove the cobbler from the oven and let cool on a wire rack. Serve warm in a bowl with vanilla ice cream.

CHEF'S TIP ❯ Now that we're making peach cobbler, let's talk about late harvest versus early harvest peaches. No other fruit has such a long growing season. From late May to early September, fresh peaches are available throughout the South. However, the flavor and texture of peaches changes during the growing season. For the best flavor, make this dish when peaches are at their peak in July and August.

PASSION FRUIT MOUSSE

This mousse is one of the most requested desserts at Seviche, particularly in the summertime. Guests love the light texture combined with the tangy flavor of the passion fruit; the mousse is not too sweet and has a bit of a surprise that lingers on the back of the palate—a touch of heat from ground habanero. Start with a smaller amount of the ground habanero if you're timid; taste, and then add more if you like the heat. There's a saying I came up with years ago about cooking with peppers and adding heat to your food: "If you're scared, go to church." Don't be frightened by the ground habanero in this dessert. It's what makes it unique. This mousse is incredibly easy to prepare and can be made early in the day or the evening before you plan to serve it.

Be sure to use a pure passion fruit purée, not one with added sugar. You can also use the purée in my recipe for Passion Fruit Caipirinha (p. 24). The brand we like is The Perfect Purée of Napa Valley (see Resources on p. 277). These products combine pure fruit with filtered water—with nothing else added. The unused portion can be frozen. If you do choose to use purée with added sugar, then you will not need to add much, if any, sugar to the recipe.

SERVES 6

1 cup passion fruit purée (I like Perfect Purée of Napa Valley)

1½ cups granulated sugar (use much less sugar if you are using a passion fruit purée with sugar added)

1½ cups heavy cream

Pinch of kosher salt

1 envelope (¼ ounce) unflavored gelatin (I use Knox®)

¼ cup water

⅛ teaspoon habanero powder, or less to taste

Fresh whipped cream, seasonal berries, and mint leaves, for garnish

In a large bowl, combine the passion fruit purée and sugar and mix well with an electric handheld mixer fitted with wire beaters or by hand with a whisk until the sugar is dissolved. Add the heavy cream and salt and blend well.

Meanwhile, in a small saucepan over low heat, dissolve the gelatin in the ¼ cup water. Bring to a boil, then remove from the heat and let cool to room temperature.

Whisk the cooled gelatin into the passion fruit–cream mixture until thoroughly combined. Add a pinch (half of the ⅛ teaspoon) of habanero powder and taste. If you like a little more heat, go ahead and add the remaining amount. Whisk again to combine well.

Portion the mixture among six dessert glasses or pour it into a small serving dish. Cover with plastic wrap and chill for at least 6 hours or overnight.

To serve, garnish with fresh whipped cream, seasonal berries, and mint leaves.

TWO BOURBON LEGENDS >
CHRIS MORRIS _{WOODFORD RESERVE} & JULIAN P. VAN WINKLE III _{OLD RIP VAN WINKLE DISTILLERY}

FROM ANTHONY

Since my relocation to Louisville, "Kentucky Brown Water" and I have become friends. Honestly, we've shared many moments together—at times, too many! I first met Chris Morris, the Master Distiller of Woodford Reserve, at the Woodford Reserve Culinary Challenge in 2003, when I won the competition with my Pork Tenderloin with Smoked Cheddar Chipotle Sweet Corn Cakes. I had the opportunity to spend more time with Chris when Gwen and her husband Roger brought their culinary tour to Kentucky and Woodford Reserve was a stop on the tour along with lunch and a bourbon tasting at the distillery.

Bourbon as a culinary ingredient continues to grow in importance, but bourbon for sipping is a Kentucky tradition that has spread around the world. The most sought after bourbon is that of my friend, Julian P. Van Winkle III, the proprietor of Pappy Van Winkle bourbon.

FROM CHRIS

I remember Anthony's dish well at our first Woodford Reserve Challenge. His Latin flavors were an unexpected surprise in the Bluegrass State and caught the judge's attention. Over the years we have had the opportunity to work with Anthony on several dinners and events.

Kentucky is known for its bourbon. The history goes back almost 200 years, when it is believed that the first distillery was started in the 1820s in Bardstown, Kentucky. In the early days, distillers differentiated their bourbons by how long it was aged in the barrel and the amount of alcohol in the final product. Over the years, innovation in how bourbon is made has brought new grains, new fermentation processes, redesign of pot stills, and different styles of oak wood as well as the seasoning and toasting of the wood to the industry. It's fair to say bourbon has become more complex, and

with that complexity different bourbons deliver very different tastes.

Bourbon has a wide range of flavors represented by wood, grain, fruit and floral, sweet aromatics, and spices. Most bourbon is unbalanced, with a taste driven by one primary flavor, such as oak or vanilla and caramel or leather. It's not bad that bourbon is unbalanced. It offers something unique. However, our product tends to be right down the middle with the various flavors discernable but not overwhelming.

Bourbon has always been a part of Southern cooking, but it was when fusion cooking became popular and we were demonstrating the use of Woodford with its complexity and flavor profile that many chefs realized its potential. We can say that we were the first to start the modern movement toward culinary bourbon. Its use in cooking has grown across the country and it shows up in everything from soups and starters to desserts.

FROM JULIAN

Many people in the bourbon business can trace their heritage back through generations of distillers. My grandfather started as a whiskey salesman at the end of the 19th century. He was considered an outsider in the industry because he didn't have ancestors in the business, but after 15 years working in the business, Pappy, my grandfather, became one

of the owners. He put his own mark on how bourbon is made as well as the integrity of the product and in doing business with him. Since that time, we've been making Pappy Van Winkle bourbon and doing business the same way my grandfather did.

Bourbon has become very popular and there has been an explosion in new distillers bringing innovation in style and types of whiskey, but Pappy is about consistency and always producing fine bourbon. There was a time during the last World War that my father, who took over the business from my grandfather, could have made a lot of money selling bourbon by taking shortcuts, but he never compromised on how he made his whiskey.

Our aging process produces very unique bourbon with a depth of flavor and finish that many say is the finest in the world. That would certainly be what Pappy had expected. Today, we find bourbon being used in all kinds of foods and chefs creating recipes that are enhanced by bourbon. It takes 15 to 23 years for us to produce the various bottlings of Pappy, so when you have a bourbon like Pappy Van Winkle, which is in short supply due to the small volumes and long aging time, we say sip it, sip it very slowly and enjoy all the beautiful flavors. It's most enjoyable when shared with friends and chefs like Anthony, who appreciate its rarity and uniqueness.

KENTUCKY APPLE AND BOURBON PECAN BREAD PUDDING

With the arrival of fall in Kentucky, varieties of local heirloom apples begin to make their appearance in farmers' markets and grocery stores around Louisville. They are the inspiration for new dishes for our fall menu at Seviche and will appear in both savory dishes and desserts at the restaurant. This recipe is our version of a favorite Southern dessert, bread pudding, made with tart Granny Smith apples, some expected spices like cinnamon and nutmeg, but some unexpected surprises, like a bit of kick from Kentucky bourbon and crunch from toasted Georgia pecans.

The apples are sautéed with butter and then deglazed with bourbon and cooked with brown sugar to make a rich and sweet syrupy addition to the bread pudding. We prefer to use Woodford Reserve bourbon in our recipes because it's a great culinary bourbon and carries through the notes of vanilla and caramel in the dessert, however, any good wheat-based Kentucky bourbon to add sweetness or a rye bourbon to add spice will work. At Seviche, we serve the bread pudding warm, topped with our Bourbon Dulce de Leche, freshly whipped cream, and micro mint. Talk about a decadent dessert…this one is it.

SERVES 8

8 tablespoons unsalted butter, plus more for the baking dish

2 large Granny Smith apples, peeled, cored, and sliced

3 teaspoons kosher salt, divided

¼ cup Kentucky bourbon (I prefer Woodford Reserve)

¼ cup light brown sugar

1 quart heavy cream

8 large eggs

¾ cup granulated sugar

1 tablespoon ground cinnamon

1½ teaspoons freshly grated nutmeg

1 French baguette (approximately 12 to 14 ounces), cut into 1-inch cubes, lightly toasted

½ cup golden raisins

½ cup pecans, toasted and roughly chopped

Bourbon Dulce de Leche (p. 275), whipped cream, and micro mint (or fresh mint), for garnish

Position a rack in the center of a convection oven and heat the oven to 350°F. Grease a 9 x 13 x 2-inch baking dish with softened butter and set aside.

In a large skillet over medium heat, melt the 8 tablespoons butter until the foaming begins to subside and then add the apple slices in a single layer. Sprinkle the apples with 1 teaspoon of the salt and sauté until they are just beginning to soften, 3 to 4 minutes. Add the bourbon, remove the pan from the heat, and flambé the apples. When the flame dies down, add the brown sugar and return the pan to the heat. Stir for a few more minutes, just until a nice caramel sauce is formed; do not overcook the apples. Set aside.

In a large bowl, combine the heavy cream, eggs, sugar, the remaining 2 teaspoons salt, and spices. Mix with an electric handheld mixer fitted with wire beaters until the sugar is dissolved and everything is blended together. Add the bread cubes to the liquid, pushing them down so they can soak through, for 5 to 10 minutes, or until the cubes are saturated.

→

Slightly warm the apple mixture over medium heat if the caramel sauce has separated. Remove just the apple slices from the pan and add them to the custard. Gently fold the apples into the mixture, then add the raisins and nuts, and fold in gently.

Pour the mixture into the prepared dish, pushing the bread down into the custard, then drizzle the caramel sauce from the apples over the top. Bake for 35 to 45 minutes, or until the custard is set and the top is browned. Serve warm, topped with Bourbon Dulce de Leche, whipped cream, and micro mint (or fresh mint).

WARM MILK CAKE WITH BOURBON DULCE DE LECHE

Tres leche, the Spanish term for "three milks cake," is the inspiration for this cake. Tres leche was always one of my favorite desserts growing up in California, and it's very popular in Latin communities. It is usually served with a topping of whipped cream, but we put a different spin on the dessert and top it with Bourbon Dulce de Leche (facing page). After all, everything is better with bourbon and rich, thick caramel.

This wonderfully moist cake will keep for several days, covered, in the refrigerator.

MAKES ONE 9 X 13 X 2-INCH CAKE

Nonstick cooking spray or softened butter, plus flour, for the pan

FOR THE CAKE
6 large eggs, separated
2 cups granulated sugar
1 teaspoon pure vanilla extract
½ cup half-and-half
2 cups all-purpose flour
2 teaspoons baking powder

FOR THE CREAM TOPPING
One 14-ounce can evaporated milk
One 14-ounce can sweetened condensed milk
1 cup half-and-half

Bourbon Dulce de Leche (see the facing page) and fresh whipped cream, for serving

Position a rack in the center of a convection oven and heat the oven to 325°F. Lightly grease and flour a 9 x 13 x 2-inch glass baking dish.

MAKE THE CAKE

In the bowl of a stand mixer fitted with the whisk attachment, beat the egg whites on low speed until soft peaks form. With the mixer running, gradually add the sugar and beat to stiff peaks. Add the egg yolks, one at a time, incorporating well after each addition. In a small bowl, stir together the vanilla and half-and-half.

Sift together the flour and baking powder and add to the egg mixture, alternating it with the half-and-half mixture. (Do this quickly so the batter does not lose volume.) Pour into the prepared pan and bake until the cake is golden and a toothpick inserted near the center comes out clean, about 45 minutes. Remove from the oven and move to a wire rack.

MAKE THE CREAM TOPPING

In a high-speed blender, combine the evaporated milk, condensed milk, and half-and-half and process on high speed.

FINISH THE CAKE

While the cake is still warm, use a wooden skewer to poke holes all over the top. Pour the cream mixture evenly over the cake. Let sit and cool to room temperature. Cover and refrigerate until well chilled, at least 4 hours or overnight.

Serve portions drizzled with warm Bourbon Dulce de Leche and garnished with a dollop of fresh whipped cream.

BOURBON DULCE DE LECHE

· ·

MAKES 4 CUPS

4 cups heavy cream	2 tablespoons Kentucky bourbon
4 cups granulated sugar	(I like Woodford Reserve)

In a heavy medium saucepan, combine the heavy cream and sugar. Bring to a low boil over medium heat, stirring to dissolve the sugar. Reduce the heat and simmer, uncovered, for 1½ to 2½ hours, stirring frequently, until it's the desired consistency, thickened, and caramelized. Remove from the heat, let cool slightly, and then add the bourbon. Stir to combine well. Serve slightly warm or refrigerate, covered, for several weeks.

· ·

CHEF'S TIP ❯ Dulce de Leche holds for a couple of weeks in the refrigerator. You can cut this recipe in half, but it takes several hours to prepare, so why not make the whole batch and have leftovers. I really enjoy having it around for a while. Top your favorite vanilla ice cream or other desserts, like the Double Chocolate Espresso Brownies with Toasted Georgia Pecans (p. 260), with a little, or sneak a spoonful from the fridge every now and then. I do.

› RESOURCES ‹

The following sources carry recommended ingredients and kitchenware.

SPECIALTY FOODS & ARTISAN PRODUCTS

Amigo Foods, Inc.
Miami, FL
www.amigofoods.com
Latin food products

Anson Mills
Columbia, SC
www.ansonmills.com
Carolina Gold Rice, Sea Island Red Peas, and other heirloom ingredients

Benton's Bacon
Madisonville, TN
www.bentonscountryhams2.com
Smoky Mountain country ham and bacon

Border Springs Farm
Patrick Springs, VA
www.borderspringsfarm.com
Fresh lamb

Bourbon Barrel Foods
Louisville, KY
www.bourbonbarrelfoods.com
Bluegrass Soy Sauce and other bourbon-inspired products

Boyajian
Canton, MA
www.boyajianinc.com
Lemon and orange oils

Capriole, Inc.
Greenville, IN
www.capriolegoatcheese.com
Farmstead goat cheeses

Earthy Delights
Okemos, MI
www.earthy.com
Pawpaw purée and fresh pawpaws (in season)

Kenny's Farmhouse Cheese
Austin, KY
www.kennyscheese.com
Farmhouse cheeses

Manchester Farms, Inc.
Columbia, SC
www.manchesterfarms.com
Premium quail

Maple Leaf Farms
Leesburg, IN
www.mapleleaffarms.com
Premium duck

Newsom's Country Hams
Princeton, KY
www.newsomscountryham.com
Aged country ham and prosciutto

The Perfect Purée of Napa Valley
Napa, CA
www.perfectpuree.com
Passion fruit and other pure fruit purées

Rancho Gordo
Napa, CA
www.ranchogordo.com
Heirloom beans

Rappahannock Oyster Co.
Topping, VA
www.rroysters.com
Fresh oysters

The Spice House
Milwaukee, WI
www.thespicehouse.com
Premium spices and dried peppers

Terra Spice Company
North Liberty, IN
www.terraspice.com
Premium spices and dried peppers

Weisenberger Mill
Midway, KY
www.weisenberger.com
Stone-ground grits, cornmeal, and flour

Woodford Reserve
Versailles, KY
www.woodfordreserve.com
Kentucky bourbon

KITCHEN & COOKWARE ITEMS

Anova Culinary
Stafford, TX
www.anovaculinary.com
Sous vide circulators

Korin
New York, NY
www.korin.com
Japanese chef knives

Le Creuset
New York, NY
www.lecreuset.com
French cookware and bakeware

Lodge Manufacturing
South Pittsburg, TN
www.lodgemfg.com
Cast iron cookware

Magimix by Robot-Coupe
www.magimix.com/usa-canada
Multifunctional food processors

Steelite International
New Castle, PA
us.steelite.com
Dinnerware and glassware

Vitamix
Cleveland, OH
www.vitamix.com
High-speed blenders

› METRIC EQUIVALENTS ‹

LIQUID/DRY MEASURES

U.S.	METRIC
¼ teaspoon	1.25 milliliters
½ teaspoon	2.5 milliliters
1 teaspoon	5 milliliters
1 tablespoon (3 teaspoons)	15 milliliters
1 fluid ounce (2 tablespoons)	30 milliliters
¼ cup	60 milliliters
⅓ cup	80 milliliters
½ cup	120 milliliters
1 cup	240 milliliters
1 pint (2 cups)	480 milliliters
1 quart (4 cups; 32 ounces)	960 milliliters
1 gallon (4 quarts)	3.84 liters
1 ounce (by weight)	28 grams
1 pound	454 grams
2.2 pounds	1 kilogram

OVEN TEMPERATURES

°F	GAS MARK	°C
250	½	120
275	1	140
300	2	150
325	3	165
350	4	180
375	5	190
400	6	200
425	7	220
450	8	230
475	9	240
500	10	260
550	Broil	290

> INDEX <

Early Praise for *Southern Heat*

"*Southern Heat* showcases the great potential for diversity in American cooking. Its recipes are resplendent with chiles, but anchored in the history of the regional foods of Kentucky."

—Hugh Acheson, Chef and Author

"A personal and delicious journey showcasing the ever-changing state of southern food. *Southern Heat* is filled with an inspiring mashup of two of my favorite cuisines. This book will make you want to cook all day and all night."

—Sean Brock, Chef/Owner, Husk

"I've cooked with and against Anthony Lamas more than a few times and finally have his secrets in his first book. *Southern Heat* is an American treasure with a Latin beat."

—Bobby Flay, Chef

"If there is one chef who captures the essence of the emerging multi-cultural South and our evolving cuisines, it is Anthony Lamas. This book reflects the exciting evolution in our food and our culture by beautifully blending heritages into a very personal and passionate style of cooking. In Gwen Pratesi, Anthony has found a magnificent person to translate that passion and perspective into something all of us can enjoy."

—John Fleer, Chef/Owner, Rhubarb

"*Southern Heat* brings the fire in classic Anthony Lamas style! His southern favorites like Shrimp and Grits and Pecan Brittle, spiced up with the bold flavors of the Latin American larder, are irresistible and destined to become new standards in your kitchen. Cook this book deeply, and often."

—Matt Lee and Ted Lee, Authors of *The Lee Bros. Charleston Kitchen*

"There are few chefs I have encountered on my travels who approach sub-Mason Dixon cuisine with the skill or the imagination of Chef Anthony Lamas. Anthony balances impeccable technique and his passion for the South with Latin energy and a level of creativity that makes his cooking a genuinely one-off proposition. *Southern Heat* is the perfect balance of culinary location and culinary heritage."

—Simon Majumdar, Author and Broadcaster

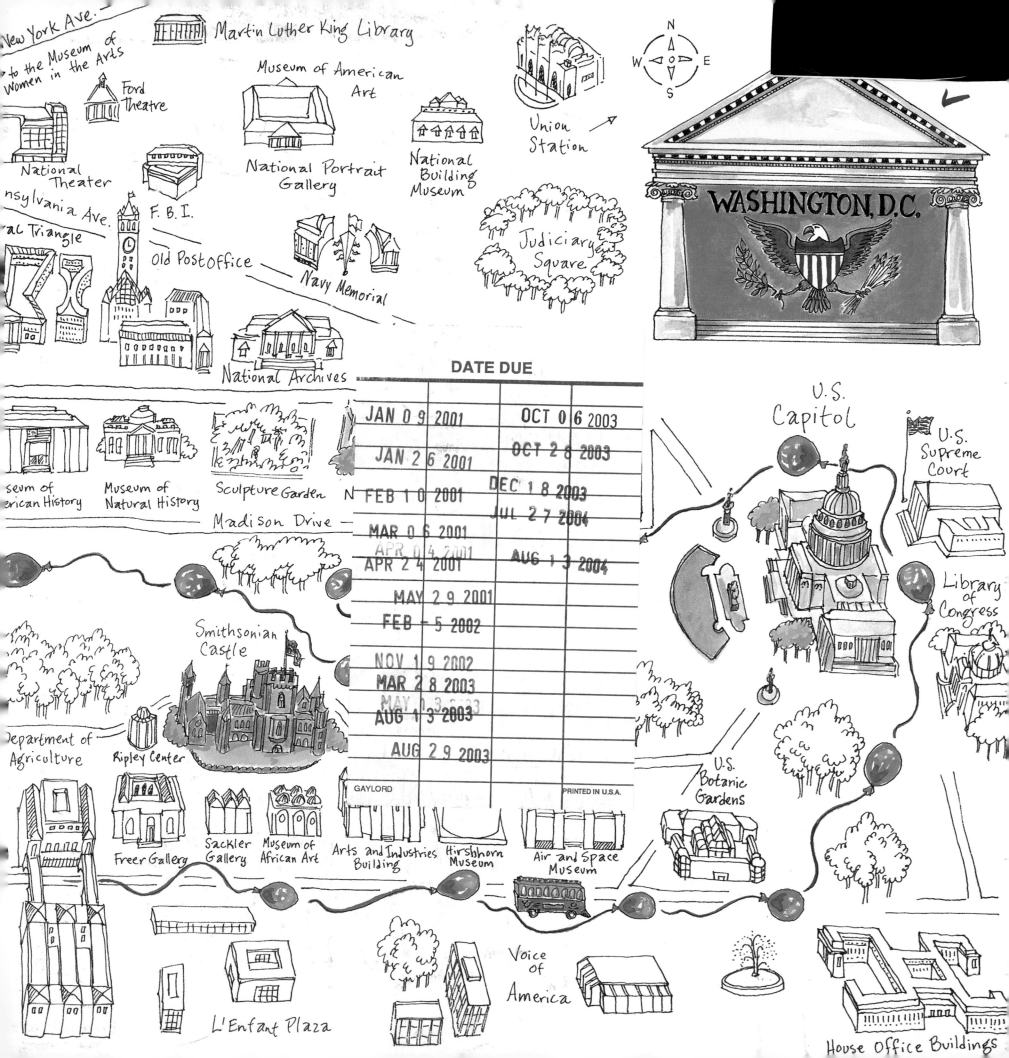